International Journal on Advances in Security

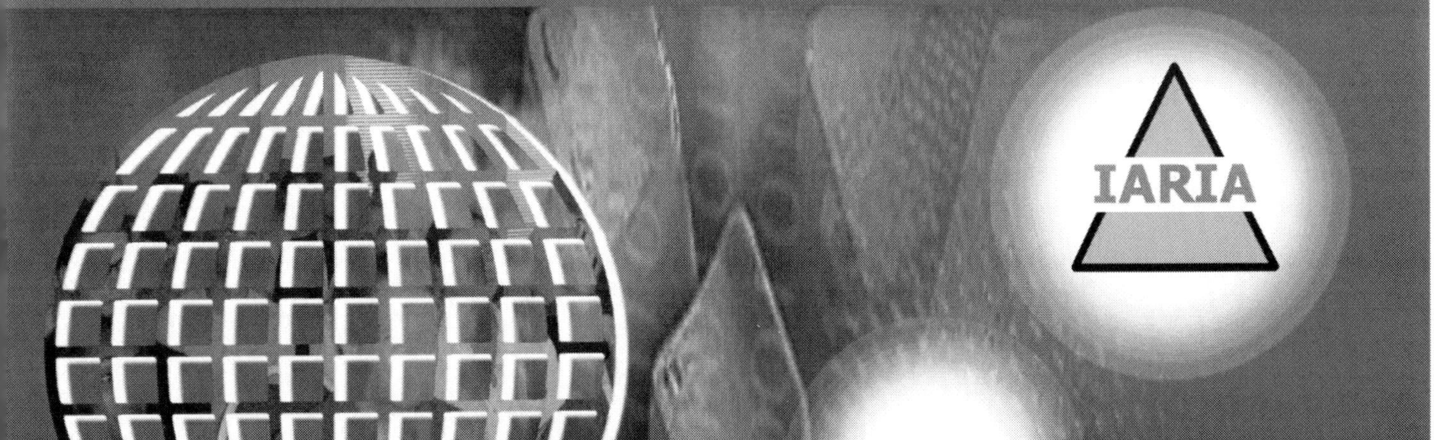

2017 vol. 10 nr. 3&4

Printed from e-media with permission by:

Curran Associates, Inc.
57 Morehouse Lane
Red Hook, NY 12571

CURRAN ASSOCIATES INC.
proceedings
.com

Some format issues inherent in the e-media version may also appear in this print version.

Printed by Curran Associates, Inc. (2018)

International Academy, Research, and Industry Association (IARIA)
412 Derby Way
Wilmington, DE 19810

Phone: (408) 893-6407
Fax: (408) 527-6351

petre@iaria.org

Additional copies of this publication are available from:

Curran Associates, Inc.
57 Morehouse Lane
Red Hook, NY 12571 USA
Phone: 845-758-0400
Fax: 845-758-2633
Email: curran@proceedings.com
Web: www.proceedings.com

The *International Journal on Advances in Security* is published by IARIA.
ISSN: 1942-2636
journals site: http://www.iariajournals.org
contact: petre@iaria.org

Reference should mention:

> *International Journal on Advances in Security, issn 1942-2636*
> *vol. 10, no. 3 & 4, year 2017, http://www.iariajournals.org/security/*

Reference to an article in the journal is as follows:

> *<Author list>, "<Article title>"*
> *International Journal on Advances in Security, issn 1942-2636*
> *vol. 10, no. 3 & 4, year 2017, <start page>:<end page> , http://www.iariajournals.org/security/*

Sponsored by IARIA
www.iaria.org

International Journal on Advances in Security
Volume 10, Number 3 & 4, 2017

Wolfgang Boehmer, Technische Universitaet Darmstadt, Germany
Alexis Bonnecaze, Université d'Aix-Marseille, France
Carlos T. Calafate, Universitat Politècnica de València, Spain
Juan-Vicente Capella-Hernández, Universitat Politècnica de València, Spain
Zhixiong Chen, Mercy College, USA
Clelia Colombo Vilarrasa, Autonomous University of Barcelona, Spain
Peter Cruickshank, Edinburgh Napier University Edinburgh, UK
Nora Cuppens, Institut Telecom / Telecom Bretagne, France
Glenn S. Dardick, Longwood University, USA
Vincenzo De Florio, University of Antwerp & IBBT, Belgium
Paul De Hert, Vrije Universiteit Brussels (LSTS) - Tilburg University (TILT), Belgium
Pierre de Leusse, AGH-UST, Poland
William Dougherty, Secern Consulting - Charlotte, USA
Raimund K. Ege, Northern Illinois University, USA
Laila El Aimani, Technicolor, Security & Content Protection Labs., Germany
El-Sayed M. El-Alfy, King Fahd University of Petroleum and Minerals, Saudi Arabia
Rainer Falk, Siemens AG - Corporate Technology, Germany
Shao-Ming Fei, Capital Normal University, Beijing, China
Eduardo B. Fernandez, Florida Atlantic University, USA
Anders Fongen, Norwegian Defense Research Establishment, Norway
Somchart Fugkeaw, Thai Digital ID Co., Ltd., Thailand
Steven Furnell, University of Plymouth, UK
Clemente Galdi, Universita' di Napoli "Federico II", Italy
Emiliano Garcia-Palacios, ECIT Institute at Queens University Belfast - Belfast, UK
Birgit Gersbeck-Schierholz, Leibniz Universität Hannover, Germany
Manuel Gil Pérez, University of Murcia, Spain
Karl M. Goeschka, Vienna University of Technology, Austria
Stefanos Gritzalis, University of the Aegean, Greece
Michael Grottke, University of Erlangen-Nuremberg, Germany
Ehud Gudes, Ben-Gurion University - Beer-Sheva, Israel
Indira R. Guzman, Trident University International, USA
Huong Ha, University of Newcastle, Singapore
Petr Hanáček, Brno University of Technology, Czech Republic
Gerhard Hancke, Royal Holloway / University of London, UK
Sami Harari, Institut des Sciences de l'Ingénieur de Toulon et du Var / Université du Sud Toulon Var, France
Dan Harkins, Aruba Networks, Inc., USA
Ragib Hasan, University of Alabama at Birmingham, USA
Masahito Hayashi, Nagoya University, Japan
Michael Hobbs, Deakin University, Australia
Hans-Joachim Hof, Munich University of Applied Sciences, Germany
Neminath Hubballi, Infosys Labs Bangalore, India
Mariusz Jakubowski, Microsoft Research, USA
Ángel Jesús Varela Vaca, University of Seville, Spain
Ravi Jhawar, Università degli Studi di Milano, Italy
Dan Jiang, Philips Research Asia Shanghai, China
Georgios Kambourakis, University of the Aegean, Greece

International Journal on Advances in Security
Volume 10, Numbers 3 & 4, 2017

CONTENTS

Steffen Fries, Siemens AG, Germany
Rainer Falk, Siemens AG, Germany
Chaitanya Bisale, Siemens AG, Germany

Cancelable Hand Geometry-Based Biometric Authentication System Using Steganography Techniques

Louis-Philip Shahim, Dirk Snyman, Tiny du Toit, Hennie Kruger
School of Computer-, Statistical- and Mathematical Sciences
North-West University,
Potchefstroom, South Africa.
e-mail: LP.Shahim6@gmail.com; {Dirk.Snyman, Tiny.DuToit, Hennie.Kruger}@nwu.ac.za

Abstract – **Complex methods are often used in an attempt to rectify basic security aspects that should be prevalent in all authentication systems, but are lacking. Biometric information remains unique to each individual and it is for that reason that it should be protected, and yet many developers neglect the importance of securing biometrics effectively. This research presents a novel approach for authentication systems to protect biometric information using a combination of transformation techniques and steganography encryption methods. A leap motion controller captures user-specific biometric information. Once this information is retrieved, it is transformed or made "cancelable." This ultimately prevents a third party from reconstructing the information to its original state. The concept of obfuscating biometric information seems inadequate without storing this information so that users may be authenticated. The shortcomings of storing this information become apparent should an attack occur on the database that holds the biometric information. One can breach a database and expose all the users' personal information by simply gaining access to a username and password. To counter this threat, the use of image steganography to store user-biometric information in various pixels throughout an image is presented. By using cancelable biometrics combined with image steganography, biometric information can be safeguarded against reconstruction and possible identity theft prevented. The resulting framework presented in this paper shows promise to a novel cancelable biometrics approach using steganography.**

Keywords- cancelable biometrics; information security; leap motion controller; multifactor authentication; steganography.

I. Introduction

Biometrics have long been used as an accepted user authentication method and have been implemented as a security measure in many real-world systems including personal computers, mobile devices (cell phones and tablets), and also physical access control systems [1]. Biometrics are the digitalization and analysis of a person's innate physical or biological characteristics and the use thereof to distinguish between persons that are to be afforded access to specific systems, information or physical areas [1][2]. By encoding a person's physical attributes the disadvantages of traditional password based security, like passwords being lost or stolen, can be overcome [1][3]. One of the factors that hampers the acceptance of biometric authentication systems is that the cost of the development and implementation has traditionally been high due to factors such as biometric hardware, computational processing power, infrastructure integration, user training, and research and testing [1][3]. Furthermore, biometric systems present a unique challenge in terms of user privacy due to the personal nature of the biometric information that is stored in and used by the system [4].

The cost factor is one that decreases as continued development in the related hardware takes place. Alongside this development of dedicated biometric hardware there is an influx of new augmented computer interaction possibilities (i.e., new and non-traditional ways to control computers), a wide range of technological facets such as voice-, imaging- and movement control are receiving a lot of attention [3][4]. Image-control typically refers to facial recognition implementations, retina scanners and/or eye-tracking software that implement infrared imaging. In order to facilitate these interactions, the hardware is implicitly working with information that can be harnessed for biometric authentication. Hardware peripherals (like the leap motion controller (LMC)) that extend the basic functionality of computers to include support for voice and imaging facets are becoming more commonplace [2]. These peripherals are even used in biometrics research. For instance, Chan *et al.* [5] used an LMC for hand scanning and biometric authentication whereby a user would be able to gain access to a system, physical area or information by having their hand geometry scanned and analysed. They also posit the use of an LMC in multifactor authentication systems in combination with traditional passwords and PIN approaches.

Typically, this type of biometric authentication process follows the protocol of matching prior biometric templates (i.e., digitally formatted biometric features) that are stored within a database to the biometrics that are presented to the system during the biometric scanning process. This study proposes a system that expands on the existing techniques for biometric authentication with an LMC. This expansion uses techniques from steganography to store binary representations of the biometrics within an image as a biometric template alternative. The system does not merely store the raw biometric data within the image, but rather applies transform parameters to it. Only once the transform parameters have been added to the original biometrics are they stored/matched to authenticate and authorize the user. This ensures that each user's biometric information is neither compromised, nor exposed. Cancelable biometrics refers to protecting the biometric information from third party scrutiny by obfuscating this information (see Section II-A). This addresses the challenge of privacy of biometric information as mentioned above.

The objective of this research is to present the planning and development of a framework for a novel LMC hand-geometry authentication system that ensures the cancelability of biometric information by employing steganography techniques. Furthermore, this research also aims to present an illustrative example of the implementation of the steganography techniques for a cancelable biometric authentication system.

The remainder of this paper will be organized as follows: in Section II, background literature on the various related topics to this particular system will be discussed. Within Section III the proposed framework will be discussed, followed by an illustrative example in Section IV. In Section V, conclusions will be drawn and possible future work will be discussed. The final conclusion to the paper will be presented in Section VI.

II. Literature Study

Within this section, the topics of *cancelability*, *steganography* and the use of an *LMC* for biometric authentication will be discussed in more detail. This section attempts to provide the reader with a better understanding of the individual topics and techniques before they are combined to create the proposed authentication system.

A. Cancelability

With the use of authentication systems becoming more prevalent, a primary concern becomes real-time processing of transmitted information as to verify a user's identity. The authentication process itself within traditional systems has evolved and often resorts to biometric information rather than passwords, tokens and/or secret keys [3]. This is primarily due to the inability of these traditional schemes to differentiate between an authentic user and an impostor. By authenticating users using biometric information the privacy of biometric data becomes important. Should attackers manage to gain access to the recognition system and its underlying data, the user-specific biometric information becomes readily available for identity theft. The biometric information should be protected. A possible solution would be to use multifactor biometric authentication with two or more biometric traits being employed. However, by adding more biometric features it will only add to the possible losses (should the system be compromised). Within the information security industry, one of the long acclaimed benefits of using biometric authentication has been that with post-enrolment biometric templates, user-specific biometric information (matching the stored template) could not be reconstructed. The benefit was refuted and once biometric templates become compromised, the biometric template is rendered useless [2]. This is because unlike passwords, biometric templates cannot simply be re-assigned due to their personal unique nature. Considering the susceptibility of such biometric authentication systems an approach to enhance the robustness can be used that is known as cancelable biometrics (CB). This approach improves upon standard encryption algorithms that expose biometric templates during the authentication attempt by not supporting the comparison of templates within the encrypted domain [2]. Simply put, the encrypted domain referred to by CB ensures that data will remain secure in transit and in storage. Furthermore, CB allows for re-issuing and/or regenerating biometric information with a unique and independent identity. The process of transforming or repeatedly distorting the biometric feature using transform parameters that are predetermined rather than using the original biometric achieves this [1]. As to meet some of the major requirements regarding biometric information protection, biometric cryptosystems (BCS) and CB are designed so that biometric features are [2][3]:

- *Diverse* – Unable to be applied in multiple applications;
- *Reusable* – Reused/replaced in the event of compromise; and
- *Irreversible* – Computationally challenging to reconstruct the original biometric template, but simultaneously rudimentary to generate the protected biometric template.

Various approaches may be adopted when considering an implementation schema for biometric systems. However, one must consider the alternatives to an approach as to ensure that the chosen method is feasible. Thus, both BCS and CB are presented in order to gain an objective understanding.

BCSs are systems designed so that digital keys can be directly bound to a particular biometric [2]. One BCS approach is relevant to this particular study, namely biohashing, which implements a biometric key-generation. However, Rathgeb and Uhl [2] state that an implementation should not exist that directly generates keys from biometric templates. They elaborate that biometric features cannot provide sufficient information to reliably obtain lengthy and renewable keys without relying on helper data. Helper data is public information that is used within the key generation/retrieval process in a BCS [2]. This is useful to the study because helper data can be used to transform and obscure biometric information. Another approach to BCS is a biometric key-bind cryptosystem. This involves a secret key that relates to a biometric model by using helper data. To successfully implement this approach, facts regarding both the biometric model and the secret key may not be disclosed [6]. According to [2][7], implementation of key-binding cryptosystems can occur through a fuzzy commitment and a fuzzy vault. The concept of fuzzy incorporates the generation of helper data extracted from biometric features using a secrecy key. The abovementioned helper data, combined with the secrecy key are then both encrypted and stored in the database. In order to authenticate a user, the helper data then uses the model and biometric features to rebuild the key and match the generated template to the secure template [6]. Finally, if the templates match then the result will be positive and the user will gain access.

Having considered a BCS, one needs to weigh up the options regarding the possible approaches to cancelability and implementations thereof. Cancelability, too, has the sole purpose of ensuring computational challenges when attempting to retrieve/recover the original biometric data by a third party [2]. The focal point regarding cancelability remains that biometric characteristics should remain innately robust so that even when transform parameters are applied the biometric features do not lose value/individuality. Among individuality, by transforming biometrics one should ensure tolerance to intra-class variance so that the false rejection rate is not too high. Another important feature that cancelability has to offer is unlinkability [2]. This ensures that multiple transformed templates do not reveal any information relating to the original biometrics. In the unlikely event (assuming successful implementation) of data compromise, the transform parameters are simply altered, which simultaneously implies biometric template updates.

With regards to transforms within a CB implementation, two categories remain forthcoming, namely [2]:

- Non-invertible transforms; and
- Biometric salting.

The abovementioned approaches differ in performance, accuracy and security. Depending on the system that is to be implemented, a weighted feasibility analysis should be conducted on those particular factors in order to select the most suitable approach. These approaches are briefly discussed below.

1. Non-invertible transforms

This approach involves the use of a non-invertible function that is applied to the biometric template. By applying this function, stored templates can be updated when transform parameters are modified [2][8]. Therefore, security is increased due to the inability to reconstruct the biometric data even though transforms may have been compromised. With this advantage comes an equal and opposite disadvantage. A loss of accuracy and a performance decrease is the disadvantageous result thereof. This is due to transformed biometric templates becoming laborious in comparison processing, which ultimately provides fewer biometric results to process during matching (thus, influencing the accuracy thereof).

2. Biometric salting

Biometric salting commonly involves biometric template transforms that are preferred invertible as opposed to the non-invertible approach (abovementioned). The term *"salting"* refers to the act of merging specific data (such as passwords) with unique random values ("salt") in order to make all of the original data distinct [9]. In this particular context, this technique may be applicable when a 4-digit PIN is used as the salt to be combined with the hand geometry vector prior to hashing the combination of data. This means that regardless of what biometric feature vector is chosen, the biometric template extraction cannot be reconstructed to the original biometric template [2][7]. This commands that transform parameters have to remain private. Variations of the approach may appear if user-specific transforms are applied. However, this demands that each authentication attempt requires transform parameters, which may result in discrepancies if attackers successfully attain transform parameters. Ultimately, a decrease in performance is likely if the system implementation does not contain efficient biometric algorithms with high accuracy regarding private transform parameters. In contrast to non-invertible transforms, this approach maintains high recognition performance, however, the latter excels in terms of security [2][10].

According to Rathgeb and Uhl [2], even though it seems to be common to adopt non-invertible approaches to system implementation schemes, biometric salting seems superior. Not only does biometric salting increase performance, but in user-specific transform applications by incorporating two-factor authentication one can improve both security and accuracy.

To conclude this subsection, the aim is to combine the key-binding capabilities of a BCS with the biometric salting of CB. Once the user-specific biometric information has been transformed and is secure, it is ready for storage. In order to store this sensitive biometric information, rather than using a conventional database (due to its vulnerabilities, i.e., username/password exploits) a technique known as *steganography* was utilized.

B. Steganography

According to Kishor *et al.* [11], secret information is hidden using a type of communication, known as steganography. This is done through the use of multimedia files in cohesion with secret keys to embed information within these multimedia files. Steganography came about when it was realised that cryptography itself was incapable to securely transmit various forms of information across the Internet [12]. The word steganography can be translated from Greek into "covered writing" [13]. When hiding sensitive information, the information in question is typically concealed using an alternative format to that of its original. This is done through regeneration of data using multimedia formats. Some of these formats include text, image, audio and even video. For the purposes of this particular study, focus will be maintained upon image steganography and the shrouding of sensitive biometric information by means of bit encryption within the cover object (image). While cryptography disguises only the meaning of a message using code, steganography aims to hide the entire message from possible attackers [11][14].

The conventional flow of image steganography (as seen in Figure 1) follows a combination of encryption and decryption (just as cryptography does), but aims to use a confidential communication channel while secretly storing data and protecting the alteration of that data. Other applications that also make use of similar techniques, which are crucial to this particular study, include steganography as a conventional database alternative [13], and encryption method for user authentication data [15].

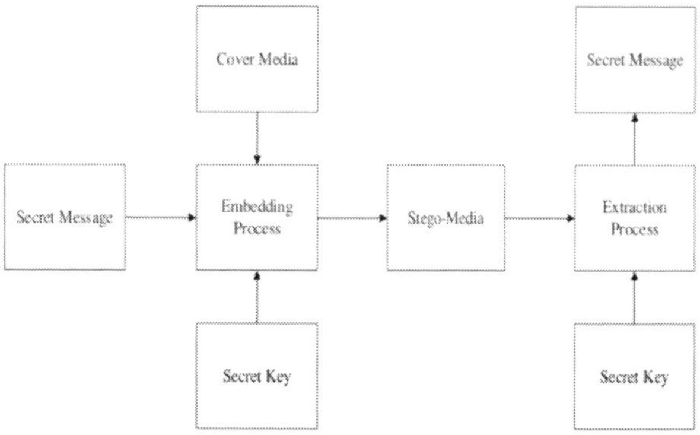

Figure 1. Conventional image steganography flow

In image steganography, both the encryption process and the decryption process involve the use of a cover image and a stego-image. In short, the difference between the two is merely that the stego-image contains the sensitive information, while the cover image can be seen as an empty data storage location for the sensitive information. In Figure 1, the steganography process requires sensitive information that is to be stored within the cover media (in this case, the image). This sensitive information is embedded into the image during the embedding process with the use of a secret key and a cover image to hide the information in. With the embedded information, the image is then referred to as the "*stego-image.*" The sensitive information can then only be extracted if the secret key is known.

Steganography can be implemented in various ways. However, the two major techniques that will be discussed regarding image steganography involve the following [4][14]:

- Spatial domain technique; and
- Transform domain technique.

The main difference between the two techniques is that when implementing a spatial domain steganography, the pixels within the image are directly manipulated. This is juxtaposed to the transform domain steganography that uses distinct transformations to allow image transformation in the transform domain and then only is the sensitive information stored with the image [14][16].

The purpose of modern steganography is to allow the host image protection so that the image itself, as well as the sensitive data it holds may not be recovered from the stego-image. By achieving this, the technique implemented is classified as irreversible steganography. The aforementioned objective is typically partnered with the ability to conceal sensitive information in a natural image in such a way that distortion of that image is minimal.

It is important to maintain that this particular study focusses on cancelable biometrics being stored using steganography techniques. This implies that the image may be distorted because even if an attacker manages to access the stego-image, he/she should not know what type of information is being stored, nor how to recover to biometrics after the transforms.

According to [12][14], steganography techniques are evaluated using various criteria. However, evaluation criteria that is relevant to this particular study are the following:

- *Hiding capacity* – This is the maximum amount of data that can be stored within an image with reference to bits per pixel (bpp). Comparatively speaking, a larger hiding capacity means the steganography technique is better.
- *Security Analysis* – The technique should be able to withstand attacks to the image that include any attempt to alter the image.
- *Robustness* – By being robust against attempts to attack the image statistically, as well as image manipulation attacks, the technique alone provides protection to the sensitive information hidden within the image.
- *Computational complexity* – With an algorithmic implementation, it is always important to take into consideration the time and space complexity.

An image can be seen as a two-dimensional function, where the $F(x, y)$ is the image pixels that can be represented as a grid. Each pixel contains ARGB (Alpha-Red-Green-Blue) values. Alpha values represent the pixel's opacity and RGB values represent a particular colour within the colour system. These ARGB values range from (0, 0, 0, 0) to (255, 255, 255, 255). To embed data, one can either store information sequentially or randomly among various image pixels using the $F(x, y)$ grid layout. By using sequential embedding of data one makes the data more susceptible to steganalysis detection by clustering the sensitive information within the image grid [17]. Randomly embedding data complicates the detection process by scattering the data using a random number sequence. The proposed system aims to use steganography techniques in the storage and obscuring of sensitive biometric information within (an) image(s) once the biometric information has been transformed using CB techniques. In the next subsection, the means by which biometric information will be extracted using an LMC as the biometric scanner will be discussed.

C. The leap motion controller

With the LMC's advanced hand and finger tracking capabilities, the position, velocity and orientation of all ten fingers, supplemented by hand geometry information, are reported upon with accuracy and reduced latency [8]. Chan *et al.* [5] presented the implementation of an LMC to assume the role of a biometric authentication device by harnessing the abovementioned information. The low-cost factor of this device makes this implementation even more favorable in situations where cost is of substantial concern. One drawback of this approach is that the LMC is a peripheral device that still requires a computer system to connect it to as the device cannot function in a stand-alone way. This disadvantage will add to the associated cost of implementation.

The LMC is able to scan a human hand at approximately 100 frames per second (FPS). With the use of an LMC it is possible to extract all finger/bone measurements of any given hand during a scan. Any given combination of these measurements should be unique to every person [5]. The infrared scanner is then able to capture metrics relating to the hand and/or bones within the hand. As seen in Figure 2, a model of the hand is then created based on the readings taken by the LMC.

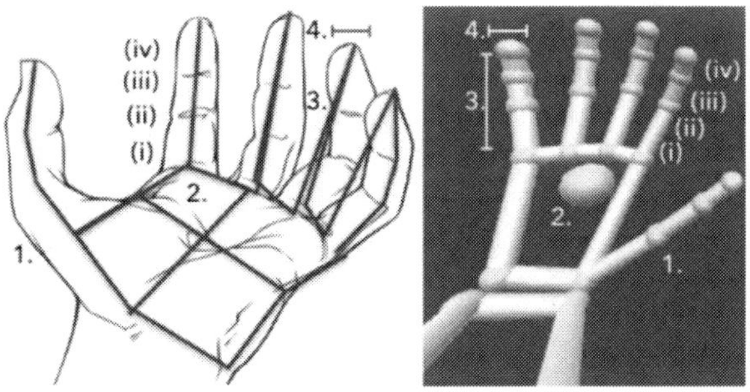

Figure 2. Example of LMC generated hand model

Information retrieved from the hand scans can be seen in Table I. The LMC is capable of acquiring numerous metrics relating to any presented hand. A combination of Figure 2 and Table I provides an overview of the metrics that are relevant to the proposed system. It must be stated that i-iv can be further explained as the acquired lengths and widths of each of these bones.

Table I. Relevant LMC readings

	Readings		Bone
1.	Left/Right (Hand)	(i)	Metacarpal
2.	Palm Width (Hand)	(ii)	Proximal
3.	Length (Fingers)	(iii)	Intermediate
4.	Width (Fingers)	(iv)	Distal

All of the above information becomes relevant when attempting to authenticate users based on their hand-geometry. Although the LMC maintains great accuracy when gathering information regarding to the presented hand, the readings tend to differ depending on the position of the hand in relation to the LMC device itself. The readings show minimal discrepancy; however, this could become an issue when statistically analysing the false acceptance rate and false rejection rate of the final authentication system [18].

While scanning the hand using an LMC one can vary the length of the scans to acquire a larger data set for each user reading during the enrolment and storage phase. This allows for the system to iterate through the hand and its 19 bones (four bones per finger, except for the intermediate bone, which is non-existent in the thumb) within the fingers and retrieve the lengths of each of those bones.

With the use of an LMC, features can be extracted from presented hands, transformed to implement CB and stored using steganography techniques. A proposed framework to implement such a system is discussed in the following section.

III. Proposed Framework

The prevailing architectures of biometric authentication systems consist of two main phases. These phases involve *enrolment* and *authentication*. The reason these two phases are required is so that during the authentication phase, the system has a biometric to compare to the biometric currently being presented to the system. This comparative biometric is typically referred to as a *biometric template*. During the enrolment phase, the biometric template is created for the user and then stored in a database. The manner within which the biometric template is created consists of several images being taken of the hand and then algorithmically extracting features from those images to create a final model for the specified user [19]. This entire enrolment phase can be simplified through the use of an LMC due to its ability to extract hand features from the internal LMC hand model that is created upon presentation of the hand. In order to comply with CB practices, this hand model has its features transformed mathematically, such that the original biometric information is not used in the transit/storage processes. The authentication phase simply compares the presented hands' extracted features to those of the models within the database. This authentication process would, therefore, also need to transform the presented biometrics in order to match it to the stored model.

Figure 3 represents the information (system structure) flow within the authentication system. The LMC initiates the information flow for the system when the hand is presented and immediately extracts features therefrom. Once the features are extracted, they can be transformed mathematically allowing for the enrolment phase to commence. In an attempt to further secure the biometric information, the decision was made to implement two-factor authentication. This is done by issuing a 4-digit PIN to each new user that is enrolled into the system. For implementation purposes, the use of 4-digit PINs allows for a maximum unique user capacity of nine thousand users (randomly generated and numbered from 1000 to 9999). The issued user PIN will determine where in the stego-image the biometric information is stored. By taking this approach, the system is then able to use two different images for storage (one for PINs and one for the biometrics).

In order to generate stego-images for sensitive information storage, one needs to specify exactly what images are made

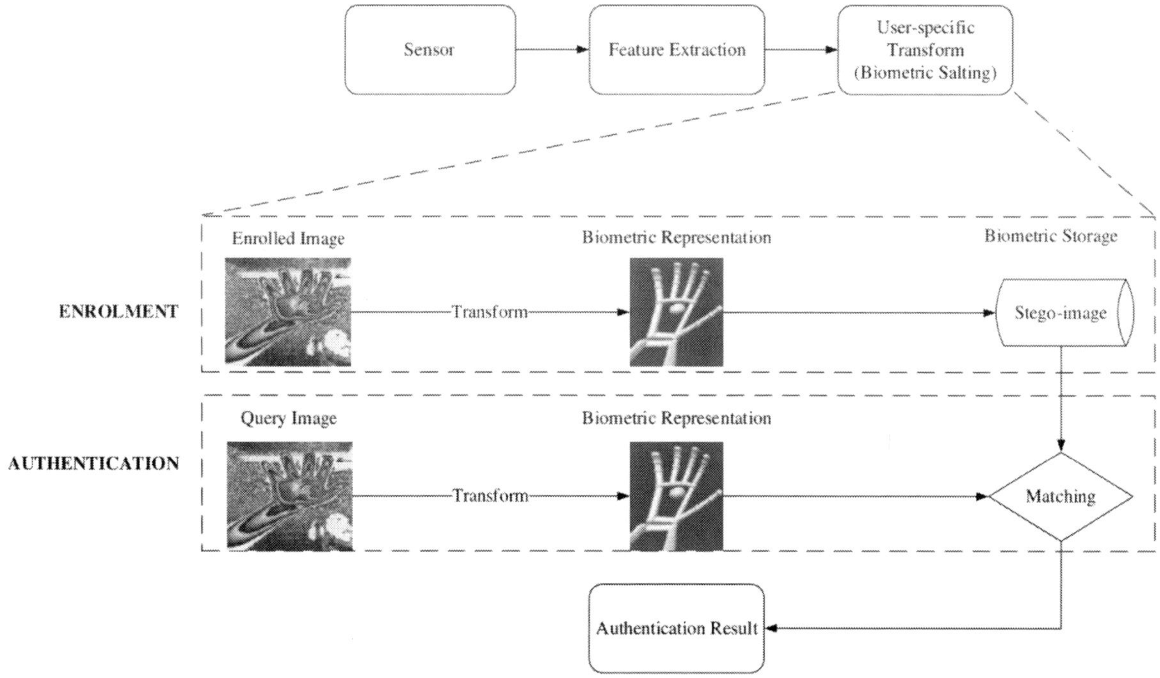

Figure 3. System structure flow diagram

up of, how they are processed and how to programmatically generate them.

A. *Stego-image contextualisation*

An image can be seen as a two-dimensional matrix that is made up of pixels containing information about the colours within each particular pixel. This pixel information can be used to store sensitive biometric information. Using steganography techniques to store the transformed biometric models in an image involves that in order to store these models, each models' bit-data would have to be processed. All electronic information is essentially made up of 1's and 0's (or bits). This means that the models that are generated need to be manipulated in such a manner that each user model's bit data can be extracted for processing thereof. Once this bit data is processed, it can then be stored within an image to correspond to a particular user.

With two-factor authentication being applied, both the PIN and the hand geometry need to be stored. Using one image to store the PIN, the system can then use the stored PIN to enrol/locate a user in a second image. This can be likened to a one-to-one relational database model. To illustrate this concept, Table II shows how PIN information in the first image can be used to correspond to the hand geometry stored in the second image. For instance, in the first block of Table II, the bold number (**1**) represents the user ID slot number while 3648 is the user PIN. The corresponding slot in the second stego-image is then used as the storage location for the user hand geometry data.

In order to standardize the amount of data that can be used to store information within the pixels, the system uses 32bpp (bits per pixel) image formatting. This ensures that within each pixel of the image, 32 bits of information can be held. These 32 bits are made up of A (8 bits), R (8 bits), G (8 bits), and B (8 bits) values. Due to the fact that the number of bits used to store a 4-digit PIN would vary depending on the value, it was decided to also standardize the number of bits used during PIN storage per user. To do so, a hash-function is used [20].

The hash-function ensures that regardless of what the PIN is, the length of the hash representation will be similar. A SHA256 (Secure Hashing Algorithm 256-bit) function was chosen. This is because it is the successor of SHA1, which was compromised [21], and addresses the issues prevalent in SHA1.

Each PIN is made up of 256-bits (8 pixels, if one pixel = 32bpp), leading to 8 pixels to store user their information within both images. Referring back to the earlier statement of using two images with a one-to-one relationship, a user PIN can be mapped and correlated directly to the hand geometry in the second image using the hash function prior to enrolling the user.

Table II is an example illustration of user ID slots in correlation to the image pixels with an image resolution of 80 X 5. The first image is used to store hashed user PINs.

To generate the stego-image, the PINs are shuffled to ensure that the PIN-ID combination is not sorted such that PIN 1000 is stored in the first 8 pixels using the ID slot 1 etc.

B. Random PIN generation

To counter the threat of reverse-engineering the generated PINs, a program was written that generated 9 000 (unsorted) unique 4-digit PINs and mapped each PIN to an ID that ranged from 1-9000. An example of such a mapping is demonstrated using Table II to illustrate that PIN 3648 correlates to the user ID of 1. With this information generated and stored locally, using a conversion to bit data, stego-image 1 was generated so that all of the hashed PINs were stored and mapped. Stego-image 1 will, thus, remain unaltered after it has been generated. Stego-image 2 can then be altered during the enrolment phase. This is further explained below.

C. Stego-image generation

Stego-image 2 is a randomly generated image that will be altered as users enrol into the system. During the enrolment phase, users will be issued a PIN. Depending on the PIN he/she receives, a user ID correlating to that PIN is known by the system. Once the system has calculated the user ID based on the PIN that was entered by the user, the pixels within stego-image 2 can be altered using the hashed hand geometry of the enrolling user. By altering stego-image 2 in this way using stego-image 1, the authentication phase become more efficient because the pixels containing the biometric information can be directly read due to the mapping. The authentication process would be inefficient if the system had to search through the entire image each time a user presented their hand. Since an image can be seen as a matrix with 9 000 users, the complexity to compare and authenticate the presented hand geometry to the image would be $O(n^2)$ each time.

In order to gain a better understanding of how the system operates, the pseudo-code for the system is discussed.

D. Pseudocode for system algorithm

Keeping in mind the abovementioned information flow, as well as the mapping and stego-image generation, this pseudo-code should verify the exact functioning of the authentication system.

The pseudo-code below (Algorithm 1) aims to provide an overview of what input is retrieved within the system and to clarify how the two phases of biometric systems are applied based on the input retrieved from the user. As seen above, if the user is enrolled, the system merely transforms the presented hand geometry and authenticates the user by comparing the transformed information to that stored in stego-image 2.

Algorithm 1: Pseudocode for system algorithm

```
Input: PIN, Biometric Features {handID (hID),
array[boneType (bT), boneWidth (bW), boneLength
(bL)]}

Output: User-specific HashID for Steganography

function cancelableTransform(PIN, array[]
fingerBoneInfo) returns HashID;
    If (PIN == hID) && (enrolled == true)
    Then
        handGeo = Transform(fingerBoneInfo);
        Authenticate(getPixels(map),handGeo);
    Else
        newUser = Transform(fingerBoneInfo);
        EnrolUser(PIN, newUser);
return HashID;
```

Table II. Stego-image 1: User IDs vs. their pixel correlation (10 IDs x 8 pixels per ID x 5 rows)

1, 3648	**2,** 7896	**3,** 5091	**4,** 4948	**5,** 3102	**6,** 7500	**7,** 1651	**8,** 6765	**9,** 6865	**10,** 7677
11, 5153	**12,** 1782	**13,** 2922	**14,** 2183	**15,** 1817	**16,** 6372	**17,** 1621	**18,** 8283	**19,** 2845	**20,** 6931
21, 2608	**22,** 3587	**23,** 6231	**24,** 5373	**25,** 3594	**26,** 1877	**27,** 3867	**28,** 1080	**29,** 2807	**30,** 6143
31, 7362	**32,** 4162	**33,** 8075	**34,** 8742	**35,** 7851	**36,** 3653	**37,** 8431	**38,** 4352	**39,** 1238	**40,** 2128
41, 7673	**42,** 2513	**43,** 8825	**44,** 5110	**45,** 5701	**46,** 6623	**47,** 5963	**48,** 1703	**49,** 3697	**50,** 2073

However, if the user has not been enrolled, he/she then is issued a PIN and the presented hand geometry is transformed and stored within stego-image 2, correlating to the issued PIN location.

Next, the advantages and disadvantages of the system will now be discussed.

E. Advantages/Disadvantages

The use of the current implementation of this authentication system has its advantages and disadvantages.

Advantages of the proposed system include:

- The low-cost factor;
- Ease of use and convenience;
- The security aspects are superior when compared to passwords because authentication is based on a combination of PIN and hand information that cannot be stolen or guessed; and
- Auditability in terms of being able to connect users to a specific event or activity.

The disadvantages include:

- The technology is still in its infancy and is not mature;
- While system performance for authentication is expected to be high for small organizations, it may pose a problem should more users need to be enrolled; and finally
- Error incidence due to changes in a person's hands due to injury, old age, or illness.

The following section will provide an illustrative example of the system.

IV. Illustrative Example

In this section, a simplified example of a user being authenticated is presented in order to provide a holistic view to the combination of the topics discussed in previous sections.

With each hand that is presented to the LMC a model is created that is either used for enrolment or for authentication. Assuming that the user-hand that is presented has already undergone enrolment, the LMC will create a model using a particular transform parameter to compare this model to the binary representation of the hand already stored within stego-image 2. By using the PIN that is entered prior to hand scanning, the system ensures that the users' transformed biometric representation can efficiently be compared to the newly transformed model. This is efficient because the system has mapped the PINs to pixel IDs, rather than having to search the entire image for the corresponding biometric representation.

Consider the explanation on the next page of the illustrative example shown in Figure 4.

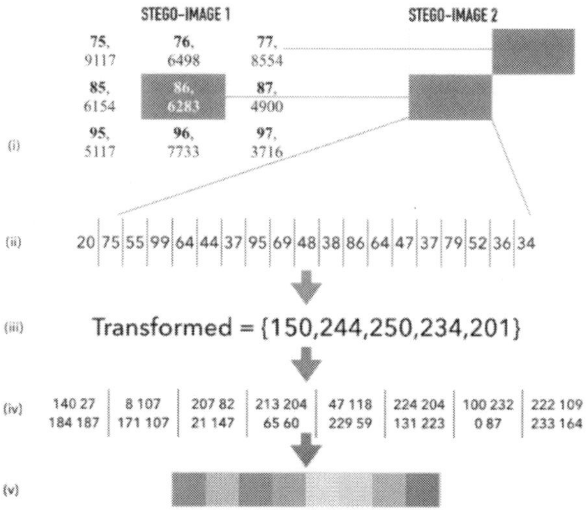

Figure 4. Example of biometric vector reading and transformation

(i) Assume the user was presented with the PIN **6283** during enrolment. The user would then have a dedicated storage section with the ID of **86** in both stego-image 1 and in stego-image 2. During the authentication phase the user will have his/her hand geometry scanned to compare the presented hand to the binary representation stored within stego-image 2.

(ii) During the abovementioned scan, the hand geometry of the user is mathematically generated by using various combinations from the thousands of readings gathered to form one vector (readings for each of the 19 individual bones in his/her hand).

(iii) By using the vector created in (ii), the system then transforms the biometric vector once more in order to implement CB (as discussed in Section II-A). In this particular example, the vector was simply transformed by adding each finger's bone readings together (3 readings for the thumb and 4 readings for all the other fingers). It should be noted that more complex mathematical transformations are recommended for the actual implementation.

(iv) The system further protects the biometric information by applying a SHA256 hash function to the vector. This vector is then represented as a byte array consisting of 32 values from the 256-bit hash function. Ultimately, this ensures that each user only uses 8 pixels within both the stego-images.

(v) Once the byte array has been generated, it can then be compared to the stored biometric representation within ID **86** consisting of 8 pixels.

Upon completion of the abovementioned process, the system will either accept the user as successfully authenticated, or the system will reject the user and ask for the hand to be re-scanned.

By using steganography techniques, the system ensures imperceptibility and cancelability. Figure 5 provides a comparative view of two generated images for their use in this context.

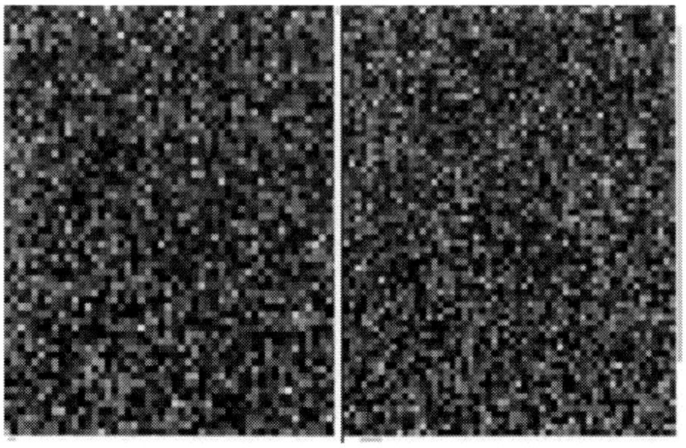

Figure 5. Randomly generated image versus stego-image

The image on the left was randomly generated, while the image on the right contains sensitive biometric information. To the human eye one cannot easily infer that these two images differ, however, upon closer inspection one may realize differing colour mappings but cannot differentiate between sensitive data and just another randomly generated image.

Ultimately, cancelability can be concluded due to the biometric information being transformed and obscured prior to storage. This means that should an attacker find these two images in a compromised system, he/she will not know what information was used to generate these images, nor how the information was transformed prior to storage. In fact, without prior knowledge he/she will not even know to expect hidden data in said images.

V. Evaluation and Discussion

In an attempt to quantify the performance of the proposed system, a threefold evaluation was instantiated and conducted. This is presented in terms of the consistency of the LMC, followed by a comparative vector tolerance analysis and finally, the overall system accuracy. Thereafter a discussion is presented. The following evaluation and discussion are based on sample data that was collected through the scanning (enrolment and authentication) of forty candidates.

A. *LMC performance evaluation*

To illustrate the efficiency and reliability of the LMC, the data that was collected from one randomly selected, five second hand geometry scan is presented in both Table III and Figure 6 below.

In order to present a visualisation with a high enough resolution to be able to see the variance in the scan readings, only the three fingers most similar in length are shown (i.e., the index, middle, and ring fingers).

Table III. Standard deviation of finger readings (mm)

Thumb	Index	Middle	Ring	Pinkie
0.197203783	0.424346553	0.464246258	0.438259197	0.35738522

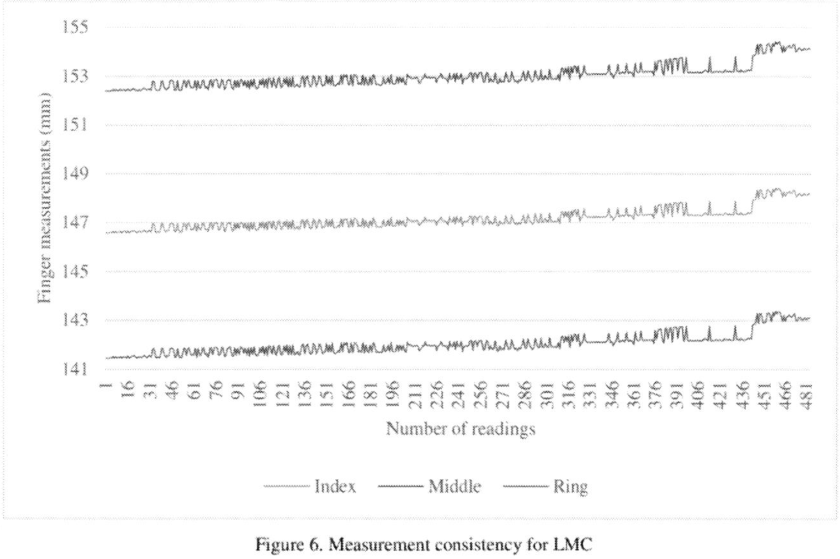

Figure 6. Measurement consistency for LMC

The significance of this data is prevalent when taking into consideration the distribution throughout the scan. It is of utmost importance to conistently extract concise data readings throughout the length of the scan. Thus, the standard deviation of the raw data correlating to the plotted data was calculated in an attempt to demonstrate the consistency that the LMC provides (see Table III).

It is interesting to note that the longer the scan has progressed, the more varied the readings become. This is attributed to the instability that is associated with an unsupported hand being held in mid-air for any given period of time.

B. Comparative vector tolerance

Despite the abovementioned LMC consistency, the system shows slight deviation from one scan to the next. To provide an explicit limit regarding the deviation of the readings during a scan, it was decided to measure a tolerance range.

The manner within which this tolerance range was calculated involves comparing test data from user enrolment scan to that of the associated authentication scan. This data includes all of the users and their transformed vector combinations. With this data, the maximum tolerance range was extrapolated based on the variations produced by the system. As seen in Figure 7 below, it was concluded that the maximum tolerance range for this data set is 5mm.

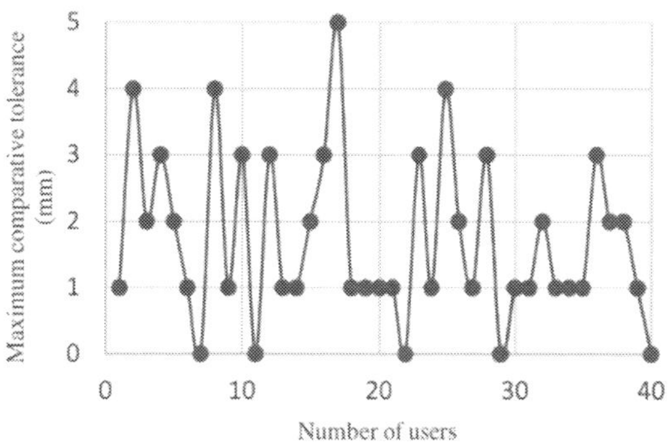

Figure 7. Maximum comparative tolerance levels

Upon further evaluation, with the tolerance range at a maximum of 5mm, the acceptance rates exponentially improved. This, however, increased the processing time to find a positive match within the tolerance range of the transformed vector.

C. Overall system evaluation

As deduced from Figure 8, a zero-tolerance rate resulted in only a 12.5% true acceptance rate. If this tolerance is then increased, the true acceptance rate also increases (e.g. 97.5% with a 4mm tolerance) until a 100% true acceptance rate is obtained at 5mm tolerance.

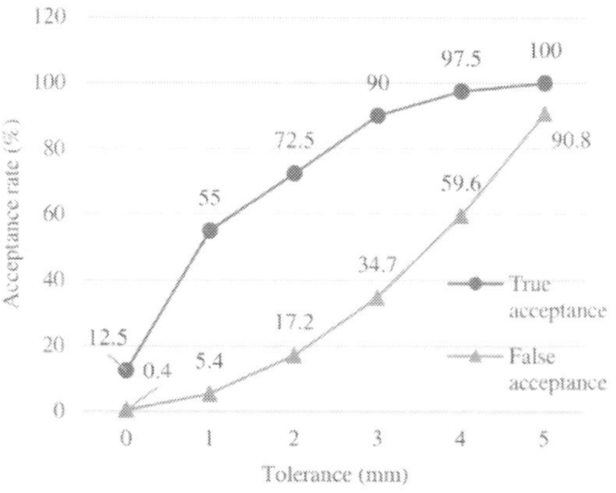

Figure 8. Acceptance rates based on dynamic tolerance range

When considering implementing this particular system approach, one needs to determine what risk factor is suitable within the authentication scenario. If the users that need to be authenticated are to be granted access to sensitive data/areas, then the tolerance range should be adjusted accordingly. The acceptance rate is drastically affected when using the maximum tolerance range. With such a high tolerance range, the false acceptance rate is also dramatically increased, but because of the two-factor authentication provided with the allocated PIN, the users are authenticated correctly.

D. Discussion

The proposed technique has revealed several promising advantages by using a combination of the techniques specified in Section II. The LMC was found to be a stable and efficient hand geometry scanner. Also, the steganography techniques used in this paper were relatively easy to implement for use in this particular instance. By using PINs (to implement two-factor authentication) the security is enhanced and aids in achieving cancelability for storing biometrics. The proposed framework ensured that the system provided results that were reliable and efficiently obtained.

Bearing in mind the abovementioned advantages, one must acknowledge some disadvantages are present when using this approach. This system was only exposed to limited testing and the authentication accuracy and robustness will need to be measured using a formal evaluation. In order to fully explore the system's functionality, one would have to extensively test the use of this framework on a larger scale. This will form part of the ongoing research.

VI. Conclusion

This paper presented the planning and development of a framework for a novel LMC hand-geometry authentication system that ensures the cancelability of biometric information by employing steganography techniques. The research presented favours authentication using intrinsic and distinctive traits of each system user's biometric information with multiple advantages over conventional password-based authentication systems. With the use of this novel approach the privacy concerns mentioned earlier are addressed by implementing CB techniques; paired with steganography techniques that have consistently been used to conceal sensitive information. The resulting stego-image generation and biometric storage process shows promising results in achieving biometric cancelability.

REFERENCES

[1] L. Shahim, D. P. Snyman, J. V. Du Toit, and H. A. Kruger, "Cost-Effective Biometric Authentication using Leap Motion and IoT Devices," *Secureware2016*, pp. 10–13, 2016.

[2] C. Rathgeb and A. Uhl, "A survey on biometric cryptosystems and cancelable biometrics," *EURASIP J. Inf. Secur.*, vol. 2011, no. 1, pp. 1–25, 2011.

[3] G. Verma and A. Sinha, "Digital holographic-based cancellable biometric for personal authentication," *J. Opt.*, vol. 18, no. 5, 2016.

[4] P. P. Paul and M. Gavrilova, "Multimodal Cancelable Biometrics," in *2012 IEEE 11th International Conference on Cognitive Informatics and Cognitive Computing*, 2012, pp. 43–49.

[5] A. Chan, T. Halevi, and N. Memon, "Leap Motion Controller for Authentication via Hand Geometry and Gestures," in *International Conference on Human Aspects of Information Security, Privacy, and Trust*, Springer Internation Publishing, 2015, pp. 13–22.

[6] P. Eng and S. B. Sadkhan, "Enhance Security of Cryptosystems," 2016.

[7] P. P. Paul, M. Gavrilova, and S. Klimenko, "Situation awareness of cancelable biometric system," *Vis. Comput.*, vol. 30, no. 9, pp. 1059–1067, 2014.

[8] E. Piciucco, E. Maiorana, C. Kauba, A. Uhl, and P. Campisi, "Cancelable biometrics for finger vein recognition," in *2016 First International Workshop on Sensing, Processing and Learning for Intelligent Machines (SPLINE)*, 2016, pp. 1–5.

[9] S. Syed Ahmad, B. Mohd Ali, and W. A. Wan Adnan, "Applications As Access Control Tools of Information Security," *Int. J. Innov. Comput. Inf. Control*, vol. 8, no. 11, pp. 7983–7999, 2012.

[10] N. Radha and S. Karthikeyan, "An evaluation of fingerprint security using noninvertible biohash," *Int. J. Netw. Secur. Its Appl.*, vol. 3, no. 4, 2011.

[11] S. N. Kishor, G. K. Ramaiah, and S. A. K. Jilani, "A review on steganography through multimedia.," in *Research Advances in Integrated Navigation Systems (RAINS), International Conference on*, 2016, pp. 1–6.

[12] R. Jain and J. Boaddh, "Advances in Digital Image Steganography," *Int. Conf. Innov. Challenges Cyber Secur.*, no. Iciccs, pp. 163–171, 2016.

[13] A. S. Pandit and S. R. Khope, "Review on Image Steganography," vol. 6, no. 5, pp. 6115–6117, 2016.

[14] A. Pradhan, A. K. Sahu, G. Swain, and K. R. Sekhar, "Performance Evaluation Parameters of Image Steganography Techniques," in *International Conference on Research Advances in Integrated Navigation Systems*, 2016.

[15] M. Dlamini, M. Eloff, J. Eloff, H. Venter, K. Chetty, and J. Blackledge, "Securing Cloud Computing ' s Blind -spots using Strong and Risk-based MFA," in *International Conference on Information Resource Management*, 2016, p. 58: 1-28.

[16] R. Roy and S. Changder, "Quality Evaluation of Image Steganography Techniques : A Heuristics based Approach," *Int. J. Secur. Its Appl.*, vol. 10, no. 4, pp. 179–196, 2016.

[17] S. A. Laskar and K. Hemachandran, "Steganography based on random pixel selection for efficient data hiding," *Int. J. Comput. Eng. Technol.*, vol. 4, no. 2, pp. 31–44, 2013.

[18] A. Nagar and A. K. Jain, "On the security of non-invertible fingerprint template transforms," in *Information Forensics and Security, 2009. WIFS 2009. First IEEE International Workshop.*, 2009, pp. 81–85.

[19] P. Varchol and D. Levický, "Using of hand geometry in biometric security systems," *Radioengineering*, vol. 16, no. 4, pp. 82–87, 2007.

[20] Y. Kashyap and R. Sharma, "A survey on various authentication attacks and database secure authentication techniques," *Int. J. Multidiscip. Educ. Res.*, vol. 5, no. 15, pp. 67–81, 2016.

[21] R. Brandom, "Google just cracked one of the building blocks of web encryption (but don't worry) - The Verge." [Online]. Available: https://www.theverge.com/2017/2/23/14712118/google-sha1-collision-broken-web-encryption-shattered. [Accessed: 27-Aug-2017].

Usability Enhancement on the Privacy-Preserving Online Monitoring Framework for E-Health Applications

Youna Jung and Minsoo Kim
Department of Computer and Information Sciences
Virginia Military Institute
Lexington, Virginia, United States
e-mail: {jungy, kimm}@vmi.edu

Abstract— **Many e-health applications are currently using online monitoring services to improve the accuracy and quality of services. Privacy concern is however one of the biggest obstacles in widespread adoption of e-health applications. To address the privacy issue on e-health applications, we have preliminarily developed the privacy-preserving online monitoring framework (PPoM) that enables healthcare providers and patients to specify their own privacy policies without professional knowledge and skills and enforces patients' privacy policies during monitoring in systematic manner. The prototype successfully protects patients' privacy against unwanted data disclosure but its complex user interfaces reduce the performance of the PPoM. In this paper, we describe how we improve the PPoM to address the usability issue and present the enhanced version of the PPoM.**

Keywords - Privacy; policy-based protection; online monitoring; framework; e-health; usability.

I. Introduction

User monitoring on e-health application is a controversial issue. In order to assess and improve the performance of e-health applications, monitoring is one of the essential techniques. It tracks and analyzes patients' online activities (e.g., mouse clicks, frequency of use, time spent in a particular page, media viewed, page navigation sequences, content entered into a textbox, location, whether a mobile device is being used, etc.) on e-health applications.

In case of e-health applications that often deal with sensitive information, however, the protection of user privacy is critical. Indiscriminate monitoring without control over the sharing of patients' sensitive data may cause serious privacy problems (i.e., private health data may be used for unwanted purposes and/or shared with unknown people) [1][2][3][4]. It is therefore urgent and critical to facilitate online monitoring without privacy loss.

To this end, we have preliminarily proposed the PPoM framework [5] and the Privacy Policy Language that complies with the Health Insurance Portability and Accountability Act (HIPAA) [6] for e-health Applications. The PPoM framework enables healthcare providers to collect necessary information without violation of patient's privacy preferences and HIPAA regulations by enforcing patients' privacy preferences on the user side, not application side. To realize the proposed idea, we developed a prototype [1].

The prototype benefits both healthcare providers and patients. For healthcare provides, it offers an intuitive way to describe privacy policies for their e-health applications, monitor patients' activities, and collect patients' data without serious privacy breach. At the same time, for patients, it provides a way to verify an application's compliance with HIPAA and policies that are mutually agreed with patients, and if necessary, rigorously protect patients' private data based on their preference on the user side. However, in the previous development in [1], we focused on the feasibility and the performance of the prototype and did not deeply concern its usability. The usability is a critical issue because the PPoM aims at non-IT patients and healthcare providers. To address the limitation, in this paper, we present an enhanced prototype having improved user interfaces (UIs) and describes Human-Computer Interaction (HCI) techniques that are used in this enhancement.

The rest of this paper is organized as follows. In Section II, our preliminary work on the PPoM is introduced and the enhanced development is described in Section III with details and examples. In Section IV, we present evaluation results and in Section V, describe our conclusion and future work.

II. Preliminary Work

The PPoM framework has been proposed to address the privacy issues on e-heath applications conducting online monitoring [5]. In this section, we briefly introduce our preliminary work on the PPoM. As shown in Fig. 1, the PPoM framework consists of four components: the *HIPAA Profile*, the *PPoM Service*, the *PPoM Browser*, and the *PPoM Tools* (PPoMT).

- *HIPAA Profile* [6] – It is a policy profile that enables both patients and e-health providers to specify a privacy policy related to health data and HIPAA regulations. It has been proposed to address the lack of considerations on health-related data of existing general-purpose policy languages (e.g., P3P [7], APPEL [8], and XPref [9]). All patients by law have a right to know if an e-health application is compliant with HIPAA and Service-Level Agreements (SLAs). To this end, they need to publish their privacy preferences on health data first. However, it is a herculean task for non-IT people to specify and verify privacy policies on health-related data using existing languages because in order to so, they have to create their own data schema for health data. To address the limitations of existing languages, the PPoM employees the *HIPAA Profile* [6] that provides the *Health* data schema and extensions to P3P.

The *Health* data schema, an addition to the existing P3P data schemas, aims to describe a patient's health status. It contains sixteen health terminologies that can be widely acceptable in a variety of e-health applications: *height, weight, hearing-acuity, visual-acuity, blood-type, blood-pressure, allergies, blood-sugar-level, cholesterol-level, family-medical-history, disease-history, disabilities, immunization-history, healthcare-providers, medication*, and *lab-tests*. By using the *Health* data schema, patients and healthcare providers can specify their privacy preferences on health data and HIPAA regulations. In addition, the *HIPAA Profile* also prevents us from having inconsistent schemas across different patients and e-health applications.

In addition to the *Health* data schema, the profile provides several extensions to P3P, which allows specifying HIPAA-friendly privacy policy. It is critical for healthcare providers to ensure full compliance with HIPAA regulations because HIPAA is the most stringent rules for privacy protection against indiscriminate disclosure of health data. To this end, e-health providers need a privacy policy language that deals with terminology and rules in HIPAA. Towards this end, the *HIPAA Profile* provides extensions to the POLICY element of P3P (represented as <POLICY>) [6].

- *PPoM Browser* – It is a user browser having the PPoM plugin. It protects patients' privacy, even if a patient is exposed to untrustworthy e-health applications that conduct indiscriminate monitoring in violation of a patient's privacy policies. To do so, the *PPoM Browser* understands a patient's privacy preferences, presents all user data being monitored, and blocks outgoing messages that contain data he/she does not want to disclose.

- *PPoMT* – It is a toolkit that helps non-IT healthcare providers develop PPoM-enabled applications. Although patient monitoring is essential, it is quite difficult for healthcare professionals to develop e-health applications conducting online monitoring based on application policies. To overcome the difficulty, the *PPoMT* provides several tools that enable them to specify application policies and convert existing applications into PPoM-enabled applications without professional IT knowledge and skills.

- *PPoM Service* – It is an online monitoring service that gathers only authorized user/usage data that users allow to monitor. By specifying user policies, patients can determine which data can be monitored. Then, the *PPoM Service* selectively collects user/usage data based on user policies. Unlike the existing monitoring services where user data are collected based on applications' preferences, the *PPoM Service* provides a way to refer user policies during online monitoring in a systematic manner, rather than simply presenting a written agreement.

In the PPoM, a healthcare provider first needs to upload the source code or enter the URL(s) of his/her e-health application to the PPoMT and then select objects to be monitored and the corresponding privacy policies through the user-friendly interfaces generated by the In-page Selector. The Privacy Policy Generator then creates the application's policies by analyzing selected monitoring data and policies, while the Application Converter produces updated source code by inserting monitoring code generated by the Monitoring Code Generator into the original source code. The provider then needs to deploy the generated application policies and updated source code in the application's server.

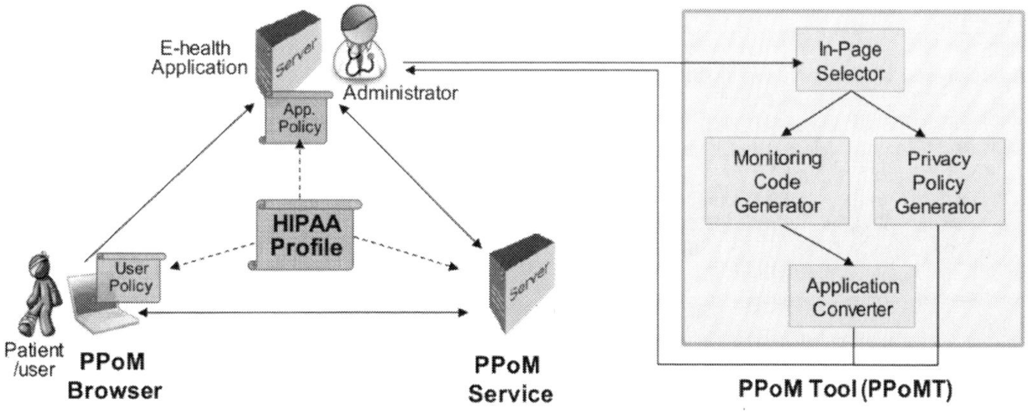

Figure 1. Overall Architecture of the PPoM Framework

When a patient enters a URL of e-health applications, his/her *PPoM Browser* compares user policies and application policies. If they match, the application server sends PPoM-enabled pages, which privacy-aware monitoring code is embed in. While the patient interacts with the application, the *PPoM Browser* displays all user/usage data being monitored so that the patient can verify privacy protection during online monitoring. The monitoring code inserted in webpages checks user policies prior to monitoring and collects only authorized user/usage. If any violation is suspected, the *PPoM Browser* will block outgoing messages to a monitoring server.

III. Enhancement on the PPoM Framework

To realize the proposed idea described above, we developed a prototype [1]. During our tests on the prototype, we found some usability issues. The usability is indeed a critical issue because the PPoM platform targets at non-IT users. In this section, we describe our improvement on each component of the PPoM in detail. Note that we developed the PPoM using PHP and JavaScript. We use PHP to develop the backend of the PPoM Browser and the *PPoMT* and JavaScript, HTML5, and CSS3 to develop the user interfaces (UIs). MySQL is used for a database of the *PPoM Service*.

A. *HIPAA Profile*

As mentioned above, the PPoM uses the *HIPAA Profile* to allow specifying privacy preference on data related to health and HIPAA regulations. To describe operations of each component in the PPoM, we use two examples of *HIPAA Profile* policy, a user policy shown in Fig. 2 and an application policy shown in Fig. 3. The examples are upgraded version of the previous examples in [6].

Fig. 2 shows an example of a patient's XPref policy specified using the *HIPAA Profile*. The user policy indicates that a patient allows a first party clinic to use his/her health data, except his/her *disability status* and *family history*, for a HIPAA-regulated retention period if the data collection is not for *telemarketing* purpose. This agreement is subject to an application's compliance with HIPAA regulations that stipulate healthcare providers must guarantee patients' access right.

```
<RULESET>
  <RULE behavior="block" condition="/POLICY[ACCESS/*
    [name(.) != "HIPAA-compliant-access"]
  <RULE behavior="block" condition="/POLICY/STATEMENT
    [PURPOSE/*[name(.) = "telemarketing"] or
    RECIPIENT/*[name(.) !="ours"] or
    RETENTION/*[name(.) !="HIPAA-compliant-retention"]]"/>
  <RULE behavior="block" condition="/POLICY/STATEMENT
    /DATA-GROUP/DATA [@ref="#health.disability" or
    @ref="#health.family-medical-history"/]
  <RULE behavior="request" condition= "true"/>
</RULESET>
```

Fig. 2. An example of a user policy specified using the HIPAA Profile

A sample application policy shown in Fig. 3 is generated for the *Daily Weight Tracker*, an e-health application that we developed as a testbed. The policy indicates that the tracker collects *weight*, *disability status*, *blood sugar level*, and *family medical history* of obese patients for the application's *healthcare operations* and *telemarketing* purposes. The collected health data will be disclosed to only the first party, the obese patient clinic that owns the online tracker. The clinic guarantees patients' right to access their health data and will retain monitoring data according to HIPAA regulations.

```
<POLICIES xmlns="http://www.w3.org/2002/01/P3Pv1">
 <POLICY discuri=http://dailyweighttracker.com/privacy.html
   name="policy">
   <ENTITY>
    <DATA-GROUP>
     <DATA ref="#business.contact-info.online.uri">
     http://dailyweighttracker.com/ </DATA>
     <DATA ref="#business.name"> Daily Weight Tracker
     </DATA>
    </DATA-GROUP>
   </ENTITY>
   <ACCESS> <HIPAA-compliant-access/> </ACCESS>
   <STATEMENT>
    <CONSEQUENCE>We collect health data of obese patients.
    </CONSEQUENCE>
    <PURPOSE> <healthcare-operation/> <telemarketing/>
    </PURPOSE>
    <RECIPIENT> <ours/> </RECIPIENT>
    <RETENTION> <HIPAA-compliant-retention/>
    </RETENTION>
    <DATA-GROUP>
     <DATA ref="#health.weight">
       <CATEGORIES> <health/> </CATEGORIES> </DATA>
     <DATA ref="#health.disabilities">
       <CATEGORIES> <health/> </CATEGORIES> </DATA>
     <DATA ref="#health.blood-sugar-level">
       <CATEGORIES> <health/> </CATEGORIES> </DATA>
     <DATA ref="#health.family-medical-history">
       <CATEGORIES> <health/> </CATEGORIES> </DATA>
    </DATA-GROUP>
   </STATEMENT>
 </POLICY>
</POLICIES>
```

Fig. 3. An example application policy specified using the HIPAA Profile

B. *PPoM Browser*

To protect user privacy, the *PPoM Browser* provides three ways to enable non-IT patients to: 1) specify users' privacy preferences on health data without knowledge about policy language, 2) check all usage and user data being monitored, and 3) block monitoring if a patient finds unwanted data disclosure.

First, a patient can generate user policies through user interfaces. The PPoM supports three levels of user policy: the *General Policies* (GP), the *Application-specific Policies* (AP), and the *Page-specific Policies* (PP). A *GP* describes a patient's general preference regarding data sharing and it must be applicable to all online applications. To define a *GP*, a patient needs to specify data types that a patient allows or disallows to be monitored across different applications. An *AP* is generated for a particular application and it affects all webpages in an application. Unlike *GP* and *AP* that describe preferences on data types, in a *PP*, we can describe privacy policies for designated web objects and values. A *PP* is applied to only a particular webpage of an application. To specify an *AP* or a *PP*, a patient needs to enter an application's url in a *PPoM Browser* as shown in Fig. 5. If two or more policies conflict, then the most specific policy takes precedence. Note that the prototype of the current version of the *PPoM Browser* only supports the *AP*s and the *PP*s.

As we can see in Fig. 4, the interface of the previous prototype displayed many buttons and colorful checkboxes in one page in order to receive a user's selection of data and policy. However, such complicated interface increases task complexity, and in turn, reduced the usability of the *PPoM Browser*. To address the usability issue, we improve the browser's interface using dynamic menus. According to the study of Stefan Leuthold et. al., dynamic menus significantly reduce task complexity and increase retention rates [10]. By leveraging the results of the study, the enhanced *PPoM Browser* displays a main menu and limited number of sub-menus, as shown in Fig. 5.

Figure 4. A complex UI of the previous PPoM Browser

The sub-menus displayed in a screen are dynamically determined depending on a user's current task and context. Fig. 5 shows a UI with five sub-menus (e.g., *Select All*, *Deselect All*, *Block Selected*, and *Allow Selected*), when a user clicks the *Block Selected* button on the main menu to select data to be protected. By using dynamic menus, the enhanced *PPoM browser* can provide more simple and intuitive interface.

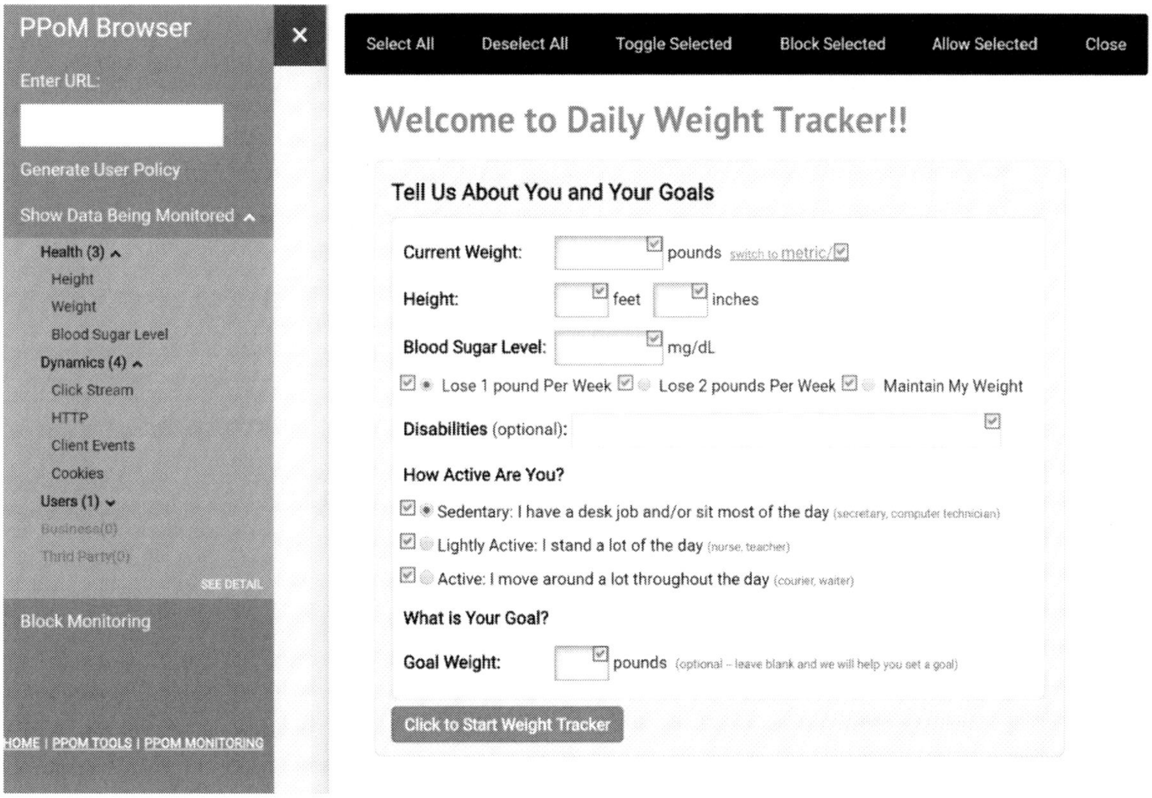

Figure 5. An improved user interface of the PPoM browser that uses dynamic menus

Second, the *PPoM Browser* displays all data being monitored when a patient uses an e-health application. Although a patient agrees to an application's policies, it is critical to verify the application's compliance with the mutually agreed SLA. To do so, a user needs to turn on the privacy-preserving mode by clicking the purple icon on the left top corner and select the *Show Data Being Monitored* menu. Then, a patient can easily figure out that what usage/user data are being monitored.

In the previous prototype, all monitoring data and recipients are displayed using different-colored checkmarks in one page as shown in Fig. 4. The *red* checkmarks mean that the data are protected and there is no recipient. The *orange* checkmarks mean that only the first party (for example, an e-health application that a patient is using) is receiving the data. The *green* checkmarks mean that third parties (for example, advertisement companies, payment companies, and other healthcare providers referred by the first party) are also receiving monitoring data. A summary of monitoring data, including not only general usage and user data defined in P3P and but also health-related data defined in the *HIPAA profile*, is displayed in the status bar.

a) PPoM Browser displaying no data

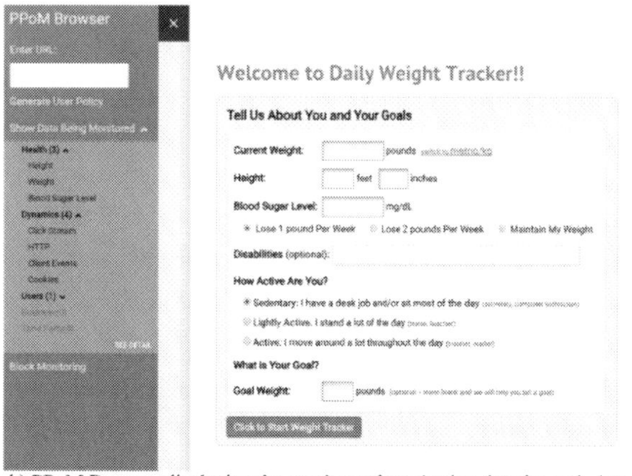

b) PPoM Browser displaying the numbers of monitoring data for each data schema (Health, Dynamics, User, Business, and Third Party)

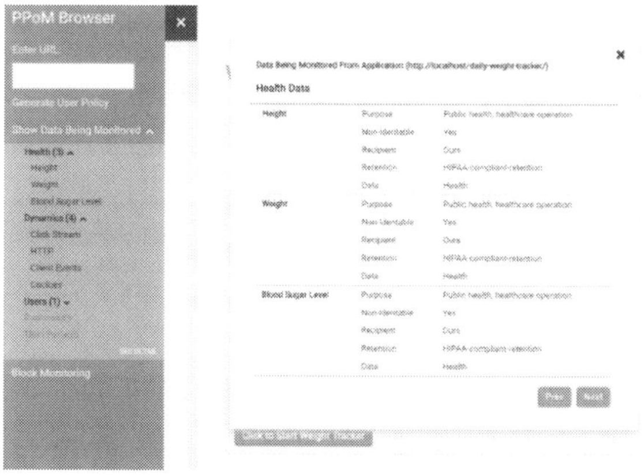

c) PPoM Browser disaplying all the data being monitored and its recipients

Figure 6. Three different levels of data display on the enhanced PPoM Browser

As pointed out above, however, displaying different types of information within a page may increase the task complexity and cause confusion to non-IT patients. Therefore, the enhanced browser only shows data that a user is interested in at that moment, rather than all the monitoring data. Fig. 6 (a) shows the enhanced browser's UI that does not display anything except the PPoM icon on the left top corner. If a patient does not want to see monitoring data, he/she can use the browser as an ordinary browser.

When a user needs to check data being monitored, clicks the icon and then the *Show Data being Monitored*. Then, the user can see the number of monitoring data for each data schema. If a user clicks on a particular schema, then specific data types are listed. Fig. 6 (b) indicates that three types of health data (*Height*, *Weight*, and *Blood Sugar Level*) are being monitored on that page. To check all monitoring data and recipients regardless of data schema at once, a user needs to click the *See Details*, and then a summary will be popped up, as shown in Fig. 6 (c).

Third, the *PPoM Browser* enables a patient to stop monitoring if he/she finds out fraud activities that are against the patient's preferences. To this end, a user needs to click the *Block Monitoring* in the main menu. Then, the browser renders all clickable web objects (e.g., buttons and objects handled by JavaScript click-event handler) and input HTML elements (e.g., textbox and checkbox), and creates checkboxes for each of them. By checking or unchecking the checkmarks, a patient can easily select data. At this time, a patient has multiple options for selecting objects: 1) select all clickable and input elements, 2) select all clickable elements, 3) select all input elements, 4) select an individual (clickable or input) element, or 5) select *None*. After selecting objects, the patient must decide whether or not to allow monitoring on those objects by clicking the *Allow Selected* button or the *Block Selected* button on the sub-menu.

To block monitoring, a *PPoM Browser* needs to generate and run JavaScript codes based on a patient's selection in real-time. Before explaining the blocking process further, let us assume that the main functionalities of an e-health application do not depend on JavaScript. To block online monitoring on a particular web element, a *PPoM Browser* disables JavaScript event handlers that are associated with the selected web elements, and in turn, a monitoring JavaScript using those handlers will be disabled. For example, if a patient selects the *Disabilities* textbox and clicks the *Block Selected* sub-menu. Then, the following JavaScript code is generated to disable the PPoM monitoring JavaScript on the *Disabilities* textbox (The ID of the textbox element is "DISABILITIESTXT"): `$("body").off("keyup keypress change click blur", "#DISABILITIESTXT")`. The generated code then removes five event handlers from 'DISABILITIESTXT' element by invoking jQuery `off` function. When the blocking code runs, none of monitoring services obtains data from that textbox.

C. PPoM Tools (PPoMT)

The *PPoMT* is a server-side toolkit that enables non-IT healthcare providers to generate application policies and monitoring codes for their own e-health applications, and in turn, upgrade their existing applications into a PPoM-enabled application, without professional skills on programming and policy languages.

As a feasibility study, we developed a prototype of *PPoMT* [1] but there was a usability issue due to high task complexity. In order to simplify user tasks, we adopt the UI design rules proposed by Shneiderman [11]. According to the rules, we use dynamic menus and breaks complicated tasks (e.g., data selection and policy specification) into several simple steps using sliders as shown in Fig. 7. The enhanced *PPoMT* shows a main menu on the left side and only if necessary, it presents sub-menus on the top. The detailed explanation for each component is below.

1) In-Page Selector

The *In-Page Selector* aims to show selectable HTML elements in webpages so that an administrator of an e-health application can select usage/user data to be monitored and policies corresponding to each web object, each page, or an entire application. Fig. 7 shows an example execution for the tracker setup page of the *Daily Weight Tracker* application. The selected data and policies are delivered to the *Privacy Policy Generator* and the *Monitoring Code Generator* for further processing.

2) Monitoring Code Generator

When receiving a set of data to be monitored and relevant policies, the *Monitoring Code Generator* produces privacy-aware monitoring codes for an e-health application. To this end, it first checks if each element selected has an ID. If not, it assigns a unique element ID and generates JavaScript code using the assigned ID. Depending on an application type, *static* or *dynamic*, ID generation processes are different.

A *static* application delivers the same HTML code stored in an application's server to all users' browsers, while a *dynamic* application dynamically generates HTML codes with different contents. If an e-health application is a *static* application, the *Monitoring Code Generator* assigns an absolute ID to an element. Let us assume that a webpage has several textboxes and its HTML code is shown in Fig. 8 (a).

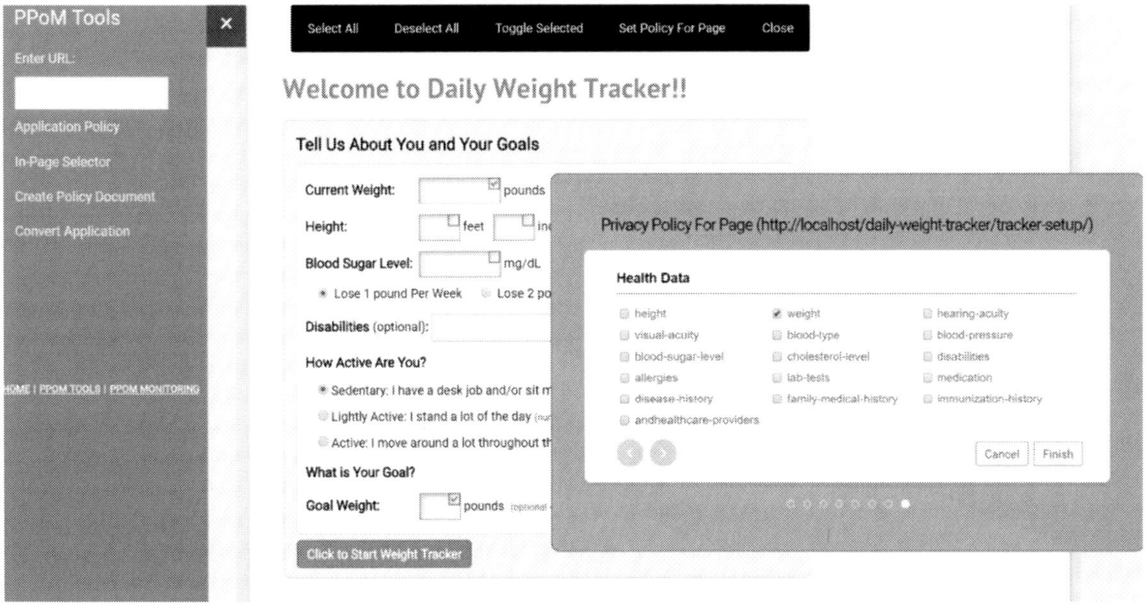

Figure 7. A screenshot of the enhnaced PPoMT (An administrator of the Daily Weight Tracker application is specifying a page policy for the Current Weight and the Goal Weight objects).

```
<body>
Current Weight:<input id="WEIGHT" type="text">lbs.
Height: <input type="text">feet
        <input type="text">inches
Blood Sugar Level: <input type="text"> mg/dL
......

<input id="BUTTON1" type="submit" value="Click to
Sart Weigt Tracker">
</body>
```

a) A code snippet of the tracker setup page shown in Fig. 6 (a)

```
<body>
Current Weight:
 <input id="WEIGHT" type="text"> lbs.
Height:
 <input id="PPOM-ELEMENT-0001" type="text"> feet
 <input id="PPOM-ELEMENT-0002" type="text">inches
Blood Sugar Level:
 <input id="PPOM-ELEMENT-0003" type="text"> mg/dL
......
<input id="button1" type="submit" value="Click to
Sart Weigt Tracker">
</body>
<script>
  $("#WEIGHT").change(function() {
     monitor($(this), "change");
  });
  $("#PPOM-ELEMENT-0001").change(function() {
     monitor($(this), "change");
  });
  $("#PPOM-ELEMENT-0002").change(function() {
     monitor($(this), "change");
  });
  $("#PPOM-ELEMENT-0003").change(function() {
     monitor($(this), "change");
  });
  ......
  $("#BUTTON1").click(function() {
     monitor($(this), "click");
  });
</script>
```

b) HTML code converted by the PPoMT in case of a static application

```
<script>
$("#WEIGHT").change(function()
  { monitor($(this), "change");});
$("input[type='text']:nth-of-type(2)").change(function()
  { monitor($(this), "change");});
$("input[type='text']:nth-of-type(3)").change(function()
  { monitor($(this), "change");});
$("input[type='text']:nth-of-type(4)").change(function()
  { monitor($(this), "change"); });
......
$("#BUTTON1").click(function()
 { monitor($(this), "click"); });
</script>
```

c) HTML code converted by the PPoMT in case of a dynamic application

Figure 8. An example of application conversion by inserting monitoring code generated by the Privacy Policy Generator into an exisitng application code.

In this example, the *Current Weight* textbox has its ID ("WEIGHT") but other three textboxes (e.g., the *feet*, the *inches*, and the *Blood Sugar Level* textboxes) do not have their IDs. If the webpage is a *static* page, then the *Monitoring Code Generator* automatically creates IDs for three textboxes. For example, "PPOM-ELEMENT-0001", "PPOM-ELEMENT-0002", and "PPOM-ELEMENT-0003" for the *feet*, the *inches*, and the *Blood Type* textbox, respectively. The generated monitoring code using the absolute IDs is shown in Fig. 8 (b).

On the other hand, if an application is a *dynamic* application, a path of an element from a root of a Document Object Model (DOM) object is used as a unique ID because an element's path is unique and unchangeable. As you can see in Fig. 8 (c), except the pre-defined ID of the *Current Weight* textbox, for other three textboxes that do not have IDs, their paths are used to identify each textbox. For example, "input[type=text]:nth-of-type(2)" and "input[type=text]:nth-of-type(3)" for the *feet* and *inches* of the *Height* textbox and "input[type='text']:nth-of-type(4)" for the *Blood Type* textbox. Note that the PPoMT uses the PPoM Service so privacy-aware monitoring script code is generated as default, but it is possible to use different monitoring services such as *Google Analytics*.

3) Privacy Policy Generator

The *Privacy Policy Generator* generates an application's policies using the *HIPAA Profile*. To do so, an administrator needs to enter a url of an application and click *Create Policy Document* on the main menu. Alternatively, he/she needs to click *Set Policy For Page* after *In-Page Selector*.

When an administrator selects a web element or a group of elements, a slider is overlapped as shown in Fig. 7 to allow him/her to specify a privacy policy about the selected element(s). Each slide in the slider focuses on one element of a policy (e.g., *Purpose*, *Non-Identifiable*, *Recipient*, *Retention*, *Data Category*, or *Data Type*). This approach significantly reduces task complexity compare to the previous *PPoMT* that displayed all child elements in one page. Such advance in UIs allows more simple and intuitive use of the PPoMT.

4) Application Converter

This component produces a PPoM-enabled application by inserting monitoring codes generated by the *Monitoring Code Generator* into DOM objects for each webpage in an application. A conversion process may be different depending on an application's type. In case of a *static* application, the *Application Converter* can generate the updated HTML code systematically. However, the *PPoMT* provides monitoring script code only if an application is a *dynamic* application. In that case, an administrator must insert the generated monitoring code into the server-side program manually.

D. PPoM Service

The *PPoM Service* provides APIs for privacy-aware monitoring to applications' administrators so that they can embed the APIs in the webpages of their applications. Note that the APIs enable them to specify the type of data to be monitored, including health-related data types defined in the *HIPAA Profile*. Once deployed in an e-health application, the APIs check a patient's user policies, not an application's policies, and collect data that the patient allows to disclose. It does not collect data if a patient prefers not to disclose it, even if a monitoring code is inserted in webpages. By doing so, the *PPoM Service* provides a way to protect a patient's privacy from indiscriminate monitoring.

Monitoring data contain general usage data (e.g., *device category*, *operating systems*, *event*, *time*, etc.) and user data including health data. All data collected are encoded in JavaScript Object Notation (JSON), a lightweight data interchange format, and sent by a patient's web browser to the *PPoM Service* server. The structure of a JSON monitoring data is shown in Fig. 9.

[ELEMENT_ID|ELEMENT_PATH] [EVENT_TYPE] [TIME] [DATA_TYPE] [DATA] [DEVICE_INFORMATION]

- *ELEMENT ID*: It is a unique ID of a HTML element.
- *ELEMENT_PATH*: In case of dynamic webpages, a path from the root element is used as an ID if an element does not have ID. The path is unique for each element.
- *EVENT_TYPE*: It denotes that a type of an event occurred. The set of event types are as follows: {*entering a page*, *leaving a page*, *clicking an element*, *filling an element*}.
- *TIME*: It denotes the occurring time of an event
- *DATA_TYPE*: It is a type of monitoring data and it must be specified based on the data types in the P3P data schema and the HIPAA Profile.
- *DATA*: It is an actual value of monitoring data.
- *DEVICE_INFORMATION*: It includes a device's *category*, *operating system*, *language*, and *browser information*.

Figure 9. The structure of a JSON object for monitoring data

```
<input id="bloodtype" type="text"
      data-type ="health.bloodtype"/>
```

a) HTML code for the Blood Type textbox

```
{"ELEMENT_ID": "bloodtype",
 "EVENT_TYPE": "TEXTINPUT",
 "TIME": "2016-07-15T12:45:07"
 "DATA_TYPE": "health.bloodtype",
 "DATA": "Type A",
 "DEVEICE_INFORMATION":
  { "DEVICE_CATEGORY":"DESKTOP","OS": "WINDOWS",
    "LANGUAGE": "ENGLISH","BROWSER": "FIREFOX"} }
```

b) JSON Object of the Raw Monitoring Data

Figure 10. Examples of monitoring data.

Let us assume that a patient enters "*A*" in the *Blood Type* textbox, which its HTML code is shown in Fig. 10 (a). Then, the monitoring data captured on that textbox is encoded a JSON object as shown in Fig. 10 (b). At this time, the values of *EVENT*, *TIME*, and *DEVICE_INFORMATION* are automatically collected by JavaScript's Built-in functions. Note that *blood type* is one of the health data type defined in the *Health* data schema.

To obtain monitoring data, the `monitor` JavaScript function presented in Fig. 11 (a) must be embedded in webpages of an e-health application prior to monitoring. When a target event is occurred, the `monitor` function captures monitoring data and creates a JSON object. To do so, the function gathers necessary information by using JavaScript built-in functions and properties. Then, it invokes the `jQuery.ajax` function to communicate with the server-side scripts (the `receiveData` function shown in Fig. 11 (b)). The `jQuery.ajax` function converts a JSON object into a string and sends it to the *PPoM Service* server through the HTTP POST method. When receiving a JSON string, the `receiveData` PHP module in the *PPoM Service* server converts the string into a JSON object and stores monitoring data in its database as shown in Fig. 12.

```
function monitor(object, event) {
  var monitoredData <= ID, EVENT_TYPE, TIME,
  DATA_TYPE, DATA, DEVICE_INFORMATION from the
  parameters object and event;
  jQuery.ajax({
     type: "post",
     url: "/PPoM/monitoring.php",
     data: JSON.stringify(monitoredData),
     contentType:"application/json; ",
     dataType: "json"                  });          }
```

a) JavaScript Function on the application side

```
function receiveData($monitoredData) {
  $object = json_decode($monitoredData);
  $link <= connection to database;
  $sql <= create INSERT query to store the
       monitored information ($object)
  mysqli_query($link, $sql);            }
```

b) PHP function in the PPoM service

Figure 11. Pseudo code of the PPoM Service that are used on both sides, the application side and the server side.

Time	Element ID	Element Path	Event Type	Data Type	Value	OS	Browser	Language
Wed Aug 09, 2017 12:26		body page_center_w page_center page_bg page_w page set7_w set7 FORM set7_sub UL LI:nth-child(1) DIV INPUT	TextInput	NUMBER	10	Windows	Chrome	en-US
Wed Aug 09, 2017 12:24		body page_center_w page_center page_bg page_w page set7_w set7 FORM set7_sub UL LI:nth-child(7) DIV INPUT	Select	NUMBER	2	Windows	Chrome	en-US
Wed Aug 09, 2017 12:12		body page_center_w page_center page_bg page_w page set7_w set7 FORM set7_sub UL LI:nth-child(3) INPUT:nth-child(4)	Select	NUMBER	0	Windows	Chrome	en-US
Wed Aug 09, 2017 12:12		body page_center_w page_center page_bg page_w page set7_w set7 FORM set7_sub UL LI:nth-child(3) INPUT:nth-child(2)	Select	NUMBER	2	Windows	Chrome	en-US
Wed Aug 09, 2017 12:12		body page_center_w page_center page_bg page_w page set7_w set7 FORM set7_sub UL LI:nth-child(1) DIV INPUT	TextInput	NUMBER	5	Windows	Chrome	en-US
Wed Aug 09, 2017 12:10	height	body page_center_w page_center page_bg page_w page set7_w set7 FORM set7_sub UL LI:nth-child(1) DIV INPUT	TextInput	NUMBER	4	Windows	Chrome	en-US
Wed Aug 09, 2017 12:10	height	body page_center_w page_center page_bg page_w page set7_w set7 FORM set7_sub UL LI:nth-child(7) INPUT	TextInput	NUMBER	5	Windows	Chrome	en-US
Wed Aug 09, 2017 12:10	weight1	body page_center_w page_center page_bg page_w page set7_w set7 FORM set7_sub UL LI:nth-child(7) INPUT	TextInput	NUMBER	100	Windows	Chrome	en-US
Wed Aug 09, 2017 12:10		body page_center_w page_center page_bg page_w page set7_w set7 FORM set7_sub UL LI:nth-child(7) INPUT	Select	NUMBER	2	Windows	Chrome	en-US
Wed Aug 09, 2017 12:10		body page_center_w page_center page_bg page_w page set7_w set7 FORM set7_sub UL LI:nth-child(3) INPUT:nth-child(4)	Select	NUMBER	0	Windows	Chrome	en-US

Figure 12. Example monitoring data stored in the database of the PPoM Service

IV. Evaluation Results

To test the performance of the prototype, we first develop two types of sample e-health applications that each has ten webpages containing different numbers of monitoring elements without IDs. As the first step, we evaluate the performance of the *PPoMT*, the *PPoM Browser*, and the *PPoM Service*, according to the evaluation plans described in [5].

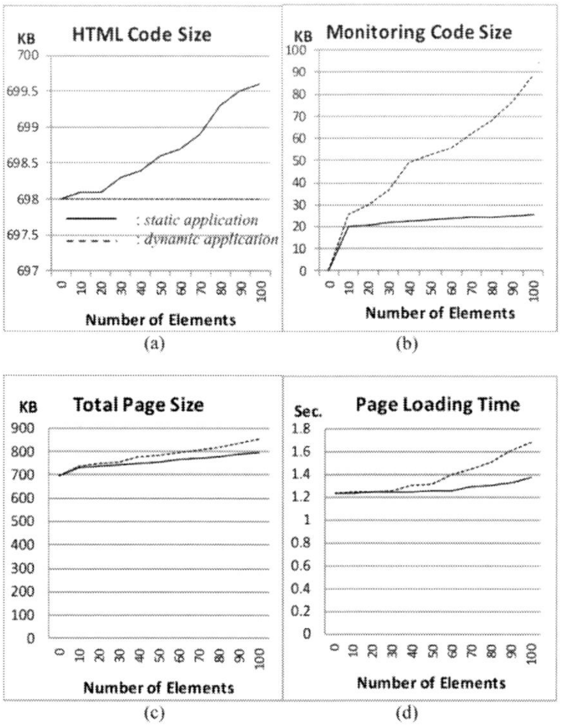

Figure 13. Evaluation Results.

As shown in Fig. 13, the size of HTML code that generated by the *Application Converter* for *dynamic* webpages is zero because the *PPoMT* will not generate HTML code for a *dynamic* application, while the size of code for *static* webpages increases linearly as the number of the monitoring elements increases (see Fig. 13 (a)).

In case of *static* webpages, the size of the generated monitoring code remains steady once it reaches a certain size, even though the number of monitoring elements increases linearly. However, the size of monitoring code for *dynamic* webpages linearly increases according to increase of the number of monitoring elements (see Fig. 13 (b)). This is because specifying paths from DOM root is costly, especially for complex web pages.

As you can see in Fig. 13 (c) and (d), in *static* webpages, the number of monitoring elements does not affect the size of converted webpages and the page loading time. However, in *dynamic* webpages, the increase in the number of monitoring elements affects the page loading time. If a *dynamic* page is complex, the loading delay becomes a big obstacle. It is one of our challenges to find out a way to minimize the loading delay caused on dynamic webpages.

To evaluate the privacy protection of the *PPoM Browser* and the *PPoM Service*, we generated five hundreds of different sets of patients' privacy preferences (i.e., allow or disallow monitoring on particular web elements) and user activities on a sample *static* application (i.e., navigating webpages, clicking buttons, or entering data in input elements). Using the sets of synthetic user policies and activities, we tested the privacy protection on the prototype. Towards this, we measured two factors: the *failure ratio* ($c/(a+c)$ in Table I) and the *successful blockade ratio* ($h/(g+h)$ in Table II).

TABLE I. FAILURE RATIO IN THE PPOM SERVICE

	Monitored	Not Monitored
Allowed	(a) 4,897	(b) 345
Not Allowed	(c) 0	(d) 3,477

TABLE II. SUCCESSFUL BLOCKADE RATIO IN THE PPOM BROWSER

	Sent	Blocked
Allowed	(e) 5,242	(f) 0
Not Allowed	(g) 0	(h) 3,477

The *failure ratio* evaluates privacy protection on the server side (the PPoM Service server) and the *successful blockade ratio* evaluates protection on the client side (the *PPoM Browser*). As shown in Table I and II, none of user/usage data that patients do not allow to be monitored was captured by the *PPoM Service* and none of the unauthorized data was sent from the *PPoM Browser*. However, as shown in Table II, we found some data loss in the *PPoM Service* server. The *PPoM Browser* sent 5,242 data ($a+b$), but the *PPoM Server* received only 4,897 data (a). It may be caused by heavy load of transactions or overheads for checking application policies and user policies. To figure out the source of the data loss, we will investigate the prototype's monitoring service in the future.

V. Conclusion

There is an urgent need for privacy protection on e-health applications. Although e-health applications can help people access healthcare service in an easy and convenient way at the reduced cost, many people hesitate to use e-health applications due to privacy concerns. To address the privacy issue, we have proposed the Privacy-Preserving online Monitoring framework, in short PPoM, and developed a prototype. In this paper, we address the usability issues on the previous prototype and describe improvements on our development with detailed examples. To achieve our ultimate goal, however, the following tasks must be completed in the future:

- A way to reduce data loss ratio on the *PPoM Service*.
- A method to reduce the size of the monitoring codes generated by the *PPoMT*, especially for dynamic applications.
- Usability test for the prototype
- Field test with actual patients and e-health applications.

REFERENCES

[1] M. Kim and Y. Jung, "A Development of Privacy-Preserving Monitoring System for e-Health Applications," Proc. the 5th international conference on global health challenges (Global Health 2016), IARIA, October, pp. 64-70, 2016.

[2] J. R. Mayer and J. C. Mitchell, "Third-Party Web Tracking: Policy and Technology," Proc. IEEE Symp. on Security and Privacy (SP '12), IEEE Press, pp. 413-427, 2012.

[3] M. Bilenko and M. Richardson, "Predictive client-side profiles for personalized advertising," Proc. ACM SIGKDD conf. on Knowledge discovery and data mining (KDD '11), ACM New York, pp. 413-421, 2011.

[4] A. McDonald and L. F. Cranor, "Beliefs and Behaviors: Internet Users' Understanding of Behavioral Advertising," TPRC 2010 Social Science Research Network (SSRN), August 16, pp. 1-31, 2010, Available from http://ssrn.com/abstract=1989092 [retrieved: 1 December, 2017].

[5] Y. Jung, "Toward Usable and Trustworthy Online Monitoring on e-health Applications," International Journal On Advances in Life Sciences, vol. 8, numbers 1 and 2, pp. 122-132, June, 2016

[6] Y. Jung and M. Kim, "HIPAA-Compliant Privacy Policy Language for e-health Applications," Proc. the 6th International Conference on Current and Future Trends of Information and Communication Technologies in Healthcare, Procedia Computer Science, Vol. 98, Elsevier, September 19-22, London, United Kingdom, pp. 283-289, 2016.

[7] P3P 1.1. http://www.w3.org/TR/P3P11/ [retrieved: 1 December, 2017].

[8] A P3P Preference Exchange Language (APPEL) version 1.0. https://www.w3.org/TR/P3P-preferences/ [retrieved: 1 December, 2017].

[9] R. Agrawal, J. Kiernan, R. Srikant, and Y. Xu, "An XPath-based preference language for P3P," Proc. the 12th international conference on World Wide Web (WWW '03), ACM, New York, pp. 629-639, 2003.

[10] S. Leuthold, P. Schmutz, J. A. Bargas-Avila, A. N. Tuch, and K. Opwis, "Vertical versus dynamic menus on the world wide web: Eye tracking study measuring the influence of menu design and task complexity on user performance and subjective preference," Comput. Hum. Behav. 27, 1, January, pp. 459-472, 2011.

[11] B. Shneiderman, "Designing the user interface: strategies for effective human-computer interaction," Pearson Education, India, 2010.

Creating and Configuring an Immutable Database for Secure Cloud Audit Trail and System Logging

Bob Duncan
Computing Science
University of Aberdeen
Aberdeen, UK
Email: bobduncan@abdn.ac.uk

Mark Whittington
Business School
University of Aberdeen
Aberdeen, UK
Email: mark.whittington@abdn.ac.uk

Abstract—**Conventional web based systems present a multiplicity of attack vectors and one of the main components, the database, is frequently configured incorrectly, frequently using default settings, thus leaving the system wide open to attack. Once a system has been attacked, valuable audit trail and system log data is usually deleted by the intruder to cover their tracks. Considering the average industry time between breach and discovery, there is often little or no forensic trail left to follow. While this presents a significant challenge to these conventional systems, when such a system uses cloud computing, the challenge increases considerably. In a conventional setting, the enterprise can use a robust firewall to afford some protection to enterprise users, however in a cloud setting, the enterprise firewall will not extend to external services, and a lot more people than are often considered can have access to cloud resources. Of equal importance is that in cloud settings, where new instances may be automatically spooled up and shut down to follow the demand curve, any data stored on the running instance before shut down will be irretrievably lost. We demonstrate how the configuration of a simple immutable database, running on a separate private system can go a long way to resolving this problem.**

***Index Terms*—Cloud security and privacy; immutable database; forensic trail.**

I. Introduction

Achieving information security is not a trivial process, and in the context of cloud computing, it becomes increasingly more difficult. Because cloud technology is enabled by the Internet, one of the key weaknesses comes from web services, which invariably are structured with a database back-end. There are a host of well understood vulnerabilities surrounding the usage of modern databases, and while there are a number of mitigating strategies that can be deployed, they seem not to be sufficient, as evidenced by their continual recurrence on annual security breach report lists. This failure to take even simple, inexpensive measures to try to mitigate the problem is tantamount to aiding and abetting the intruders. Invariably, once embedded in a system, the first goal of the intruder is usually to delete the forensic trail to eliminate all sign of their intrusion. Duncan and Whittington [1] proposed an interim solution to try to address this problem, and this paper extends that previous work.

Duncan and Whittington [2] have written about the difficulties surrounding proper audit of cloud based systems. They talked about the need for enterprises to maintain a proper audit trail in their systems, and about the weaknesses arising from poor configuration of databases, particularly in the context of cloud systems [3]. They have proposed addressing this problem through the use of an immutable database for the purpose of secure audit trail and system logging for cloud applications [4]. They used this approach to develop a proposal for using an immutable database system to log audit trail data and forensic system data [1]. The main idea here was to start with a simple, easy to configure system utilising existing technology to assist in resolving this challenging security requirement, with the intention of adapting the use of this idea to address the as yet unresolved issue of retaining cloud audit trail and forensic data.

As today's corporate enterprises evolve, there is an ever changing move to develop more and more complex software. This presents a considerable challenge in the development of ever more complex software systems, especially for configuration, because security has traditionally taken a back seat to the functionality of the software programmes. The vast majority of software and software development tools have their origin in a time when software security was not a major concern. Many of these pieces of software were developed when little thought was given to security. Before the internet took off, security was just a case of keeping the computer under lock and key. However, the internet changed all that in a big way. Anyone with access to the internet could then access any enterprise system connected to the internet, and with sufficient ingenuity, could gain access to poorly secured enterprise systems.

This is when poorly written software would come back to haunt enterprises. Few people thought about potential vulnerabilities in operating systems, or software systems — excepting potential attackers. A huge industry sprung up around finding vulnerabilities in operating systems and software systems that could be exploited. Many standards set for operating systems, software systems, systems such as email systems go back decades, back to the pre-internet days. By adding more and more complex software onto already vulnerable operating systems and software systems, the security problems are compounded. To this, we can add the lack of robustness of approach to analysing audit trail and server logs.

Some five years ago in 2012, Trustwave [5] were reporting an average time taken by enterprises of 6 months between breach and discovery. Discovery was often made by third parties external to the enterprise, rather than by the enterprise themselves. This time lag between breach and discovery has been reduced, but nevertheless remains a concern, particularly in the light of forthcoming legislation, such as the EU General Data Protection Regulation (GDPR) [6]. Looking at the latest security breach reports, the average time between breach and discovery is still in the range of several weeks to months, meaning that it is clear that many enterprises will be unable to comply with the requirement to report any breach within 72 hours. This would suggest that many firms are not monitoring their systems properly, do not maintain proper audit trails, thus leading to inadequacy in retaining a proper forensic trail to understand exactly what information has been accessed, modified or deleted.

Thus, we can see that many enterprises are adding ever more complex software on top of already weak and vulnerable systems, are often failing to analyse server logs properly, and are failing to effectively configure ever more complex systems securely, leading to an inability to understand when they have been breached.

In this paper, we outline how we might approach developing a solution to satisfy these issues and concerns. In Section II we provide some background and discuss the motivation for this work, and in Section III we discuss what an immutable database needs to be. In Section IV, where we outline how we can create and configure an immutable database using existing software, in this case we have chosen MySQL for illustrative purposes. In Section V, we discuss typical attack vectors against database systems. In Section VI, we explain the detailed mechanics of how to create and configure a secure immutable database server on which to host our proposed system. In Section VII, we discuss weaknesses, how to mitigate them, and how to move forward to provide further improved levels of security in order to minimise the possibility for attackers to succeed in any attack on this valuable resource. In Section VIII, we discuss our conclusions and future work.

II. Background and Motivation

In the early years of enterprise computing, a mainframe computer was used to process all the enterprise's information needs. Of course, this option was only open to the largest enterprises. As computer systems evolved, following the prediction of Moore's Law [7], this computing model also evolved, opening up more opportunities for ever smaller organisations to take advantage of the benefits offered by computerising their information and process systems. Once the internet arrived, opportunities increased significantly, but this brought with it additional exposure to the risks of poor security, traditionally an area given little thought.

Security practices started to evolve to try to keep up with this changing business environment, including the development of sophisticated enterprise firewalls. The development of new paradigms such as mobile computing, Bring Your Own Device (BYOD) and cloud computing, started to offer massive new opportunities, yet the increased risks associated with these practices were slow to be addressed. Assumptions such as that enterprise firewalls would protect all enterprise data, including on mobile computing, BYOD and cloud systems were erroneous. When cloud computing enabled the Internet of Things (IoT) and Big Data to gain huge traction, these erroneous assumptions continued, without considering the further increase in risks brought by the many inherent weaknesses introduced by this new technology.

As the business environment is constantly changing, so are corporate governance rules and this would clearly imply changing security measures are needed to keep up to date. Many managers are unable, unwilling or unsure of how to define proper security goals [8] [9] [10]. With more emphasis being placed on responsibility and accountability [10]–[14], social conscience [15]–[17], sustainability [18]–[22], resilience [23]–[29] ethics [17], [30]–[32] and Corporate Social Responsibility (CSR) [33]–[40], there is a need to consider more than the traditional security requirements of Confidentiality, Integrity and Availability (CIA).

Responsibility and accountability are, in effect, mechanisms we can use to help achieve all the other security goals. Since social conscience and ethics are very closely related, we can expand the traditional CIA triad to include sustainability, resilience and ethics (SRE) [41]. Thus expanding security requirements can not only help address some of the shortcomings of agency theory, but can also provide a perfect fit to stewardship theory. Stewardship carries a broader acceptance of responsibility than the self-interest embedded in agency. This breadth extends to encourage stewards to act in the interests of enterprise owners as well as society and the environment as a whole [42]. Broadening the definition of security goals provides a more effective means of achieving a successful cloud audit, although the additional complexity cloud brings will potentially complicate the audit trail.

A fundamental issue with anything cloud related is that while the software being used works well on their in-house systems, it will not necessarily be as secure when running on cloud, since enterprise firewalls will no longer provide the protection that enterprises traditionally relied on. Often, enterprises fail to realise just how many people may have access to their data in cloud based systems. While Cloud Service Providers (CSP)s often vet their staff to exacting standards, often their temporary staff providers do not. A favourite trick of attackers is to have one of their team be employed in a CSP's datacenter in order to have better access to many potential targets. Where a risk is identified, it can be quantified and properly addressed or mitigated. Whereas, an unrecognised risk can pose a very serious threat to an enterprise.

Often enterprises simply load their secure enterprise software onto cloud systems and assume they will still be secure. While the software may very well run in a functional way, the enterprise can not be assured that these systems will run securely. A major cloud issue which has yet to be resolved [43]–[45] is that once an attacker breaches a cloud system, there is nothing to stop them adjusting or deleting both the audit trail and the forensic trail of such systems. A less obvious weakness arises when systems are automatically scaled up, and down, to meet demand. Often, these systems assiduously collect server log data, including audit and forensic trail data, but fail to record this data securely elsewhere, meaning that as each instance is shut down to match falls in demand, these records are lost for ever [46].

In this paper, we use the MySQL relational database management system (RDBMS) to illustrate what is currently possible. While not all databases are identical, many exhibit similar weaknesses, often arising through improper configuration. In the next stage of our research, we will compare and test a number of SQL, NoSQL and NewSQL systems to gain a better understanding of how well each might perform for our purposes. MySQL, a RDBMS, has long been the most popular database globally, powering large scale websites such as Google, Facebook and Twitter, no doubt helped by its open source nature. The community is very well defined.

NoSQL, on the other hand, does not use SQL and can be considered a non-relational database, meaning it is table-less, the thought being it will be easier to manage. It also offers higher flexibility, newer data models, is mostly open source and low cost, offering scalability through support for Map Reduce, with no need for detailed database models. On the other hand, the community is not well defined, it is lacking in user tools, both for analysis and performance testing, and lacks standardization as well as not complying with Atomicity, Consistency, Isolation, and Durability (ACID), but instead relying on complying with **B**asically **A**vailable, **S**oft state, **E**ventual consistency (BASE). This is likely to be a major barrier to overcome when considering the importance of ACID compliance for both the audit and forensic trails.

NewSQL, on the other hand, tries to bridge the gap between SQL systems and NoSQL systems, offering to combine the ACID guarantees of SQL with the scalability and high performance of NoSQL. Again, being a relatively young technology, is suffers from many of the drawbacks of NoSQL, but does at least offer ACID compliance.

Clearly, there will be benefits and drawbacks in the case of each different database offering, and it will be necessary to clearly identify the specific details of which will offer the best utility for our purposes.

Often, the software environment chosen to integrate with the database is often subject to the same poor configuration, thus leading to the ongoing success of attackers. These weaknesses in configuration are frequently exploited by attackers, and there is often a poor understanding of how proper use of the audit trail can help to improve security significantly. Thus, we shall first discuss the purpose of audit and the significance of the audit trail.

A. Audit and the Audit Trail

There are many areas of business activity that merit diligent checking and verification by an objective person or organization from outside the organization itself. Some of these may be undertaken voluntarily by the firm, others such as the audit of financial systems and results are mandated. Clearly cloud computing audit is a new, immature field and it would be surprising if there were not lessons to learn from the experiences — and failures — of audit processes and practices that have been honed over decades if not centuries [47].

Whenever a new technical area emerges it will be difficult to find people with the appropriate skillset — a technical knowledge of the area and competency in carrying out an audit. As commercial organisations, audit firms may seek to extend their audit competence into new technical areas, not just cloud audit, but perhaps environmental audit as another example. Over a century of experience in the development of audit tools and practices then needs to be applied to a new technical domain. Alternatively, computing specialists might pick up an audit skillset. A logical outcome would be for audit firms to recruit computer cloud experts and seek to harmonise their skills with those of audit already embedded in the firm. The culture clash between accountants and cloud experts would be a potential side effect from such a strategy [1].

One tool the accountants have used for decades is the audit trail and this is a phrase already in the cloud computing literature by the National Institute of Standards and Technology (NIST) [48] for example. However, the same phrase may not carry the same meaning in both settings. Quoting from the Oxford English Dictionary (OED) [49]: "(a) Accounting: a means of verifying the detailed transactions underlying any item in an accounting record; (b) Computing: a record of the computing processes that have been applied to a particular set of source data, showing each stage of processing and allowing the original data to be reconstituted; a record of the transactions to which a database or a file has been subjected". So, disparity of definition is recognized by the OED.

Accountants are members of professional bodies (some national, some global) that limit membership to those who have passed exams and achieved sufficient breadth and length of experience that they are deemed worthy to represent the profession. Audit is a key feature of these exam syllabi and the tracing back to the source each accounting activity (the trail) is a foundational aspect of audit.

Whilst NIST [48] gave a clear explanation of an audit trail in a computing security setting and in keeping with the OED definition (b), the use of the term in research in cloud audit seems less precise and consistent. For example, Bernstein [50] sees the trail including: events, logs, and the analysis of these, whilst Chaula [51] gives a longer, more detailed list: raw data, analysis notes, preliminary development and analysis information, processes notes, and so on. Indeed, Pearson and Benameuer [52] accept that the attaining of consistent, meaningful audit trails in the cloud is a goal rather than reality. More worryingly Ko et al. [46] point out that it is quite possible for an audit trail to be deleted along with a cloud instance, meaning no record then remains to trace back, understand and hold users to account for their actions and Ko [53] then details the requirements for accountability. Indeed, the EU Article 29 Working Party [54] highlights poor audit trail processes as one of the security issues inadequately covered by existing principles.

Whilst the audit trail might seem a long and tedious list of activities and interventions, it can be of enormous value in chasing down the root of a cyber-attack, in much the same way as an accountant might use it to trace the steps and individuals involved in enabling an inappropriately authorised payment. At root, the concept should be implemented in a way that it ought even to enable the reconstruction of a system were it to have been completely deleted, not just trace an errant single transaction. The audit trail may be duplication, but it is necessary given the risk of manipulation, compromise or loss.

Our discussions with IT professionals, who have asserted their confident reliance on data backups, show a level of unmerited trust as an inappropriate intervention will be repeated in every backup until it is discovered. Backups of a corrupted system will not achieve a rebuild to an uncorrupted one — the audit trail gives this opportunity. Referring back to Ko et al. [46] establishing an excellent audit trail is worthless if it is only to be deleted along with a cloud instance. The establishment of an adequate audit trail often needs to be explicit as software frequently allows audit trails to be switched off in its settings.

Once an audit trail has been established, it contents need to be protected from any adjustment. As Anderson [55] points out, even system administrators must not have the power to modify it. Not only is this good practice even with well trained and ethical individuals, but it is always possible that a hacker might be able to attain administrator status. Therefore, the audit trail needs the establishment of an immutable database (i.e., one that only records new activities but never allows adjustment of previous ones). This is the primary goal of this first test for the successful development of a system to preserve both the audit trail and system logs. In the next section, we discuss the motivation for this work.

B. *Motivation*

Given how easily many enterprises unwittingly make life much easier for attackers, we are motivated to do something about it that should neither be expensive to implement, nor technically challenging. It is obvious from analysis of past successful attacks, that one of the key goals of the attacker is to attack both the audit trail and the system logs, in order to obfuscate, or delete all trace of their visit, and everything that they have done whilst inside the compromised system.

The lack of proper monitoring by enterprises, and the ease with which attackers can carry out this, important for them, exercise also makes it much harder for the enterprise to even know they have been breached, let alone understand what exactly has been read, modified, deleted, or ex-filtrated from their systems. Since this will form a cornerstone of the forthcoming EU GDPR, this requirement must be addressed.

Why should this be of concern? The EU GDPR has some serious teeth. Failure to report a breach within 72 hours will be a contravention, as will failure to take proper steps to protect data assets. There are serious penalties that can be enforced. A single data breach can result in a fine of up to the greater of €10 million or 2% of Global Turnover based on the previous year's accounts. Multiple breach elements can result in the fine increasing to the greater of €20 million or 4% of Global Turnover based on the previous year's accounts.

That is sure to catch the attention of enterprises, particularly in line with the current industry standard time between breach and discovery. Given that the enforcement date of the EU GDPR is 25th May 2018, and that enterprises have yet to get the time between breach and discovery down to hours, let alone days, this has to be concerning. Those enterprises who are UK based, will also have no respite, as the UK have agreed to implement the EU GDPR and continue with it after Brexit. Indeed, they propose additional changes to give users greater rights.

We strongly believe that enterprises must make provision to ensure the maintenance of both a proper audit trail, and the preservation of as much forensic evidence as possible. Users who do not, are effectively aiding and abetting attackers. For the reasons already discussed above, they must also take particular note of the need to preserve both audit trail data and systems log data when using the cloud. Thus we now take a look at one of the weakest links in this chain, the database.

The cloud paradigm is essentially web based technology, facilitated by a database back end. There are many well known web based vulnerabilities, yet it is clear from analysis of security breach reports, that many enterprises are continually failing to implement even the simplest of preventative measures to mitigate these weaknesses. In addition, it is also clear that many enterprises are failing to monitor their systems properly to detect breaches, given the disparity in time between breach and discovery. As far back as 2012, Verizon [56] highlighted the fact that discovery of security breaches often took weeks, months or even years before discovery, with most discovery being advised by external bodies, such as customers, financial institutions or fraud agencies. While improvements have been made in the intervening years, the situation is far from perfect.

It is also appropriate to consider the work done by the Open Web Application Security Project (OWASP), who carry out a survey around every 3 years in which they collate the number of vulnerabilities which have the greatest impact on enterprises globally. In TABLE I, we can see the top ten lists from 2017, 2013, 2010 and 2007:

Sitting at the top of the table for 2017, 2013, again for 2010, and in second place in 2007, we have injection attacks. It is very clear that enterprises are consistently failing to configure their database management systems properly. Injection attacks rely on mis-configured databases used in dynamic web service applications, which allow SQL, OS, or LDAP injection to occur when untrusted data is sent to an interpreter as part of a command or query. The attacker's hostile data can trick the interpreter into executing unintended commands or accessing data without proper authorization. This can lead to compromise, or deletion of data held in enterprise databases.

TABLE I. OWASP TOP TEN WEB VULNERABILITIES — 2017 - 2007 [57]

2017	2013	2010	2007	Threat
A1	A1	A1	A2	Injection Attacks
A2	A2	A3	A7	Broken Authentication and Session Management
A3	A3	A2	A1	Cross Site Scripting (XSS)
A4	A7	-	-	Missing Function Level Broken Access Control
A5	A5	A6	-	Security Misconfiguration
A6	A6	-	-	Sensitive Data Exposure
A7	-	-	-	Insufficient Attack Protection
A8	A8	A5	A5	Cross Site Request Forgery (CSRF)
A9	A9	-	-	Using Components with Known Vulnerabilities
A10	A10	-	-	Unprotected APIs

But injection attacks are not the only attacks which involve databases, numbers A3 and A8 in the 2017 column also are directly related to either missing input validation or output sanitation. Equally, databases might also be used in most of the other top ten vulnerabilities, which means database mis-configuration, failure to carry out proper input validation or failure to configure systems which use database systems properly account one way or another for most of the successful attacks.

Attackers continue to use methods which continue to work, which is clear to see from the continued success of the same attacks, year after year. Indeed the top three attacks have been around for over a decade. Thus, we consider this area to be of vital importance for ensuring that any enterprise may achieve a high level of security. And given the importance of the audit trail and system log data, we believe the best approach would be to use an immutable database to record this data properly, which we shall discuss in the next section.

III. WHAT IS AN IMMUTABLE DATABASE?

We can describe an immutable database as a secure database implementation capable of meeting the criteria for a proper audit trail, namely, that it should only be capable of being read by a restricted number of authorised users. It must not permit the editing of any transactions, and must not allow any transaction to be deleted. Only new records can be added, no modifications are permitted, and no deletions may take place, thus preserving the original input for subsequent examination.

There are many ways that we might approach developing an immutable database beyond the MySQL route. We could use new database technology such as NoSQL [58], [59] and NewSQL [60], or we could take the blockchain/bitcoin approach [61]–[63]. These approaches do show some promise, but are out of scope for this current paper, which concentrates on a pragmatic and simple approach. We do, however, include them for consideration in our future work as outlined in Section VIII.

Looking at the fundamental requirements of the audit trail in Section II-A, it is clear that a conventional database structure fails to deliver on a number of these requirements. A conventional database structure allows any records to be seen, by anyone authorised, or an attacker able to gain adequate credentials to do so. Worse, there is nothing to prevent modification, or deletion of these records. Thus a conventionally set up database is totally unsuitable for an audit trail. The same argument holds for system logs, which should have the same characteristics as an audit trail.

Thus, an audit trail and system log database must have the same characteristics as the manual system, namely restricted access to view the audit trail, with NO option to add, modify or delete records [3]. Naturally, in a cloud setting, as there may be anything from a single instance up to many thousands of instances running at any given time, it would be sensible to host the logging systems on a completely different server or servers at a location remote from the cloud instances, such that all the instances will have their audit trail and system logging data stored in the remote system. This can reduce the probability that a successful attack on the cloud instance can be leveraged to attack the logging database. Ideally, the logging server or servers should be dedicated entirely to running a secure immutable database, with preferably no direct means of public access.

We accept that this means that the logging database is likely to become a prime target for attack. Thus the logging database should be protected with the highest level of security settings, and should be subject to special monitoring to provide instant warning of any attack.

We made the decision that there would be insufficient time to consider writing bespoke software for our purposes. Thus we would restrict ourselves in this work to evaluating what we could do with an existing system. In [3], we observed that short of writing new bespoke database software, or making serious modifications to existing database software, we would be left with three options we could use to meet our objective:

1) Remove all user access for all users to modifying or deleting records and the database itself;
2) Remove the Modify Record and Delete Record command from the software;
3) Use an Archive Database.

In the next section, we examine the pros and cons of each option, in order to come up with the best practical solution to this problem.

IV. CREATING AN IMMUTABLE DATABASE

Having decided that we would not consider writing some bespoke software, but instead would see how we could configure something utilising existing software, we then evaluated the three options listed in Section III.

1) On the positive side, this option is the simplest to configure, does not involve any software modification, and will not impact on software updates. On the negative side, should an attacker gain access to the database and be able to escalate privileges, there would be nothing to prevent them from reversing the restrictions;
2) On the positive side, this option would take away the ability of an attacker, should they get in to the database

and be able to escalate privileges, to reverse the restrictions. On the negative side, this could complicate software updates;

3) On the positive side, this presents an extremely simple solution, no software needs modifying, and there is nothing for the attacker to reverse. On the negative side, the Archive Database does not support key searching. This is likely to make searches cumbersome. However, in the short term, we could resolve this issue by extracting a copy of all the data into a conventional database with full key search capabilities for rapid examination.

Thus, we took the view that for the purposes of this work, we would use option 3, using the Archive Database option, in order to create the system logging and audit trail databases. We assume the application database will run using conventional settings, although it is important to take account of the following four weaknesses in conventional systems.

First, default logging options can result in insufficient data being collected for the audit trail. Second, since there is often a lack of recognition that the audit trail data can be accessed by a malicious user gaining root privileges, we recommend the audit trail and system logs should be sent to the external immutable database, set up using the Archive Database configuration, for this purpose. Third, failure to ensure log data is properly collected and moved to permanent storage can lead to loss of audit trail data, either when an instance is shut down, or when it is compromised. Sending all audit trail and system log data to the external immutable database/s will ensure that the data will not be lost when the instance is closed down. Fourth, the recommended mitigation techniques suggested by OWASP should be implemented in the main web application software.

Now, we consider the minimum audit trail data we would wish to collect. MySQL offers the following audit trail options:

- Error log — Problems encountered starting, running, or stopping mysqld;
- General query log — Established client connections and statements received from clients;
- Binary log — Statements that change data (also used for replication);
- Relay log — Data changes received from a replication master server;
- Slow query log — Queries that took more than long_query_time seconds to execute;
- DDL log (metadata log) — Metadata operations performed by Data Definition Language (DDL) statements.

By default, no logs are enabled, except the error log on Windows. Some versions of Linux send the Error log to syslog. Thus for a straightforward implementation, we would wish to collect the Error Log, the General query log, the Binary log and the Slow query log. Where replication is in use, adding the Relay log is recommended. Where DDL statements are used, then the DDL log should also be activated.

While Oracle offer an audit plugin for Enterprise (paid) editions of MySQL, which allows a range of events to be logged, by default most are not enabled. The MariaDB company, whose author originally wrote MySQL, have their own open source audit plug-in, and offer a version suitable for MySQL. It has the following functionality:

- CONNECTION — Logs connects, disconnects and failed connects (including the error code);
- QUERY — Queries issued and their results (in plain text), including failed queries due to syntax or permission errors;
- TABLE — Which tables were affected by query execution;
- QUERY_DDL — Works as the 'QUERY' value, but filters only DDL-type queries (CREATE, ALTER, etc);
- QUERY_DML — Works as the 'QUERY' value, but filters only Data Manipulation Language (DML) DML-type queries (INSERT, UPDATE, etc.).

Where an enterprise falls under the provisions of the new EU GDPR regulations, using the MariaDB audit trail plug-in and turning on ALL 5 logging options would be a prudent move. Admittedly this would require a considerable increase in storage requirements for the log output. However, since they would then be in a position to provide full disclosure to the regulator of all records accessed, tampered with or deleted, this would go a very long way to mitigate the amount of fine they might be subject to, which could be as high as 4% of their global turnover.

Thus, this approach will address the first problem, that of insufficient audit trail and system logging data being collected. If the data is sent to a well protected external database, an attacker who has compromised the running instance will not be able to cover their trail. The system logs could be retained on the instance to make the attacker think that they have covered their tracks. Thus, the second point is addressed. By sending a copy of all log data to the secure immutable database, we can address the third point, thus ensuring no data is lost on shut down of the instance. Finally, if the OWASP mitigation techniques are used to harden the web application, there will be less likelihood of a successful breach taking place. Plus the immutable database on the secure external server satisfies the requirements of a proper audit trail [55].

There is also no doubt that adding an Intrusion Detection system (IDS) is also a useful additional precaution to take, and again, this should be run on an independent secure server under the control of the cloud user.

Equally, where the MySQL instance forms part of a LAMP server, then it would also be prudent to make some elementary security changes to the setup of the Linux operating system, the Apache web server, and to harden the PHP installation.

There is one additional task that would be very worthwhile. That is to set up an additional control instance to monitor every new instance added to the application, which regularly checks whether the instance is still functioning as expected. This would allow this system to warn of instances unexpectedly being closed down, which might be a sign of an attack. In addition, the log files in the immutable database could be monitored for specific patterns, which might indicate the possibility of an attack.

One of the biggest issues is the fact that there is such a lag between breach and discovery, and this approach could provide much earlier warning of such an event. However, of greater interest, is the fact that a full forensic trail would be instantly available for immediate investigation. And it would be possible to disclose the extent of the breach well within the required disclosure time of 72 hours from the time of breach to disclosure.

As we see from [64], see Figure 1, that in 2015, 75% of breaches happened within days, yet only 25% of discoveries are actually made within the same time-frame. This still leaves a large gap where compromised systems may still be under the control of malicious users. Our proposed approach would go some way to reducing this problem.

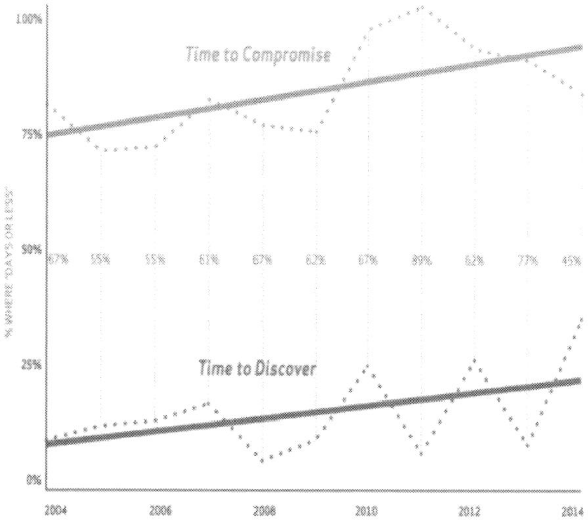

Fig. 1. The Lag Between Breach and Discovery © 2015 Verizon

This presents a clear indication that very few firms are actually scrutinising their server logs. We take a quick look at some typical database attacks and possible mitigation for these attacks in the next section.

V. Typical Database Attack Methodologies

SQL injection attacks are relatively straightforward to defend against. OWASP provide an SQL injection prevention cheat sheet [65], in which they suggest a number of defences:

- Use of Prepared Statements (Parameterized Queries);
- Use of Stored Procedures;
- Escaping all User Supplied Input;

They also suggest that enterprises should enforce least privilege and perform white list input validation as useful additional precautions to take.

For operating system injection flaws, they also have a cheat sheet [66], which suggests that LDAP injection attacks are common due to two factors, namely the lack of safer, parameterized LDAP query interfaces, and the widespread use of LDAP to authenticate users to systems. Their recommendations for suitable defences are:

- Rule 1 Perform proper input validation;
- Rule 2 Use a safe API;
- Rule 3 Contextually escape user data.

And for LDAP system injection flaws, their cheat sheet [67] recommends the following injection prevention rules:

- Defence Option 1: Escape all variables using the right LDAP encoding function;
- Defence Option 2: Use Frameworks that Automatically Protect from LDAP Injection.

These preventative measures suggested by OWASP are not particularly difficult to implement, yet judging by the recurring success of these simple attacks year after year after year, enterprises are clearly failing to take even the simplest of actions to protect themselves against them.

In addition to making the simple suggestions we propose above, cloud users should also make sure they actually review the audit trail logs. IF you do not review the logs, how will you know whether you have been breached? It is vital to be able to understand when a security breach has occurred, and exactly which records have been accessed, compromised or stolen. While we recognise that this is not a foolproof method of achieving cloud security, it is likely to present a far higher level of affordable, achievable security than many enterprises currently achieve.

Implementing these suggestions will not guarantee security, but will make life so much more difficult for the attacker that they are more likely to move on to easier 'low hanging fruit' elsewhere. There is currently an abundance of other options for them to choose from.

However, the enterprise must remain vigilant at all times. It would be prudent to subscribe to security feeds, and follow leaders in the field to ensure they remain aware of all the latest security vulnerabilities and exploits. Of course, enterprises must realise that the threat environment is not restricted to outside parties alone. A greater concern is the threat posed by malicious internal actors, which can be even more serious where they act in concert with outside parties. This presents one of the most serious weaknesses to the security of an enterprise. Equally, laziness on the part of staff or lack of knowledge, particularly where they have not been regularly trained to provide them with full awareness of all the latest threats, including social engineering attacks, and the consequence of falling victim to them, can also pose an extremely serious risk to enterprise security.

In the event of a security breach, not if, but rather when it happens, it may be necessary to conduct a forensic examination to establish how the enterprise defences were breached. With traditional distributed systems, there is usually something for the forensic computer scientists to find, somewhere in the system. They are completely accustomed to dealing with being able to find only partial traces of events, from which they can build a forensic picture of the breach. This becomes more problematic the longer the time between breach and discovery.

However, once an enterprise adopts cloud use, this becomes far more problematic. While forensic computer scientists can work wonders with a range of partial discoveries, deleted or otherwise, once a cloud instance is shut down, there is virtually zero chance of regaining access to the shut down system. The disk space used by that system could be re-used, literally within seconds, and where the time interval between breach and discovery is considerably longer, as is generally the norm, then this opportunity becomes a physical impossibility. Thus, for forensic purposes, enterprises need to pay far more attention to what is actually going on in the cloud.

The suggestions we make can go a long way to providing a greater level of security, and perhaps more importantly, can ensure there is actually a forensic trail to follow in the event of a breach.

VI. Creating and Configuring Securely an Immutable Database System

From Section IV, we can see how to create an immutable database. We do not want to install this in the same cloud system we are trying to protect, as this would leave the immutable database open to direct attack by the successful intruder. Rather, we would wish to place this into a dedicated server, preferably installed in a secure system under the control of the enterprise. However, in some circumstances, it may be necessary to run the immutable database in a cloud system, and in this case, we strenuously recommend that a different CSP is chosen. Our preference is, of course, for an in-house dedicated secure server, so we shall start by outlining the requirements for that system first. Later in this section, we will consider what special measures might need to be taken for setting up this system in a cloud environment, and we finish off with a comparison between the two options.

A. *The In-House Secure Server*

This server should be placed behind the enterprise firewall and an Intrusion Detection System (IDS). There should be no direct external web access to this system. There should be no external login to a shell allowed to this system. It is necessary to remove as many toys as possible from the attacker to limit the scope for attack. Clearly, once the attacker discovers the presence of this system, it is likely to become a prime target for attack. Thus we must remove as many routes in as we possibly can to this system. Direct web access is an attacker's dream. Removing this option makes life far more difficult for the attacker, and that is precisely what we want to achieve.

This server should have no wireless components attached, especially for connection to the network, as wireless can be readily subject to attack. For a paranoid approach, the server can be placed inside a locked room, with keyboard, video screen and mouse removed from the server and stored in a locked cabinet installed for the purpose, meaning it will then be physically impossible to interact with the server. The key should not then be available to the system administrator for this server. Only collected data from the cloud source will be allowed in through the hard wired internet connection. The bandwidth and speed of this connection will have to be more than adequate to service the projected needs of the required data flow. Also, the server will require to have sufficient performance and permanent storage for the collected data that will require to be stored over time.

When installing the operating system for this server, the operating system software must be analysed and ALL unneeded software should be removed. Similarly, only the immutable database software should be installed, with no other software installed on this system. All open ports must be closed, both on the server and on the network configuration. The immutable database server systems administrator should not be granted any privileges on the immutable database. The administrator for the immutable database should not be granted root access for the immutable database either. Once the immutable database has been set up by a user who is granted root privilege through a dongle to be inserted solely for that purpose, the dongle and the access credentials should also be securely locked away in the secure cabinet. Access to the cabinet should be through two members of senior management, with their keys securely stored elsewhere. In Unix based systems, Cron is a time-based job scheduler in an operating system, designed to carry out specific tasks at specific times. The Cron can handle a multiplicity of commands (or shell scripts) over time, thus ensuring the right tasks are carried out at the right time. Thus maintenance routines can be set as Cron jobs to run tasks which can be performed by the server itself at fixed times, dates, or intervals.

Server software updates can either be set to operate automatically, or can be done under controlled conditions by the system administrator. Similarly, database updates can either be set to operate automatically, or can be done under controlled conditions by the database administrator.

For a super paranoid approach, this system can be replicated elsewhere, and the data mirrored as it is streamed, whereby it is operated under the same conditions with no physical access for anyone involved in the system that is being protected.

For extreme levels of paranoia, Write Once Read Many (WORM) times hard drives might be used. This is already well established technology for CD disks, DVD disks and RDX disks. These are usually considered too slow for enterprise use. While conventional hard disks are available to use in a WORM high security Network Attached Storage (NAS) configuration, they are still expensive and not super fast yet.

We earlier mentioned that this immutable database server could be configured to operate in the cloud, and in the next sub-section we note how this can be achieved, bearing in mind that so doing will introduce additional vulnerabilities.

B. *The Cloud Based Immutable Database Server*

The first point to stress with a cloud based immutable database server, is that it will be considerably less secure than the in-house version. This is due to the inherently less secure nature of cloud technology, which is why we are attempting to resolve this problem in the first place. On the plus side, it will be considerably more pragmatic in use, since it will be impossible to lock up the server and remove keyboard, video screen and mouse.

Taking all of that into account, on the plus side, the instance will be capable of scaling easily to meet demand. On the negative side, it will be much easier to attack. However, since it will not have direct web access, this will present a much greater challenge to the attacker. Also, it will not be set up with the same CSP as the main system, which means unless the intruder gets far enough into the main system, it will take some figuring out. But it would not be impossible, and therefore the immutable database will become a very promising target.

Everything that can be done in Sub-Section VI-A, with the exception of the physical tasks can be carried out in this case. Careful setup of who is allowed to access this system can help control who can gain access to the system, and with no direct external web access to this system and only tightly restricted login to a shell available, this will make the attacker's job much more difficult. But, you must always remember it is running on a cloud system, and is therefore subject to the same pitfalls as the main system you are trying to protect.

This means that in addition to IDS systems, you will also require to have a seriously good monitoring system in place. It will be vital to understand who is in your system and what they are trying to do. In fact, let us re-phrase that. Other than receiving the data you expect — anyone inside your system is an intruder, so you need to have instant warning, bells ringing, lights flashing, klaxons blaring — whatever it takes, in order that the intruder can instantly be dealt with.

C. A Comparison Between the Two Options

Before attempting to make a decision between the two options, we must first consider the pros and cons of each system.

For the in-house immutable database system option:

Pros:

- In-house will be more secure than cloud-based;
- In-house offers the advantage of extra physical security;
- In-house will be fully under the control of the enterprise;
- In-house will gain protection from enterprise firewall and IDS;
- In-house system will benefit from not requiring external web access;
- In-house system will benefit from no wireless access.

Cons:

- Lead time for implementation and expansion increases can be a factor;
- Insufficient internet bandwidth could adversely impact on performance;
- In-house costs may be greater than for cloud-based systems;
- In-house system will become a highly attractive target.

For the cloud-based option:

Pros:

- Cloud-based systems are simple to implement and can be rapidly deployed;
- Cloud-based systems respond well to changes in demand;
- Cloud-based systems cope well with increased volumes of data storage.

Cons:

- Cloud-based systems will be less secure than in-house;
- Cloud-based systems will become a highly attractive target;
- Cloud-based systems will be easier to attack than in-house systems;
- Cloud-based systems will need to ensure that all data from closed down instances are permanently stored.

Thus it is clear that compromises will have to be made depending on which route is chosen to store the data collected into the immutable database. However, being able to understand the pros and cons of each option provides a good basis on which to evaluate the impact of either on the enterprise, thus leading to the right decision for the enterprise.

Regardless of which system is chosen, either will require the installation of a good monitoring system. In the next sub-section, we consider the requirements for a suitable monitoring system.

D. Monitoring the Immutable Database Server

The data contained in the main system is very valuable to an enterprise. The data collected and contained in the immutable database is also extremely valuable to both the enterprise and to law enforcement. Under conventional attack scenarios, the audit trail and forensic trail are usually modified or deleted by the intruder, in order to cover their trail. Without proper audit trail or forensic data, it becomes very difficult to understand what records have been accessed, modified or deleted. When this concerns data covered by the EU GDPR, this brings a serious problem to bear on the enterprise — the potential impact of fines. Thus the audit trail and forensic trail data captured in this remote server becomes an especially useful resource for the enterprise.

With conventional successful cloud systems attacks , the forensic trail is usually obliterated, or partially destroyed by the intruder, and this will be the approach for the successful attack on the main system. Very few intruders will be skilled enough to understand that there is a secret cache of forensic data. However, if an intruder is skilled enough to realise that this is the case, then they most certainly will come after the audit and forensic data, and will attempt to discover where it is and attack that system. The setup of this system means this will present a much greater challenge, which will defeat all but the most skilled intruder. This is why it is vital to have a successful monitoring system in place.

It would be sensible to use a software agent to monitor, and log, all system calls made inside the immutable database server system. Any system call made other than the writing of data to the immutable database is likely to arise from the unexpected actions of an intruder. So by monitoring and looking for system calls that do not match the expected pattern, then this provides evidence of a possible intruder in the system.

Naturally, it also makes sound sense to monitor the incoming data from the main system being protected by the immutable database. It would make sense to create another software agent, or agents, do handle these tasks also. The agents could be used to scan the incoming data to search for know patterns suggestive of the presence of an intruder. This can provide a second line of defence in the event that such agents in the main system had been knocked out by the intruders.

Monitoring of these systems is vital in order to be able to realise the moment an intruder breaches the system, particularly in the light of the stringent reporting requirements of the forthcoming EU GDPR.

VII. Discussion on Security Issues

In our quest to secure cloud based systems in the light of the forthcoming EU GDPR, we need to face facts. Achieving any kind of security in IT systems at this time is akin to trying to perform all one's daily tasks with one's hands tied behind one's back. The combination of the requirement for legacy compatibility, poor inherent security of software due to bug riddled software and insufficient testing, both the operating systems and for the ever more complex software running on these systems, coupled with insufficient understanding of how to configure all these products securely, means that there is little prospect of a successful outcome.

Also, many standards for various software implementations were developed decades ago, long before the internet opened up every user to exploitation due to non-existent or limited security. Decades of limited software testing are opening up ever more vulnerabilities for attackers to exploit. The insistence on backward compatibility of software products is a case in point. Adding a more complex system on top of an already vulnerable system is simply a recipe for disaster.

What is needed is a recognition that we are collectively going about this the wrong way. In software development, the reuse of software is a laudable software engineering goal. But the reuse of inherently insecure software systems simply perpetuates the problem. This is why we have weaknesses in operating systems, database systems, web systems, network systems, email systems, indeed pretty much all our current software systems.

A new approach is required, whereby all software systems are re-written from the ground up — to be secure. A good start would be to enforce the writing of proper secure software systems, APIs, DLLs and drivers for all new hardware being produced. A revision of email and network protocols would provide a useful improvement to reduce delivery of attack vectors for attackers. Operating systems and all other software in general should be re-written in a much more secure way. Default configuration should be "super secure", so that every software installation will be guaranteed secure. Detailed security configuration instructions should be provided with all software, to minimise the effect of mis-configuration opening up unexpected vulnerabilities.

It is comforting to note that many operating system developers have started initiatives to develop secure operating systems. Over recent years, it is clear that a lot of work has gone into this effort, but it is equally clear that it may be some time before we see a fully secure operating system available for use. Equally, many software development businesses have also started similar initiatives, which is also very welcome. Again, it may be some time before we see the full fruits of these initiatives. Solving the major cloud issue of how easily cloud audit and forensic data can be deleted remains a serious concern.

Initiatives, such as the Bright Internet [68], are also very welcome as a means of providing greater accountability by all internet service companies and users. The status quo can not continue. Last year, the global cost of cybercrime is estimated to have exceeded global income from illicit drugs for the first time. As long as the status quo remains, the impact of cybercrime will continue to climb. Add to that the cost of potential fines arising from penalties arising from cyber breaches around the globe, and it is clear that something positive needs to happen.

VIII. Conclusion and Future Work

We have considered a wide range of security issues in cloud based systems, with a view to highlighting that the attack surface of any cloud based system extends well beyond technical issues. We have identified that databases present a considerable weakness in cloud based systems, in addition to the unintended potential loss of forensic data caused by the manner in which scalability is handled in large cloud systems.

It is common for experts to recommend simple housekeeping solutions when security vendors want to sell new technology. This proposed solution is more of the former, though development of audit trail interrogation tools would help meet the tight deadlines for discovery and rectification in the GDPR. A solution based on an immutable database of an audit trail may seem a very boring and low-tech solution, but since high level technological solutions have yet to be able to resolve this very important weakness, it represents a pragmatic short term approach to addressing a serious problem with cloud. As if that were not enough to get some attention, 4% of turnover fines ought to focus minds, even if protecting customer and employee data doesn't.

We have suggested a simple approach that could be easily implemented, with minimal technical knowledge, which would offer a considerable improvement on cloud security, with the additional benefit of maintaining a vastly improved forensic trail to explore in the event of a breach. Until such time as this major cloud weakness can be properly resolved, this proposal offers an interim mitigating solution.

Equally, our proposal also offers the benefit of being able to discover precisely which records have been viewed, compromised, or deleted. This presents a means of ensuring compliance with the GDPR, which is likely to offer a significant mitigation in the event that any regulator proposes a significant fine, since the enterprise will be in a position to comply fully with the reporting requirements.

We plan to test this proposal to identify any loss in performance resulting from not being able to use key searching in the immutable database, and to identify how it will stand up to attack. In the longer term, it would be useful to develop a software solution that might add the key search capability to the immutable database.

However, as a follow through to the limited work contained in this paper, we will extend our view to include NoSQL, NewSQL and blockchain technology. We will also consider several methodologies for security the immutable database so that it might be run securely on cloud, including the use of a Unikernel solution based on UnikernelOS software. This might provide an interesting synergy for security due to both the ultra small profile that UnikernelOS offers together with the immutability of running instances.

REFERENCES

[1] B. Duncan and M. Whittington, "Creating an Immutable Database for Secure Cloud Audit Trail and System Logging," in *Cloud Comput. 2017 Eighth Int. Conf. Cloud Comput. GRIDs, Virtualization*. Athens: IARIA, ISBN: 978-1-61208-529-6, 2017, pp. 54–59.

[2] B. Duncan and M. Whittington, "Enhancing Cloud Security and Privacy: The Cloud Audit Problem," in *Cloud Computing 2016: The Seventh International Conference on Cloud Computing, GRIDs, and Virtualization*, April 2016, pp. 119-124.

[3] B. Duncan and M. Whittington, "Enhancing Cloud Security and Privacy: The Power and the Weakness of the Audit Trail," in *Cloud Computing 2016: The Seventh International Conference on Cloud Computing, GRIDs, and Virtualization*, April 2016, pp. 125-130.

[4] B. Duncan and M. Whittington, "Cloud cyber-security: Empowering the audit trail," *Int. J. Adv. Secur.*, vol. 9, no. 3 & 4, pp. 169–183, 2016.

[5] Trustwave, "2012 Global Security Report," Tech. Rep., 2012.

[6] EU, "EU General Data Protection Regulation (GDPR)," 2017. [Online]. Available: http://www.eugdpr.org/ Last accessed: 28 August 2017.

[7] G. Moore, "Cramming More Components Onto Integrated Circuits," *Electronics*, vol. 38, no. April 19, pp. 114–117, 1965.

[8] N. Papanikolaou, S. Pearson, M. C. Mont, and R. K. L. Ko, "Towards Greater Accountability in Cloud Computing through Natural-Language Analysis and Automated Policy Enforcement," *Engineering*, pp. 1–4, 2011.

[9] A. Baldwin, D. Pym, and S. Shiu, "Enterprise Information Risk Management: Dealing with Cloud Computing," *Abdn.Ac.Uk*, pp. 257–291, 2013. [Online]. Available: http://link.springer.com/10.1007/978-1-4471-4189-1{_}8 Last accessed: 30 November 2017.

[10] B. Duncan and M. Whittington, "Enhancing Cloud Security and Privacy: Broadening the Service Level Agreement," in *14th IEEE Int. Conf. Trust. Secur. Priv. Comput. Commun. (IEEE Trust.*, Helsinki, Finland, 2015, pp. 1088–1093.

[11] M. Huse, "Accountability and Creating Accountability: a Framework for Exploring Behavioural Perspectives of Corporate Governance," *Br. J. Manag.*, vol. 16, no. S1, pp. S65–S79, mar 2005.

[12] S. Pearson, "Toward accountability in the cloud," *IEEE Internet Comput.*, vol. 15, no. 4, pp. 64–69, jul 2011.

[13] D. Catteddu, M. Felici, G. Hogben, A. Holcroft, E. Kosta, R. Leenes, C. Millard, M. Niezen, D. Nunez, N. Papanikolaou, S. Pearson, D. Pradelles, C. Reed, C. Rong, J.-C. Royer, D. Stefanatou, and T. W. Wlodarczyk, "Towards a Model of Accountability for Cloud Computing Services," in *Int. Work. Trust. Account. Forensics Cloud*, 2013, pp. 21–30.

[14] W. Benghabrit, H. Grall, J.-C. Royer, M. Sellami, M. Azraoui, K. Elkhiyaoui, M. Onen, A. S. D. Olivera, and K. Bernsmed, "A Cloud Accountability Policy Representation Framework," in *CLOSER-4th Int. Conf. Cloud Comput. Serv. Sci.*, 2014, pp. 489–498.

[15] A. Gill, "Corporate Governance as Social Responsibility: A Research Agenda," *Berkeley J. Int'l L.*, vol. 26, no. 2, pp. 452–478, 2008.

[16] M. Low, H. Davey, and K. Hooper, "Accounting scandals, ethical dilemmas and educational challenges," *Crit. Perspect. Account.*, vol. 19, no. 2, pp. 222–254, Feb 2008.

[17] S. Arjoon, "Corporate Governance: An Ethical Perspective," *J. Bus. Ethics*, vol. 61, no. 4, pp. 343–352, nov 2012.

[18] C. Ioannidis, D. Pym, and J. Williams, "Sustainability in Information Stewardship: Time Preferences, Externalities and Social Co-Ordination," in *Weis 2013*, 2013, pp. 1–24.

[19] A. Kolk, "Sustainability, accountability and corporate governance: Exploring multinationals' reporting practices," *Bus. Strateg. Environ.*, vol. 17, no. 1, pp. 1–15, 2008.

[20] K. Gilman and J. Schulschenk, "Sustainability Accounting Standards Board," pp. 14–17, 2012. [Online]. Available: www.sasb.org Last accessed: 30 November 2017.

[21] R. G. Eccles, K. Perkins, and G. Serafeim, "How to become a sustainable company," *MIT Sloan Manag. Rev.*, vol. 53, pp. 43–50, 2012.

[22] R. G. Eccles, I. Ioannou, and G. Serafeim, "The impact of corporate sustainability on organizational processes and performance," *Manage. Sci.*, vol. 60, no. 11, pp. 2835–2857, 2014.

[23] F. S. Chapin, G. P. Kofinas, and C. Folke, *Principles of ecosystem stewardship: Resilience-based natural resource management in a changing world*. New York: Springer, 2009.

[24] G. Hamel and L. Välikangas, "The quest for resilience," *Harv. Bus. Rev.*, vol. 81, no. 9, pp. 52–63, 131, sep 2003.

[25] G. Sundström and E. Hollnagel, "Learning How to Create Resilience in Business Systems," *Resil. Eng. Concepts Precepts.*, pp. 1–20, 2006.

[26] J. Birchall and L. H. Ketilson, *Resilience of the Cooperative Business Model in Times of Crisis Sustainable Enterprise Programme*. International Labour Organization, 2009.

[27] G. C. Avery and H. Bergsteiner, "Sustainable leadership practices for enhancing business resilience and performance," *Strateg. Leadersh.*, vol. 39, no. 3, pp. 5–15, 2011.

[28] T. Prior and J. Hagmann, "Measuring resilience: methodological and political challenges of a trend security concept," *J. Risk Res.*, no. January 2015, pp. 37–41, 2013.

[29] V. Chang, M. Ramachandran, Y. Yao, Y. H. Kuo, and C. S. Li, "A resiliency framework for an enterprise cloud," *Int. J. Inf. Manage.*, vol. 36, no. 1, pp. 155–166, 2016.

[30] L. G. Price, "The Concept of Fiduciary Duty As a Basis for Corporate Ethics," *J. Business, Soc. Gov.*, vol. 3, pp. 21–30, 2011.

[31] B. Withers and M. Ebrahimpour, "The Effects of Codes of Ethics on the Supply Chain: A Comparison of LEs and SMEs," *J. Bus. Econ. Stud.*, vol. 19, no. 1, pp. 24–40,118–119, 2013.

[32] G. R. Weaver, "Encouraging Ethics in Organizations: A Review of Some Key Research Findings," *Am. Crim. Law Rev.*, vol. 51, no. 107, pp. 293–316, 2014.

[33] T. Hahn, F. Figge, J. Pinkse, and L. Preuss, "Editorial Trade-Offs in Corporate Sustainability: You Can't Have Your Cake and Eat It," *Bus. Strateg. Environ.*, vol. 19, pp. 217–229, 2010.

[34] A. Lindgreen and V. Swaen, "Corporate social responsibility," *Int. J. Manag. Rev.*, vol. 12, pp. 1–7, 2010.

[35] D. J. Wood, "Measuring corporate social performance: A review," *Int. J. Manag. Rev.*, vol. 12, pp. 50–84, 2010.

[36] T. Green and J. Peloza, "How does corporate social responsibility create value for consumers?" *J. Consum. Mark.*, vol. 28, pp. 48–56, 2011.

[37] A. Christofi, P. Christofi, and S. Sisaye, "Corporate sustainability: historical development and reporting practices," *Manag. Res. Rev.*, vol. 35, no. 2, pp. 157–172, 2012.

[38] N. Rahman and C. Post, "Measurement Issues in Environmental Corporate Social Responsibility (ECSR): Toward a Transparent, Reliable, and Construct Valid Instrument," *J. Bus. Ethics*, vol. 105, pp. 307–319, 2012.

[39] M. A. Delmas, D. Etzion, and N. Nairn-Birch, "Triangulating Environmental Performance: What Do Corporate Social Responsibility Ratings Really Capture?" *Acad. Manag. Perspect.*, vol. 27, no. 3, pp. 255–267, 2013.

[40] I. Montiel and J. Delgado-Ceballos, "Defining and Measuring Corporate Sustainability: Are We There Yet?" *Organ. Environ.*, pp. 1–27, 2014.

[41] B. Duncan, D. J. Pym, and M. Whittington, "Developing a Conceptual Framework for Cloud Security Assurance," in *Cloud Comput. Technol. Sci. (CloudCom), 2013 IEEE 5th Int. Conf. (Volume 2)*. Bristol: IEEE, 2013, pp. 120–125.

[42] B. Duncan and M. Whittington, "Company Management Approaches Stewardship or Agency: Which Promotes Better Security in Cloud Ecosystems?" in *Cloud Comput. 2015*. Nice: IEEE, 2015, pp. 154–159.

[43] T. Keyun, R., Carthy, J., & Kechadi, "Cloud Forensics An Overview," in *7th IFIP Conf. Digit. Forensics*, no. January, 2011, pp. 35–46.

[44] NIST, "NIST Cloud Computing Forensic Science Challenges," p. 51, 2014.

[45] S. Almulla, Y. Iraqi, and A. Jones, "A State-Of-The-Art Review Of Cloud," *J. Digit. Forensics, Secur. Law*, vol. V9N4, pp. 7–28, 2014.
[46] R. K. L. Ko, P. Jagadpramana, M. Mowbray, S. Pearson, M. Kirchberg, B. S. Lee, and Q. Liang, "TrustCloud: A Framework for Accountability and Trust in Cloud Computing," *Perspective*, pp. 1–9, 2011.
[47] B. Duncan and M. Whittington, "Compliance with Standards, Assurance and Audit: Does this Equal Security?" in *Proc. 7th Int. Conf. Secur. Inf. Networks*. Glasgow: ACM, 2014, pp. 77–84.
[48] B. Guttman and E. A. Roback, "NIST Special Publication 800-12. An Introduction to Computer Security: The NIST Handbook," NIST, Tech. Rep. 800, 2011. [Online]. Available: csrc.nist.gov/publications/nistpubs/800-12/handbook.pdf Last accessed: 30 November 2017.
[49] OED, "Oxford English Dictionary," 2016. [Online]. Available: www.oed.com Last accessed: 30 November 2017.
[50] D. Bernstein, E. Ludvigson, K. Sankar, S. Diamond, and M. Morrow, "Blueprint for the Intercloud Protocols and Formats for Cloud Computing Interoperability," in *Internet Web Appl. Serv. 2009. ICIW'09. Fourth Int. Conf.*, 2009, pp. 328—336.
[51] J. A. Chaula, "A Socio-Technical Analysis of Information Systems Security Assurance: A Case Study for Effective Assurance," Ph.D. dissertation, 2006. [Online]. Available: http://scholar.google.com/scholar?hl=en{\&}btnG=Search{\&}q=intitle:A+Socio-Technical+Analysis+of+Information+Systems+Security+Assurance+A+Case+Study+for+Effective+Assurance{\#}1 Last accessed: 30 November 2017.
[52] S. Pearson and A. Benameur, "Privacy, Security and Trust Issues Arising from Cloud Computing," *2010 IEEE Second Int. Conf. Cloud Comput. Technol. Sci.*, pp. 693–702, nov 2010.
[53] R. K. L. Ko, "Data Accountability in Cloud Systems," in *Secur. Priv. Trust Cloud Syst.* Springer, 2014, pp. 211–238.
[54] EU, "Unleashing the Potential of Cloud Computing in Europe," 2012. [Online]. Available: http://eur-lex.europa.eu/LexUriServ/LexUriServ.do?uri=SWD:2012:0271:FIN:EN:PDF Last accessed: 30 November 2017.
[55] R. J. Anderson, *Security Engineering: A Guide to Building Dependable Distributed Systems*, C. A. Long, Ed. Wiley, 2008, vol. 50, no. 5.
[56] Verizon, "2012 Data Breach Investigation Report: A study conducted by the Verizon RISK Team in cooperation with the United States Secret Service and Others," Tech. Rep., 2012. [Online]. Available: http://www.verizonenterprise.com/resources/reports/rp{_}data-breach-investigations-report-2012{_}en{_}xg.pdf Last accessed: 30 November 2017.
[57] OWASP, "OWASP home page," 2017. [Online]. Available: https://www.owasp.org/index.php/Main{_}Page Last accessed: 30 November 2017.
[58] C. J. M. Tauro, S. Aravindh, and A. B. Shreeharsha, "Comparative study of the new generation, agile, scalable, high performance NOSQL databases," Int. J. Comput. Appl., vol. 48, no. 20, pp. 14, 2012.
[59] D. G. Chandra, "BASE analysis of NoSQL database," Futur. Gener. Comput. Syst., vol. 52, pp. 1321, 2015.
[60] Y. N. Silva, I. Almeida, and M. Queiroz, "SQL: From traditional databases to big data," in Proceedings of the 47th ACM Technical Symposium on Computing Science Education, 2016, pp. 413418.
[61] D. Wilson and G. Ateniese, "From pretty good to great: Enhancing pgp using bitcoin and the blockchain," in International Conference on Network and System Security, 2015, pp. 368375.
[62] V. L. Lemieux, "Trusting records: is Blockchain technology the answer?," Rec. Manag. J., vol. 26, no. 2, 2016.
[63] E. Gaetani, L. Aniello, R. Baldoni, F. Lombardi, A. Margheri, and V. Sassone, "Blockchain-based database to ensure data integrity in cloud computing environments," in CEUR Workshop Proceedings, 2017, vol. 1816.
[64] Verizon, "Verizon 2015 Data Breach Investigation Report," Tech. Rep., 2015.
[65] OWASP, "OWASP IoT Security Guidance," 2016. [Online]. Available: https://www.owasp.org/index.php/IoT{_}Security{_}Guidance Last accessed: 30 November 2017.
[66] OWASP, "OWASP Injection Prevention Cheat Sheet," 2016. [Online]. Available: https://www.owasp.org/index.php/Injection{_}Prevention{_}Cheat{_}Sheet Last accessed: 30 November 2017.
[67] OWASP, "OWASP LDAP Injection Prevention Cheat Sheet," 2016. [Online]. Available: https://www.owasp.org/index.php/LDAP{_}Injection{_}Prevention{_}Cheat{_}Sheet Last accessed: 30 November 2017.
[68] AIS, "Bright Internet Initiative," 2017. [Online]. Available: http://aisnet.org/?page=BrightICT Last accessed: 30 November 2017.

Secrecy and Randomness: Encoding Cloud data Locally using a One-Time Pad

Paul Tobin*, Lee Tobin†, Michael McKeever‡, and Jonathan Blackledge§
* School of Electrical and Electronic Engineering
Dublin Institute of Technology, Dublin 8, Ireland
Email: paul.tobin@dit.ie
† CASL Institute Level 3, UCD Science Centre East
University College, Belfield, Dublin 4, Ireland
Email: lee.tobin@ucdconnect.ie
‡ School of Electrical and Electronic Engineering
Dublin Institute of Technology, Dublin 8, Ireland
Email: mick.mckeever@dit.ie
§ Military Technological College
Sultanate of Oman,
Email: Jonathan.blackledge59@gmail.com

***Abstract*—There is no secrecy without randomness, and we address poor cloud security using an analogue chaotic one-time pad encryption system to achieve perfect secrecy. Local encoding returns control to the client and makes stored cloud data unreadable to an adversary. Most cloud service providers encode client data using public encryption algorithms, but ultimately businesses and organisations are responsible for encoding data locally before uploading to the Cloud. As recommended by the Cloud Security Alliance, companies employing authentication and local encryption will reduce or eliminate, EU fines for late data breach discoveries when the EU implements the new general data protection regulations in 2018. Companies failing to detect data breaches within a 72-hour limit will be fined up to four percent of their global annual turnover and estimates of several hundred billion euros could be levied in fines based on the present 146 days average EU breach discovery. The proposed localised encryption system is additional to public encryption, and obeying the rules of one-time pad encryption will mean intercepted encrypted data will be meaningless to an adversary. Furthermore, the encoder has no key distribution problem because applications for it are of "one-to-cloud" type.**

Keywords*—*Secrecy; Local encryption; GDPR fines; one-time pad; one-to-cloud; key distribution problem; chaos.

I. Introduction

This paper builds on the conference paper presented at the IARIA cloud conference in Athens, Greece, February 2017, and includes new test results and concepts not included previously because of page number limitations [1]. Existing poor security of sensitive data stored in the cloud is addressed by introducing local encoding by the client. A One-Time-Pad (OTP) encryption system returns control to the client by adding an extra encoding layer of security over public encryption and makes encoded data unreadable to any adversary who gains access to a server. In May 2018, the EU introduces the General Data Protection Regulations (GDPR) which will penalise companies and organisations for late data breach discoveries more than the proposed 72-hour limit [2]. Fines up to four percent of the global annual turnover of EU and UK companies and institutions, are estimated at several hundred billion euros each year and potentially could result in some of them ceasing operation. The Cloud Security Alliance (CSA) recommends organisations should employ authentication and local encryption to protect against data breaches, and GDPR Articles 32 and 34 state why local encryption by the client will mitigate against punitive fines [3]. A two-pronged solution for inadequate cloud security and EU fines was proposed in a paper [4], where local encryption, immutable databases, and audit trail accountability, was discussed.

In this paper, we discuss further aspects of the OTP encryption system which incorporates analogue chaos oscillator sources initialised by electronic noise. For the OTP encoder, we suggest "One-To-Cloud" (OTC) applications for protecting client confidentiality, where there are no Key Distribution Problems (KDP) because the client retains the OTP key. Eliminating side-channel attacks and other less sophisticated hacking methods is not possible, irrespective of this encoding system, or that provided by the Cloud Service Providers (CSP). However, our system will make data unreadable for adversaries who do not possess the OTP key.

The paper layout is as follows: Section I introduces the concept of local encryption and OTC applications showing how it protects client data and addresses the proposed GDPR fines for late data breach discoveries. In Section II, security in the Cloud explains why local encryption will solve specific security problems. In Section III, a brief OTP history illustrates how it secured successfully, intergovernmental communications between British and American leaders in WWII, and protected world peace during the cold war period. Discussed briefly is the structure of the OTP encoder and why it is a true source of entropy.

In Section IV, modern OTP applications explain why the chaos encoder protects client confidentiality and does so with no KDP. Section V introduces chaos cryptography and describes the design of the OTP prototype comprising analogue chaos oscillators initialised with electronic noise. In Section VI, we outline a range of statistical tests carried out on the encryption prototype to ensure it meets international standards for randomness. Conclusion and future work are given in Section VII, and the Appendix contains figures to illustrate specific points in the paper.

II. Security in the Cloud

Cloud computing has many advantages, and managing information from any location is critical for efficient business operation [5][6]. However, clients are seeing cloud server attacks reported daily in the media and is causing a drop in confidence in cloud security [7]. Furthermore, these clients do not know if their data is encrypted by the CSP, or where it is stored, but encoded data should have:

- **Integrity**: Detecting unwanted modification by an adversary,
- **Confidentiality**: Ensures authorised only users can access stored information,
- **Authentication**: Guarantees the client identity and the validity of stored data,
- **Availability**: Ensures client data can be accessed at all times, and,
- **Accountability**: An audit trail which encompasses non-repudiation, intrusion detection and prevention.

Compounding poor cloud security is the possibility of backdoors in public encryption as suggested by Shumow and Ferguson in a 2007 presentation [8][9][10]. In 2013, Edward Snowden alleged backdoors were placed in public encryption systems by the National Security Agency (NSA) [11]. That said, the Advanced Encryption Standard (AES) algorithm used in cloud security, is probably secure, but nobody knows what other weaknesses exist in public encryption. Backdoors and the threat of GDPR fines for late reporting of data breaches, strengthen our argument for an extra layer of localised security using an OTP random binary number generator.

A. Localised cloud security

Localised OTP encryption for data uploaded to the cloud Infrastructure as a Service (IaaS), addresses poor security issues. Security breaches in the Cloud are rarely discovered and reported instantly, and many months elapse before discovery [12]. Although the time for detecting these breaches has been reduced, the global average is still 146 days [3]. In May 2018, the EU GDPR will replace the Data Protection Directive 95/46/ec, where it states that mandatory breach notification must be reported within 72 hours. Companies and organisations failing to meet this will be fined up to four percent of their global annual turnover [13].

Article 32 of the regulations deals with security of personal data and states, "... controller, and the processor shall implement appropriate technical and organisational measures to ensure a level of security appropriate to the risk, including the pseudonymization and encryption of personal data". Article 34 states for any company "... has implemented appropriate technical and organisational protection measures ... such as encryption", may avoid punitive breach fines. Apart from these two articles, the regulations cover little on encryption standards, but it appears to encourage companies to use local encryption. Interestingly, GDPR will apply to UK businesses post-Brexit.

Inadequate security in the Cloud is now a primary concern amongst cloud users because commercially-available encryption algorithms are not protecting stored data. The proposed hardware-based OTP random binary number generator encodes data locally by the client before uploading to the Cloud and makes data unreadable if intercepted. The encoder produces random binary sequences digits by thresholding the signal output from two analogue chaos oscillators, and software post-processing of the OTP binary stream ensures sequences from the interleaved chaos source are unbiased and statistically independent from each other.

III. One-Time Pad Encryption

A patent granted in 1917 for an OTP encryption system by Joseph Mauborgne and Gilbert Vernam, was not the first of its kind, however, because Dr Steven Bellovin discovered telegrams were encoded using OTPs many years before this. In an 1882 book, "Telegraphic Code to Insure Privacy and Secrecy in the Transmission of Telegrams", Frank Miller describes how OTPs could protect telegrams [14][15]. There is no record to show whether Miller, a successful banker, actually made an OTP generator prototype.

Modern encryption is not protecting sensitive data in the Cloud, as is evidenced by the fact that most of the greatest security agencies have been hacked, and so a new approach using the concept of OTP encryption is considered. Some cryptologists argue the OTP has no place in modern encryption because of the KDP and the large size of the OTP. However, we make the case that with modern electronics and specific applications, and the fact that it is unbreakable, makes the OTP a viable encryption method for protecting sensitive material in the Cloud.

A. Key distribution problem

The OTP is a symmetric encryption method that uses the same key for encoding and decoding but creates a KDP. Two solutions to this are: (i) Use the courier Sneakernet method of carrying the key between two people, or (ii) choose OTC applications which have no key sharing. The latter point is the focus of this paper where only one person is involved with no KDP. What we are not suggesting is to use the OTP for day-to-day Internet transactions, such as email, etc., but only for encoding sensitive data requiring extra security measures. The OTP is unbreakable provided it is used only once, is truly random, and is the same length as the data (plaintext). However, computer memory is inexpensive, so this latter point is no longer valid.

B. One-time pad history

Clarke and Turing worked in Bell Labs and were part of a team which created the 55-tonne SIGSALY encryption system for protecting conversations between Winston Churchill and Franklin Roosevelt between 1942-1946 [16]. Messages encrypted with this method were wholly secure, but the system had a KDP because noise (OTP) from a vacuum tube recorded on a vinyl record was flown across the Atlantic. Another OTP application was the famous "hotline" used during the Cuban crisis by the Russian and American governments in the 60s.

Protecting information from interception by adversaries dates back many thousands of years. The WWII German four-rotor *Enigma* encoder with 10^{113} permutations, is perhaps, the most famous encryption system and would still need a year of modern computing power to decode messages. A Polish secret service cryptanalyst, Marian Rejewski, knew wiring details of the first rotor which reduced the possible permutations slightly. He passed this information to the staff in Bletchley Park to help decode German radio messages, but in reality, the German *Enigma* operators made significant operating mistakes and was a more substantial factor for decoding the messages [17][18].

C. Rules for OTP encoding

One-to-one OTP encoding systems had a KDP and operator security problems which consigned the OTP to history and was replaced by symmetric block ciphers and asymmetrical public key algorithms [19][20]. The Soviet Intelligence used OTP encryption because of its excellent record of protecting data and distributed massive quantities of OTP keys during WW11. However, human operators distributed more than two copies of the same key - a significant factor which helped the United States and British intelligence who created the *Venona* project, to break the Soviet OTP code during this period and later during the cold war period.

Encryption algorithms and devices should adhere to the Kerckhoff-Shannon Principle, *'A cryptosystem should be secure if everything about the system except the key, is public knowledge'*, or, as Claude Shannon stated, *The enemy knows the system*, now known as Shannon's maxim [21]. Thus, an encoding system should never rely on the complexity of the encoder for secrecy and should obey the encoding algorithm operating rules to remain secret.

IV. Modern One-to Cloud OTP Applications

The OTP is making a comeback [22][23][24], and we propose OTC applications which have no KDP because the client carries the OTP key to decode data from the Cloud at other locations [25]. Figure 1 shows the first OTP encoder-decoding process for OTC applications which generates random binary sequences stored in an air-gapped computer (i.e., not connected to the Internet), or on a flash drive.

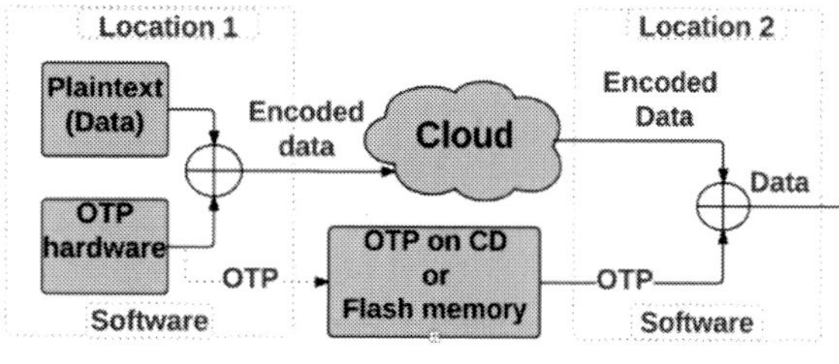

FIGURE 1. OTP ONE-TO-CLOUD ENCODING APPLICATION WITH NO KDP.

The client uses software, which exclusively OR-gates the OTP from the encryptor hardware with the plaintext data at location one. At location two, software decodes the ciphertext with the key.

A. OTP encryption and randomness

Claude Shannon described the OTP as "perfect secrecy", and is information-theoretic secure and mathematically unbreakable even if using unlimited computing power. An OTP must be truly random to protect the plaintext data from ciphertext attack because an attacker cannot determine the plaintext from the ciphertext without the key. Brute-force searching the key space by an adversary will not help because all messages are equally likely.

Figure 2 shows an Exclusive OR (EXOR) logic gate (7486) which encrypts using modulo two, the message plaintext string of bits with an OTP. The message, $m \in \{0,1\}^n$ for some n, is encoded with the secret key $k \in \{0,1\}^n$ for some n, and produces an output, $E_k(m) = m \oplus k$. The encryption function E maps the secret OTP key and the plaintext message to a ciphertext, $c \in \{0,1\}^n$ for some n and is written, $c = E_k(m)$. To recover the data a decoding function, D, reverses this by mapping the key k and the ciphertext, c, back to the plaintext message, $m = D_k(c)$.

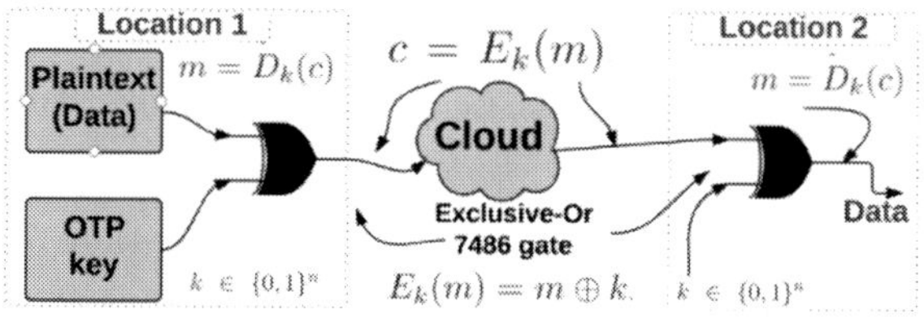

FIGURE 2. OTP ENCODING AND DECODING USING MODULO TWO ADDITION.

The following OTP applications have no KDP:

- Academics uploading exam scripts for retrieval by office staff.
- Making presentations about sensitive data away at different locations.
- Medical and legal OTC applications discussed in [26] but repeated here for completeness.

Advantages of OTC applications:

- Able to download secure data at many locations,
- Eliminates transporting of sensitive unencoded documents which could be lost in transit,
- Encrypting documents locally with an OTP prevents an intruder from understanding intercepted data, and
- Avoids the punitive GDPR fines for late breach discovery.

B. Solution to the key distribution problem

The first application for solving the KDP is an OTC medical example for encoding patient medical details displayed on medical images. Transporting medical images from the hospital to the doctor via post, or given to the patient, are insecure methods because data can be lost and compromises patient confidentiality. A better method is to encode the images and store them in the Cloud at the hospital. These can be accessed by the doctor using the OTP key given to the patient on a memory device such as a flash memory device or CD. Figure 3 shows the proposed method for storing images.

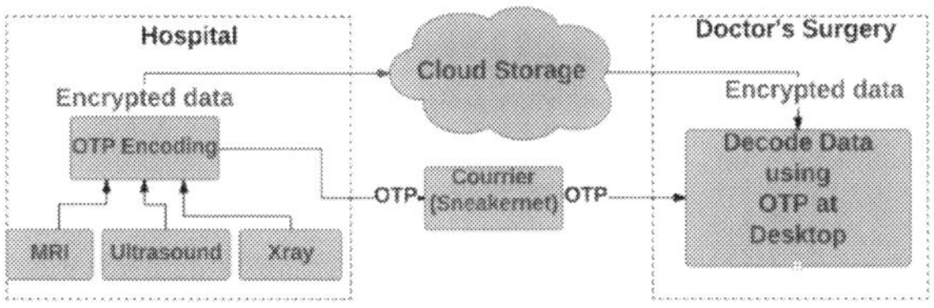

FIGURE 3. ENCODING MEDICAL IMAGES USING OTP.

Digital Imaging and Communications in Medicine (DICOM), is the international standard for distributing, processing and storing medical images, where, for example, an MRI image will display patient metadata on the image [27]. The OTP encoding system encodes the images or the metadata, to retain patient confidentiality [28]. Figure 4 for example, shows an MRI head scan image which was requested by a doctor for a patient with persistent headaches and high blood pressure. The encoded MRI image in the middle pane was processed using a JavaScript application interface written to process the OTP with the image pixel data array. The third pane is the image after processing with a deskewing algorithm described in section V.

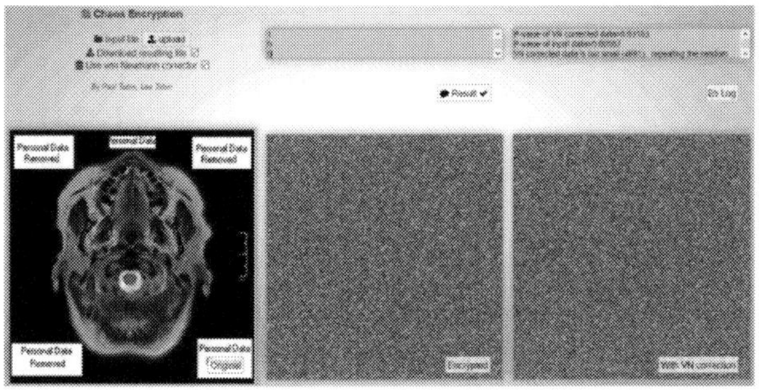

FIGURE 4. (A) DICOM MRI SCAN (B) ENCODED IMAGE (C) ENCODED IMAGE WITH VN PROCESSING.

C. *The paperless court case*

The second example concerns encrypting documents locally before a court case and introduces the concept of paperless litigation.The system in Figure 5 is similar to AES encoding used in [29] for protecting client confidentiality. At present, legal staff carry court case documentation to court in ring binders, and searching these files for case details in court is inefficient, slow, and insecure. Introducing a much more efficient data search mechanism in court is highly desirable and is achievable with the proposed encoder system.

Encoding data and uploading to the Cloud before a court case, creates a paperless environment, protects data and client confidentiality, and also provides an efficient document search mechanism. In court, the barrister downloads the encoded court case data to an Android device and decodes it using the OTP contained in a memory stick, which if lost, does not create any security issues requiring only a new key.

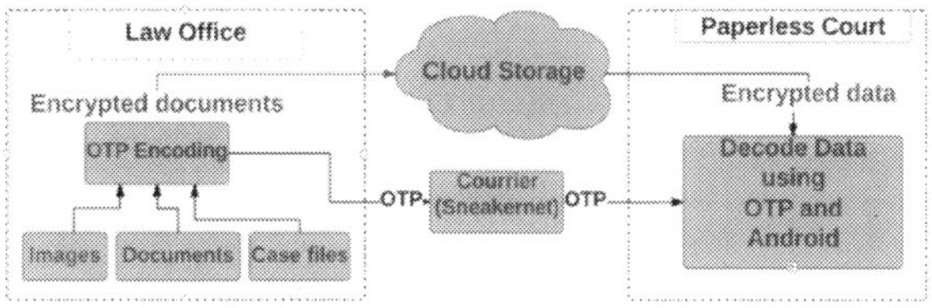

FIGURE 5. PAPERLESS LITIGATION COURTROOM USING LOCAL ENCRYPTION.

V. CHAOS CRYPTOGRAPHY

Confusion, diffusion and secrecy, are fundamental attributes of an encryption system, and comparable properties exist in chaos cryptographic systems. Claude Shannon in his 1949 paper [30], said data could be encoded by applying chaos maps in a symmetric key encryption configuration. However, Shannon's paper did not create the same interest in chaos cryptography, as did his 1945 information theory paper [31]. He discussed the relationship between chaos and cryptography and compared ergodicity and mixing in chaos to cryptographic confusion and Sensitivity to Initial Conditions (SIC) in chaos to diffusion for small changes in the key [32][33]:

"Good mixing transformations are often formed by repeated products of two simple non-commuting operations. Hopf has shown, for example, that pastry dough can be mixed by such a sequence of operations. The dough is first rolled out into a thin slab, then folded over, then rolled, and then folded again, etc. In good mixing, transformation functions are complicated, involving all variables in a sensitive way. A small variation of any one variable changes the outputs considerably".

Expanding on these comparisons: Any small change in the initial conditions will cause a chaos system to produce a different trajectory within a short time, similarly in cryptography, changing a small bit of the key will produce a different ciphertext. Public-key cryptography was established in 1976 by W. Diffie and M. E. Hellman, when "New Directions in Cryptography" was published showing secret communication was possible without transporting a secret key between sender and receiver [34]. Many papers published on chaos cryptography since 2000, demonstrated it was possible to encrypt data using chaotic maps in a multi-algorithmic format, arranged on a randomised block-by-block basis [35][36].

A. *Chaos production and Dibit forming*

Figure 6 presents an overview of the proposed encryption system for generating OTP random bit streams from analogue Chua and Lorenz chaos oscillators initialised by electronic noise. The random bit stream encodes data locally before storing in the Cloud [37]. OTP binary sequences were created by interleaving the two uncorrelated independent data streams from the Lorenz and Chua chaos sources to achieve alternate bit independence. Pairs of bits called *dibits*, are processed by a

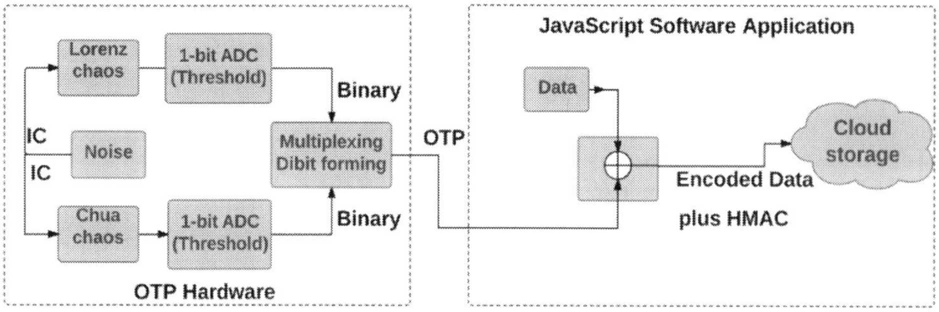

FIGURE 6. OTP RANDOM BINARY NUMBER GENERATOR WITH CHAOS SOURCES INITIALISED WITH RECEIVER NOISE. DIBIT ARE FORMED IN PREPARATION FOR THE VN ALGORITHM.

JavaScript interface through a Von Neumann (VN) algorithm. This deskewing process removes any bias that might be present and thus increases the sequence entropy. Using two uncorrelated bit streams is often overlooked, and the VN algorithm is incorrectly applied to a single data stream only.

The VN algorithm examines each dibit pair created and rejects '00' and '11' whenever they occur. Similarly, dibit '01' becomes '0' and '10' becomes '1' [38]. In this manner, the algorithm eliminates 75 percent of the data, but this just means generating more bits.

The right bottom pane in Figure 4 shows the encoded image processed with the VN but there is little discernible difference between the two encoded images because bias was not present in the OTP. Removing bias in encoded images is necessary as it makes them susceptible to cryptanalysis; otherwise, the encoded image will display patterns as shown in Figure 25 in the appendix.

B. Authentication

The Cloud Security Alliance (CSA) recommends companies add a Hash Message Authentication Code (HMAC) SHA-256 function to the encrypted data to guard against breaches and to check the integrity of the encrypted data [39]. HMAC is a unique fixed-length function derived from the plaintext and added to the ciphertext to verify the received encoded data was not changed by a third-party. The hash output ensures the clients identity is correct [40] and may be combined in several ways with the encrypted message before being sent to the Cloud.

Analogue chaos oscillator signals have infinitely many states produced from a small number of independent variables, but this is not true if created on a digital computer. Random binary sequences from analogue chaos circuits initiated with natural noise produce true random binary streams, which, in theory, will have an infinite sequence length and generate excellent keys.

Generating chaotic oscillations digitally on computers will not produce true random binary sequences because finite computer arithmetic will produce finite length sequences [41]. Similarly, random sequences from chaotic maps implemented digitally will also have repeatable sequence lengths and thus generate weaker keys [42].

Random binary streams produced from chaos sources on digital computers are called pseudo-random sequences, have a limited cycle length but are useful in many security applications.

C. The Lorenz chaos oscillator

Edward Lorenz was a meteorologist modelling weather patterns in 1963, and during one of the modelling sessions, he discovered SIC, one of the hallmarks of chaos systems. To speed up the simulation he truncated model parameters from five places of decimals to three and noticed it produced different results from a previous simulation. He simplified the original 1963 twelve equation model to three first-order coupled equations in (1) [43].

$$\begin{aligned} x &= -P \int_{t_0}^{t} \{x - y\} dt \\ y &= -\int_{t_0}^{t} \{-Rx + y + \mathbf{10}xz\} dt \\ z &= -\int_{t_0}^{t} \{Bz - \mathbf{10}xy\} dt \end{aligned} \tag{1}$$

It was necessary to scale the Lorenz second equation by ten (scale factor in bold type) to reduce signal amplitudes for electronic devices (Figure 21 Appendix). Furthermore, the equations were expressed in integral form because summing inverting integrators were used to solve the equations as shown in Figure 7. which was created and simulated using Cadence® OrCAD PSpice, v17.2.

PSpice connects parts of the circuit using net aliasing (placing names on wires) rather than actual wires, and this makes the schematic easier to read. The encoder source of randomness is supplied by analogue Lorenz and Chua chaos oscillators, both initialised by electronic noise whose ergodic properties ensure the binary streams are cryptographically-strong. Power supply decoupling components were not included in the schematic, because decoupling components are not modelled in PSpice and DC power supply lines were not shown connected directly to integrated circuits but were given alias names called POS and NEG. This simplified the circuit for easier reading.

Lorenz used B = 2.666, P = 10, R = 28 defined oscillator components: $R1$ = $R2$ = 100 kΩ, $R3$ = 36.3 kΩ, $R4$ = 10 kΩ, $R5$ = 1 MΩ, $R6$ = 10 kΩ, $R7$ = 357 kΩ, and C = 330 pF. At the testing stage, the Lorenz parameters were changed in the

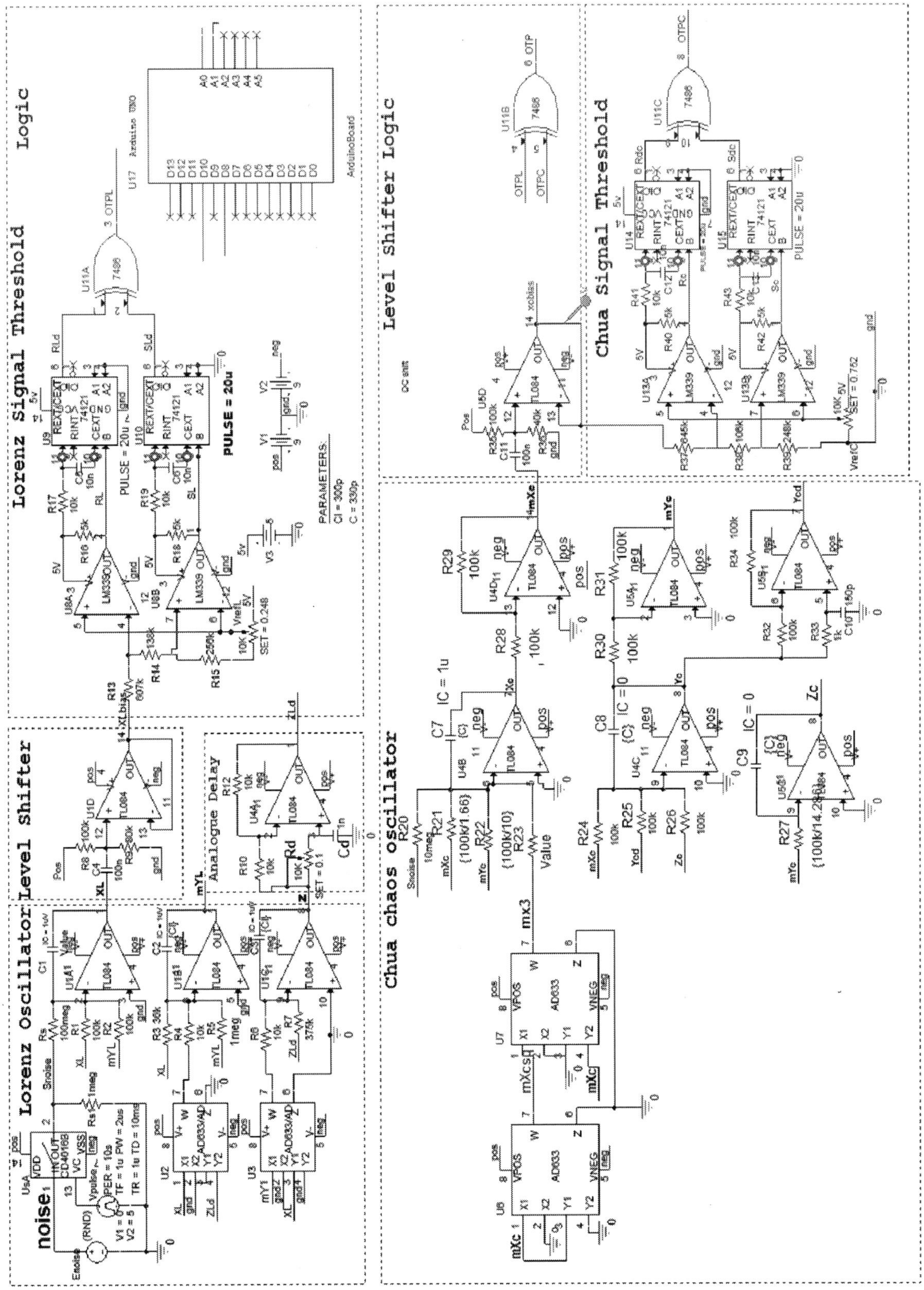

FIGURE 7. THE COMPLETE OTP CHUA-LORENZ ENCODER WITH 1-BIT ADC AND XOR LOGIC.

prototype to increase the OTP entropy as $B = 2.8$, $P = 11$, $R = 27.5$.

Analogue Behavioural Model (ABM) parts were used initially for summation, multiplication and integration for quicker simulation times and with fewer convergence problems (see Figure 22 in the Appendix). However, these parts were replaced with actual model parts after a successful proof-of-concept simulation, [44][45].

The four-quadrant AD633 multiplier integrated circuit (IC) implemented the nonlinear cross-product terms, xy and xz, such terms being necessary for chaos to exist. The general-purpose quad operational amplifier integrated circuits (TL084), were configured as inverting summing integrators to solve the equations.

D. *Thresholding the Lorenz chaos oscillator*

The OTP is a sequence of random binary numbers produced by converting the analogue chaos signal to binary. Maximum entropy binary sequences were produced by thresholding the (x) signal using a 1-bit analogue to digital converter (ADC) circuit formed from two comparators (LM339) which produced digital pulses with varying widths. It was necessary therefore to use two monostable devices to produce constant width pulses. Selecting the Fixed Points (FP) of the attractor as the suitable thresholding point on the chaos signal resulted in binary sequences with maximum sequence entropy. It was necessary to calculate the centre of these stable regions around which the trajectory of the Lorenz x signal rotates to calculate the threshold circuit values.

The set and reset pulse sequences from the two comparator outputs are superimposing on the $(x\text{-}y)$ strange attractor shown in Figure 8. It can be seen how the pulse sequence trajectories line up with the two centres (The set and reset signals are shown in Figure 20 in the Appendix).

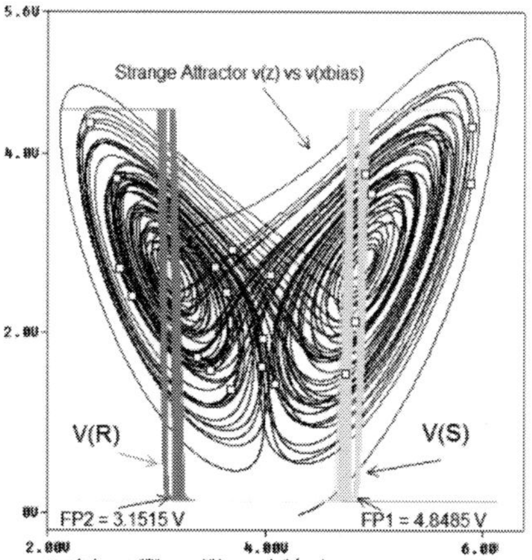

FIGURE 8. THE LORENZ STRANGE ATTRACTOR Z VS *Xbias*.

The loci centres are visited by the signal trajectory in a random fashion and the FPs of (1), where one centre loci represents a '1', when the trajectory is near that region, and a '0' for the other centre. The threshold electronic circuit is designed by determining the FPs at the centre of the strange attractor by assuming the system is approximately linear at the origin. These loci values are determined by equating to zero the first-order in (1). For example, for $x = y = z = 0$, yields $\frac{dx}{dt} = 10(y - x) = 0 \Rightarrow x = y$. Substituting this into the second equation as $\frac{dy}{dt} = 28x - x - xz = 0$, yields $z = 27$. Using this value, yields:

$$\frac{dz}{dt} = x^2 - Bz = 0 \Rightarrow = \pm\sqrt{B(R-1)} \tag{2}$$

The lobe centre coordinates, $C_{1,2}$, are calculated:

$$C_{1,2} = \{+\sqrt{B(R-1)}, -\sqrt{B(R-1)}, (R-1)\} \tag{3}$$

Substituting the standard Lorenz yielded $C_{1,2} = \{+8.48V, -8.48V, 27V\}$. It was necessary to magnitude scale the equations by ten to reduce the signal voltage amplitude suitable for electronic devices and this changed the FPs to $\pm$ 0.8485 V (see Figure 21 in the appendix). A 4 V DC bias changed the bipolar X signal to polar form and changed the upper and lower threshold levels to 3.15 V and 4.84, as shown in Figure 9.

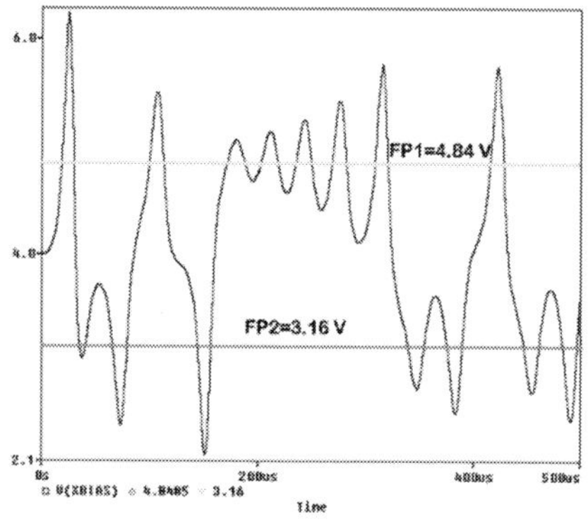

FIGURE 9. THRESHOLDS SUPERIMPOSED ON THE BIASED X SIGNAL.

Threshold component values were determined by assuming a total potentiometer value of 1 MΩ and a reference voltage of 1.24 V (Vref). Substituting these values, and the threshold values, into the following potential divider, produced values for the three resistors:

$$Vhigh = 4.84\ V = Vref\frac{R13 + R14 + R15}{R15} \tag{4}$$

Similarly,

$$Vlow = 3.15\ V = Vref\frac{R13 + R14 + R15}{R14 + R15} \tag{5}$$

The bias potential divider $R8$ and $R9$, shifts the x signal up by 4 V and U1 is a unity gain amplifier IC to buffer the biased signal. The threshold potentiometer values were calculated: $R13$ = 607 kΩ, $R14$ = 138 kΩ and $R15$ = 256 kΩ. The pair of LM339 comparators produce out-of-phase set and reset pulse sequences with pulses of varying widths because of the chaotic nature of the original signal. Hence, it was necessary to make the pulse widths constant using monostable devices (74121). The new constant-width set and reset pulses from the monostable were processed in an exclusive OR gate (XOR) (7486) to generate a controlling clock stream.

This clock stream, and the reset pulse stream from the top monostable, controlled when the OTP 'ones' and 'zeroes' were stored in Arduino memory for further processing in a JavaScript application.

E. The time-delayed feedback Lorenz oscillator

Bit stream entropy was increased by adding a time delay, τ, in the feedback path of the polar z signal in the Lorenz oscillator and modified (1) to include the delay:

$$\begin{aligned} x(t) &= -11\int_{t_0}^{t}\{x(t)-y(t)\}dt \\ y(t) &= -\int_{t_0}^{t}\{-27.5x(t)+y(t)+x(t)z(t-\tau)\}dt \\ z(t) &= -\int_{t_0}^{t}\{2.8z(t-\tau)-x(t)y(t)\}dt \end{aligned} \tag{6}$$

Adding a delay τ in the feedback path was inspired by chaotic maps such the logistic, Hénon and Lozi, which have better noise-like outputs and hence make better random number generators, but are harder to implement electronically. The normal method for introducing a delay is to use two sampling switches, i.e., a sample and hold design, but is more complex than the proposed analogue solution [46].

Figure 10 shows the analogue delay Padé approximation circuit using a passive low-pass filter. The expression for the z-transform in Digital Signal Processing (DSP), was used to obtain values for the delay [47].

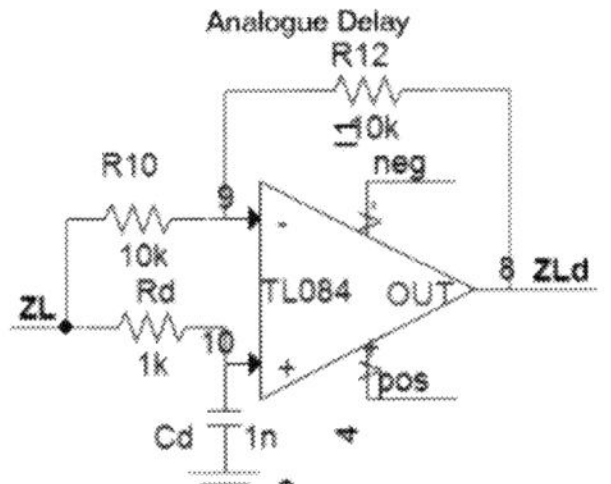

FIGURE 10. THE PADÉ DELAY CIRCUIT INCLUDED IN THE LORENZ AND CHUA OSCILLATORS.

Compare the z-transform equation to the transfer function for the analogue circuit:

$$z = e^{s\tau} = \frac{e^{s\tau/2}}{e^{-s\tau/2}} \approx \frac{1+s\tau/2}{1-s\tau/2} \tag{7}$$

The transfer function for the circuit in Figure 10, is:

$$\frac{V_{out}}{V_{in}} = -\frac{sCdRd}{1+sCdRd} \tag{8}$$

This gives an expression for the analogue delay, τ, in terms of circuit component values and substituting component values gives τ = 0.5**CdRd* = 0.5 us. The delay circuit is connected from the *Z* output via the feedback path to the input of the third integrator. Figure 11 shows the 0.5 us delay introduced to the *Z* signal, where *Zd* is the delayed signal. Chaos oscillator initial conditions were obtained from a detuned 433 MHz data FM receiver integrated circuit. Since the level of the receiver noise is random, it means an intruder cannot predict where the chaos sources start, and thus makes cryptanalysis impossible.

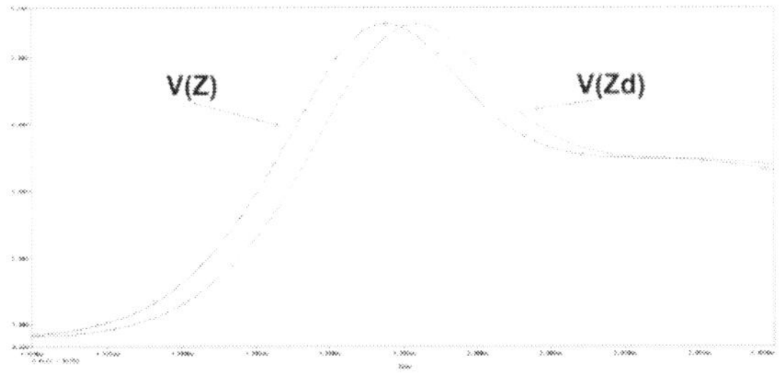

FIGURE 11. THE DELAY BETWEEN *Z* AND *Zd* IS 0.5 US

The receiver noise could be used as the primary source but external signals from an attacker, could introduce regular signals which would weaken the key.

F. The Chua chaotic oscillator

In 1983, while trying to prove the Lorenz oscillator was chaotic, Leon Chua created a new analogue chaos oscillator system defined by three first-order coupled equations as in (9). The standard Chua oscillator configuration consisted of a parallel-tuned type circuit and connected across it is a 'Chua diode'composed of segmented negative resistances achieved using operational amplifiers [48][49][50].

However, a simpler novel approach used two AD633 four-quadrant multiplier devices to implement the cubic term in (9), the term responsible for chaos [51]. An identical Padé delay to the one used in the Lorenz circuit, was also added to the y signal line to increase the signal entropy.

$$\begin{aligned} x(t) &= -\int_{t_0}^{t}\{-1.66x(t)-10y(t)+0.625x(t)^3\}dt \\ y(t) &= -\int_{t_0}^{t}\{-x(t)+y(t-\tau)-z(t)\}dt \\ z(t) &= -\int_{t_0}^{t}\{14.286y(t)\}dt \end{aligned} \tag{9}$$

The Chua attractor and signals in Figure 12, are similar to the Lorenz examined previously.

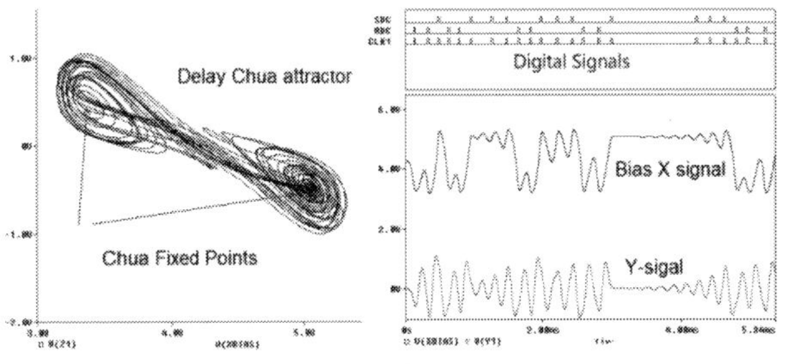

FIGURE 12. (A) THE CHUA ATTRACTOR ON THE LEFT (B) BOTTOM RIGHT PANE ARE THE ANALOGUE SIGNALS WITH THE DIGITAL SIGNALS ON TOP.

TABLE I. NIST RESULTS FOR THE COMPLETE OTP ENCODER (SHORT LENGTH OTP).

Statistical Test	*P-value natural noise*	*P-value Lorenz and Chua (XOR)*	*Pass/Fail*
Frequency	P = 0.4122	P = 0.6123	Pass
Block frequency	P = 0.1161	P = 0.1008	Pass
Runs	P = 0.7846	P = 0.0557	Pass
Block Longest Run Ones	P = 0.5388	P = 0.5850	Pass
Binary Matrix Rank	P = 0.7138	P = 0.4370	Pass
D Fourier Transform	P = 0.5206	P = 0.6840	Pass
Overlapping Template Match	P = 0.7729	P = 0.97144	Pass
Linear Complexity	P = 0.952	P = 0.4699	Pass
Serial	(P1 = 0.1971 P2 = 0.544)	(P1 = 0.0831 P2 = 0.487)	Pass
Approximate Entropy	P = 0.1143	P = 0.0603	Pass
Cumulative Sums	P = 0.4444	P = 0.6753	Pass

TABLE II. NIST RESULTS FOR THE COMPLETE ENCODER (LONG LENGTH OTP).

Random Excursion Test	*χ^2 test*	*P-value test*	*Pass/Fail*
(x =-4)	χ^2 = 3.7052	P = 0.5925	Pass
(x =-3)	χ^2 = 5.0654	P = 0.4079	Pass
(x =-2)	χ^2 = 2.1114	P = 0.8335	Pass
(x =-1)	χ^2 = 0.7659	P = 0.9791	Pass
(x = 1)	χ^2 = 1.5392	P = 0.9084	Pass
(x = 2)	χ^2 = 0.5213	P = 0.9913	Pass
(x = 3)	χ^2 = 2.2011	P = 0.8206	Pass
(x = 4)	χ^2 = 11.649	P = 0.0399	Pass

Random Excursion Variant Test	*Total visits*	*P-value*	*Pass/Fail*
(x =-9)	Total visits = 362	P = 0.0388	Pass
(x =-8)	Total visits = 412	P = 0.0645	Pass
(x =-7)	Total visits = 413	P = 0.0479	Pass
(x =-6)	Total visits = 445	P = 0.0591	Pass
(x =-5)	Total visits = 504	P = 0.1208	Pass
(x =-4)	Total visits = 525	P = 0.1228	Pass
(x =-3)	Total visits = 547	P = 0.1192	Pass
(x =-2)	Total visits = 596	P = 0.2144	Pass
(x =-1)	Total visits = 658	P = 0.6435	Pass
(x = 1)	Total visits = 673	P = 0.9565	Pass
(x = 2)	Total visits = 692	P = 0.7893	Pass
(x = 3)	Total visits = 669	P = 0.9417	Pass
(x = 4)	Total visits = 614	P = 0.5303	Pass
(x = 5)	Total visits = 620	P = 0.6178	Pass
(x = 6)	Total visits = 663	P = 0.9215	Pass
(x = 7)	Total visits = 754	P = 0.5509	Pass
(x = 8)	Total visits = 851	P = 0.2161	Pass
(x = 9)	Total visits = 899	P = 0.1392	Pass
(x = 9)	Total visits = 899	P = 0.1392	Pass

VI. TESTING THE RANDOMNESS OF THE ONE-TIME-PAD

It is impossible to say if a binary stream is random, but statistical tests such as the National Institute of Standards and Technology (NIST) suite of fifteen statistical tests (revised in 2010), can evaluate the cryptographic strength of the OTP random number sequences (see Figure 26).

These NIST Statistical null hypothesis tests examine the binary random bit stream to ascertain if the null hypothesis is verified and entails exploring the p-values to see if they are more significant than the significance level, 0.01 to 1. The test also checks the numbers produced are uniformly distributed in the interval 0:1 [52][53][54].

The NIST suite contains parameter tests to evaluate long sequences of several million bits and non-parameter tests for short sequences of 1000 bits. Table I shows NIST results for short sequences for the encoder. Included in the first column, for comparison purposes, are results from binary sequences obtained from [55]. The NIST test results for long binary sequences of several million bits are in Table II [56][57].

A. Additional randomness tests

Additional tests evaluated the entropy of the OTP for correct certification:

- Autocorrelation,
- Power Spectral Density (PSD),
- Shannon entropy,
- Kolmogorov Sinai entropy and Algorithmic Complexity,
- Histogram distribution,
- Probability Distribution Function test,
- Lyapunov exponent test, and
- Averaging test

B. Autocorrelation Test

For truly random bit sequences, the autocorrelation function test should display a Kronecker delta function over time. A display showing other correlation peaks means the stream is not truly random. The auto-correlation function for a digital sequence is the cross-correlation of a signal, $x(t)$ with a delayed version of itself, which, for intervals of rΔt, is:

$$[R_{xx}(r\Delta t) = \frac{1}{N-r}\sum_{n=0}^{N-r} x(n)x(n+r\Delta t) \quad (10)$$

Polar binary sequences meaning positive w.r.t. zero, will display a triangular shaped autocorrelation function rather than an impulse. Hence, it is prudent to subtract the mean from the series to obtain the correct impulse response shown in Figure 13 (Appendix Figure 23).

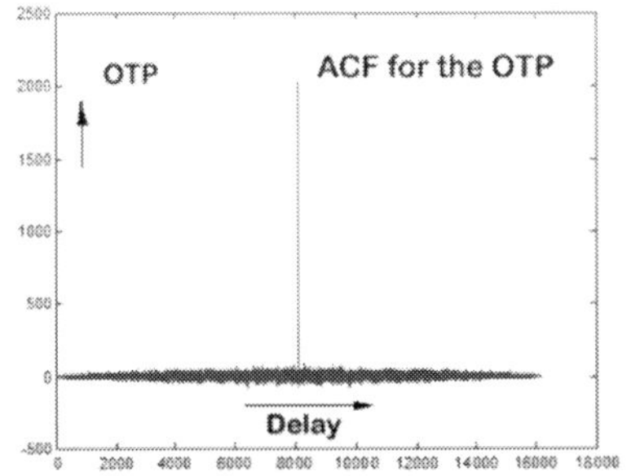

FIGURE 13. (A) THE OTP AUTOCORRELATION PLOT

C. Power Spectral Density

Spectral attacks by an adversary are possible if the Power Spectral Density (PSD) for a key is not uniform. The PSD is obtained from the absolute value of the square of the magnitude of the Fast Fourier Transform (FFT). Alternatively, apply the Wiener-Khinchine theorem to the FFT of the auto-correlation function.

$$S_x f = \lim_{T\to\infty} E\left\{\frac{1}{2T}\left|\int_{-T}^{T} x(t)e^{-j2\pi ft}dt\right|^2\right\} \quad (11)$$

Figure 14 displays Histogram and Power Spectral Density plots of the Lena bitmap image encoded by an OTP in an XOR gate. The PSD and histogram are uniform and no bias lines are in the encoded picture. The decoded Lena image in the bottom pane shows no visible degradation. Test suites such as the ENT, TestU01, CryptX, Diehard, are similar to the NIST test suite, but NIST is considered the most comprehensive [58]. Figure 26 in the appendix shows the NIST test application software used for testing the OTP binary sequence.

D. Entropy and Information

Entropy quantifies the randomness of a cipher and Shannon and Szilard showed how information and unpredictability are connected. The French Carnot family named entropy as the portion of energy which cannot do useful work in a system [59], and the German physicist, Rudolf Clausius, defined entropy S as the ratio of the heat in a system Q to its temperature T as $S = \frac{Q}{T}$. Ludwig Boltzmann formed his kinetic theory of gases and said in any closed system entropy will always increase and is a measure of the dispersal of energy

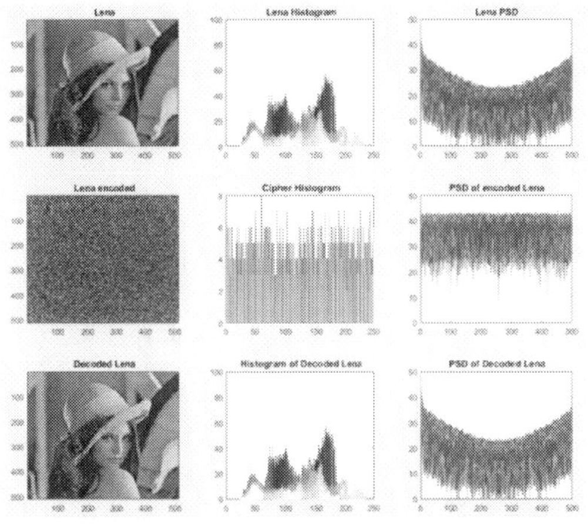

FIGURE 14. (A) THE LENA IMAGE (B) HISTOGRAM OF UNENCODED IMAGE (C) POWER SPECTRAL DENSITY OF UNENCODED IMAGE.

$S = k_B \log W$ with $k_B = 1.3806\text{x}10^{-23}$ Joules/K. Here, W is the equiprobable number of microstates with the same dimension as entropy. According to Boltzmann's hypothesis, a logarithmic relationship exists between entropy, phase space volume, k_B, and the macroscopic and microscopic states of gas [60].

A famous thought experiment by James Clerk Maxwell called Maxwell's Demon, created a paradox [61] on the entropy of gas particles in a closed system. Szilard described a sealed box containing hot and cold gas particles and a gate operated by a devil who could separate the hot and cold gas particles without expending energy.

Leo Szilard proposed a solution by associating information with entropy, because each time the demon operated the gate he collected information. Szilard argued the information balanced the overall entropy and solved the paradox. In Szilard's doctoral dissertation (1922), and a companion paper 1929 [62], he stated there was an increase of $klog2$ units of entropy in any measurement. Later, Shannon and Kolmogorov independently argued the case for a link between information and entropy.

E. Shannon Entropy

Claude Shannon discussed the relationship between entropy and information in his 1949 paper [30] and related this to the randomness of a signal. Shannon defined entropy as a measure of the amount of information to determine precisely a system state from among all possible states. Thus, the *Shannon information content* in binary digits, or '*bits*', for an outcome, x, for a random sequence, X, with n outcomes, $x_1, x_2, \ldots, x_n$, is $h(x) = \ln \frac{1}{p(x_i)}$. A measure of uncertainty for a string of length n, is the *average Shannon entropy*:

$$H(x) = -\sum_{i=1}^{n} p(x_i)\ln p(x_i)\ bits \quad (12)$$

The probability that an event x_i occurs from the number of states n, is $p(x_i)$, with each state having a probability between 0 and 1. The log of the probability yields 0 to negative infinity, but because entropy is positive a negative sign in (12) is introduced. Boltzmann and Shannon entropy equations have opposite signs and a scaling factor, *-kln2*. Shannon entropy sorts objects into N bins of size n_i and measures the amount of information required to determine precisely a system state from all possible states. The higher the entropy of a signal, the greater the amount of information and is, therefore, a measure of signal unpredictability or randomness.

F. Kolmogorov entropy and Algorithmic Complexity

The Russian mathematician, Andrei Kolmogorov suggested in 1959, a modified form of the Shannon entropy, as did Y.Sinai in the same year, hence it is known as the Kolmogorov-Sinai (KS) entropy and is an essential metric for testing the randomness of a chaotic series. For example, KS entropy is zero for a regular series, finite for a chaotic series, but infinite for a random signal [18]. Shannon and KS entropy represents the rate at which information is created and defines when a time series is chaotic.

From an observer's resolution, the partition is, $\beta = \{X_1, X_2, ..., X_m\}$, and examining the system state, x, the observer determines only the fact that $x \in X_i$ and can reconstruct the symbolic trajectory $\alpha_n = \{s_{m_1}, s_{m_2}, \ldots, s_{m_n}\}$ corresponding to the regions visited. The entropy of a trajectory α_n, with respect to the partition β, is given by

$$H_n^{\beta} = -\sum_{\alpha_n} \Pr(\alpha_n) \log_{|A|} \Pr(\alpha_n) \qquad (13)$$

where $\Pr(\alpha_n)$ is the probability of occurrence of the substring, α_n. The conditional entropy of the $(n+1)$-th symbol provided the previous n symbols are known, is defined as:

$$h_n^{\beta} = h_{n+1|n}^{\beta} = \begin{cases} H_{n+1}^{\beta} - H_n^{\beta}, & n \geq 1 \\ H_1^{\beta}, & n = 1 \end{cases} \qquad (14)$$

The entropy for a partition, β, is given by

$$h^{\beta} = \lim_{n \to \infty} h_n^{\beta} = \lim_{n \to \infty} \frac{1}{n} H_n^{\beta}$$

The KS entropy of a chaotic system is the supremum over all possible partitions.

$$h_{KS} = \sup_{\beta} h^{\beta} \qquad (15)$$

The KS entropy is zero for regular systems, finite and positive for a deterministic chaos, but infinite for a random process. It is related to the Lyapunov exponents by $h_{KS} = \sum_{1 \leq d \leq D} \lambda_d$, and proportional to the time horizon T on which the system is predictable. An important metric in cryptography which also measure randomness is the Kolmogorov Complexity (KC) created simultaneously by Kolmogorov and Ray Solmonoff but essentially is the Shannon entropy. KC specifies the minimum length to which a binary string of bits may be compressed (a truly random sequence is incompressible) [63]. A positive KS entropy is proof of chaotic behaviour and randomness and related to algorithmic complexity, where the system is ergodic. We may relate complexity and entropy as "cause and effect"- the more complex a system is, the more unpredictable its behaviour is and results in higher entropy. Complexity is considered the size of an "internal program" that generates a binary sequence, whereas entropy is computed from the probability distribution of that sequence.

G. Probability Distribution Function-Histograms

A Probability Distribution Function (PDF) is defined as a function from strings $\mathcal{L} = \{\alpha_j\}$, to nonnegative real numbers, i.e., $\Pr : \mathcal{L} \to [0, 1]$, such that $\sum_{\alpha \in \mathcal{L}} \Pr(\alpha) = 1$. A string α is truly random if, for any substring $\beta_n, \gamma_n \in \alpha$, $0 > n > length(\alpha)$ $\Pr(\beta_n) = \Pr(\gamma_n)$. We cannot predict any digit in a truly random string, i.e., for any symbol $s_i \in \alpha$, the conditional probability $\Pr(s_i|s_{i-1}, s_{i-2}, \ldots) = \Pr(s_i)$. A knowledge of a previous state has no effect on the probability of a successful prediction of the next state.

H. Lyapunov Exponential

The Lyapunov Exponent (LE) quantifies how chaotic trajectory orbits diverge with time and must be positive for the function to generate chaotic trajectories within a few iterations. The LE measures how fast two chaotic paths separate from each other, i.e., predicting the behaviour of a chaotic system in time. However, this measure has the disadvantage in that it does not consider the resolution under which the system is observed, unlike KS entropy [64][65]. Entropy and LE's in a chaotic system are approximately equal, and Pesin's theorem relates KS as the sum of positive LE's.

I. The average entropy test

Averaging the Lorenz x signal is a novel and quick test for assessing how parameter variation changes the randomness of the binary stream. A truly random signal should oscillate close to zero, but if it displays more positive than negative excursions around the zero axis, then the signal is biased. Figure 15 shows four plots for each value of *C5* and demonstrates how the delay changes the average value of the Lorenz X signal.

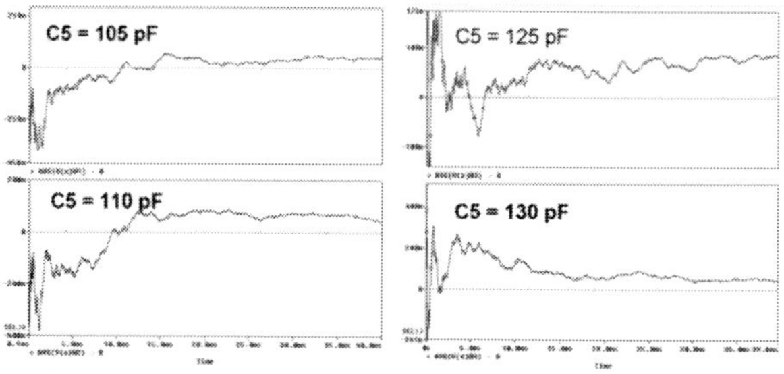

FIGURE 15. EFFECT OF C5 ON THE X SIGNAL ENTROPY.

The delay is changed by varying *Cd* or *Rd*, and observing the value which brought the average signal closest to the zero axis. In the prototype, the resistance, *Rd* was chosen as the variable parameter as it was the easier option. Averaging a non-random sequence of alternating ones and zeroes would also be plotted closest to the zero axis but the method is useful nevertheless for assessing the presence of bias. A positive start-up transient part can be observed in the average of x in Figure

16 and means the stream is biased. This necessitated rejecting the start-up transient region by the software. Figure 17 and Figure 18 show the effect of changing Lorenz parameters on the average value.

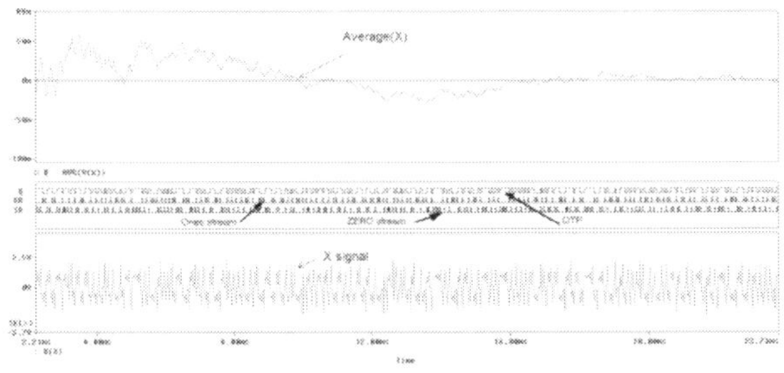

FIGURE 16. AVERAGE x FOR 0.5 US DELAY

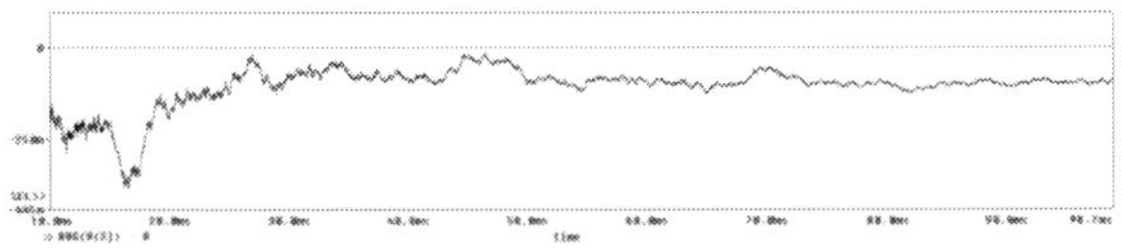

FIGURE 17. AVERAGE x FOR P = 11

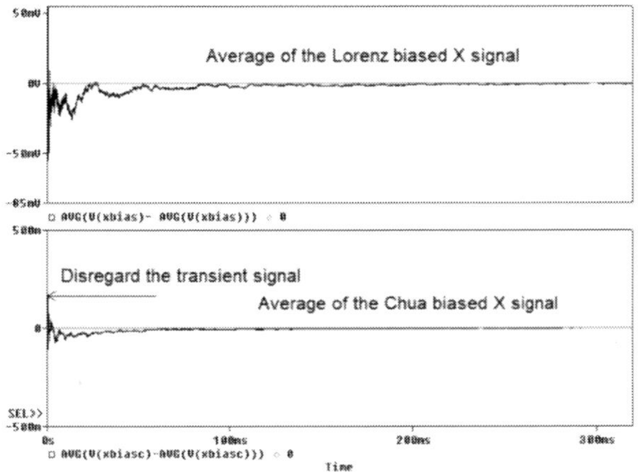

FIGURE 18. AVERAGE x FOR LORENZ AND CHUA PARAMETERS.

VII. CONCLUSION AND FUTURE WORK

Inadequate Cloud security for sensitive data stored in the Cloud was addressed by creating an extra layer of localised encoding using a truly random binary number OTP generator to return control to the client. Local encryption could reduce or eliminate, fines against companies and organisations who fail to meet the 72-hour breach deadline notification as outlined in the 2018 GDPR legislation. The proposed OTP encoder generates binary sequences from analogue chaos signals having an infinite number of states and overcome the difficulties associated with a digital implementation of an OTP which uses finite-state arithmetic and not truly random.

An analogue delay was added to the feedback paths of the Lorenz and Chua analogue oscillators to increase the OTP entropy in a novel way. Chaos sources initialised by noise from a data receiver generated truly random unlimited amounts of unbreakable binary sequences that passed the NIST statistical suite of tests. A novel testing method was developed to investigate the effect of specific parameter variation on entropy. This simple, quick test involved observing the signal average and selected the parameter which caused the average to oscillate close to the zero time axis. A JavaScript application post-processed the OTP sequences by applying a VN algorithm which maximised the sequence entropy and then combined it with the plaintext data.

A prototype printed circuit board (PCB) was tested for randomness, but future work is being planned to implement the final encoder on a Programmable System-on-Chip (PSoC) family of microcontroller integrated circuits [66]. Other planned work involves localised encryption for devices used to protect local devices used in the Internet of Things (IoT), which is growing at a fast pace and has very little security at present.

ACKNOWLEDGEMENT

The authors are grateful to Professor Michael Conlon and Dr Marek Rebow, Dublin Institute of Technology, for arranging the author's collaborative research programme.

APPENDIX

Figure 19 shows noise voltage initial conditions produce a different trajectory in the strange attractor for each noise level. This mechanism makes cryptanalysis difficult because the random nature of electronic noise produces a different value each time it is sampled.

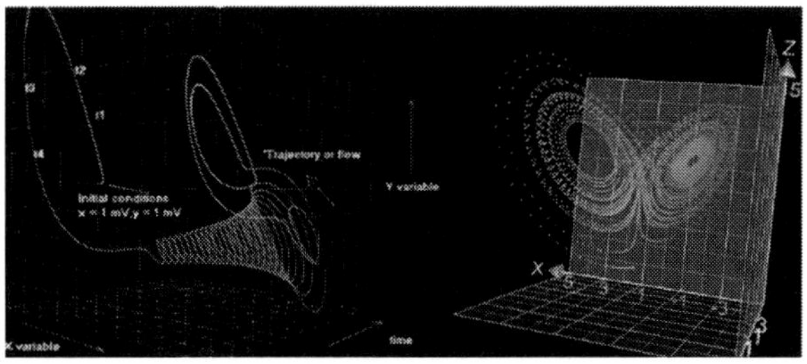

FIGURE 19. A 30D LORENZ ATTRACTOR INITIALISED BY NOISE.

Figure 20 plots a Poincaré section placed through the FPs of the attractor.

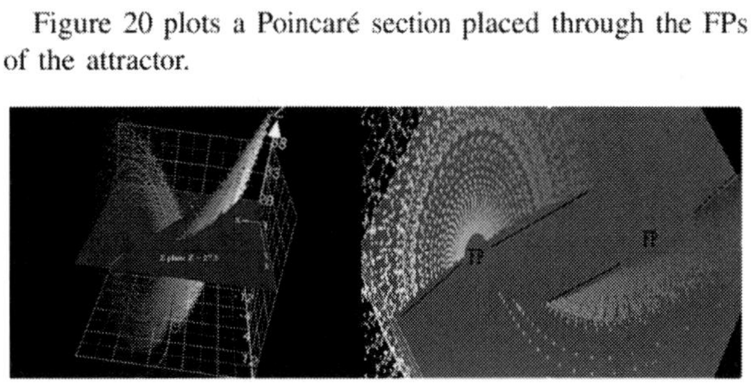

FIGURE 20. 3-D PLOT OF LORENZ ATTRACTOR.

Scaling Lorenz signals is necessary because the amplitude of the unscaled z signal shown in Figure 21 is too large at 45 V for normal electronic operation electronic implementation.

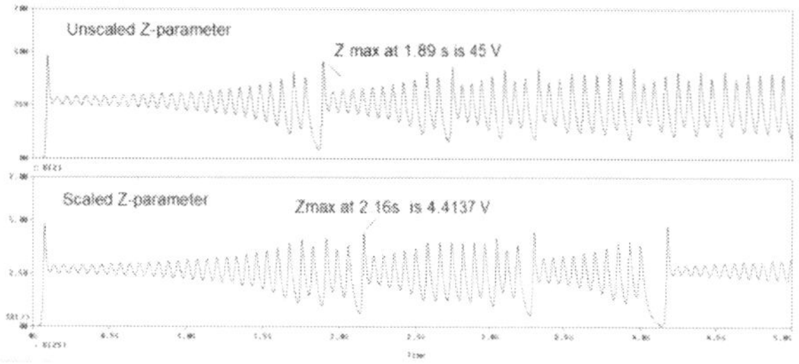

FIGURE 21. THE SCALED THE LORENZ Z SIGNAL IS IN THE LOWER PANE.

The ABM Chua circuit in Figure 22 allowed concepts to be simulated quickly and without the convergence problems of model integrated circuits. The nonlinear Chua chaos parameters are different to the previous values used. The ABM SUM, MULT, INTEG, and GAIN parts implement mathematical arithmetical functions, with a PARAM part to define any variables used.

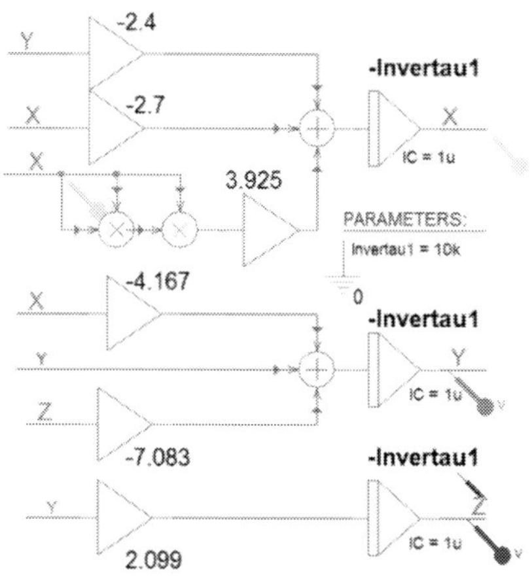

FIGURE 22. A CHUA ABM CHAOS OSCILLATOR

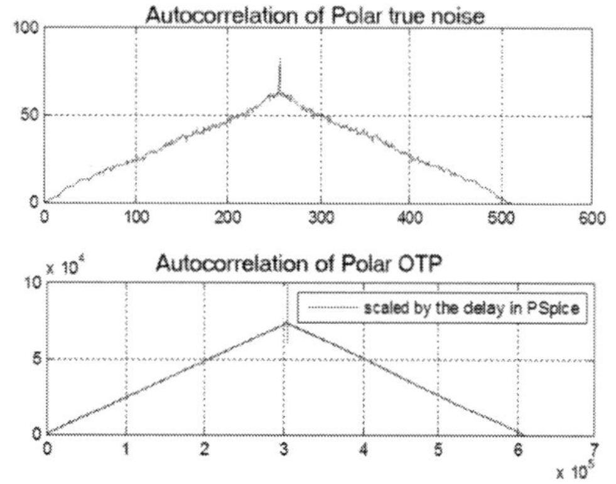

FIGURE 23. AN AUTOCORRELATION PLOT OF A POLAR NOISE SIGNAL.

The autocorrelation plots for noise and the OTP in Figure 23 shows an impulse on a triangle which is caused by the DC of a polar OTP.

Removing the average DC will display the classic impulse autocorrelation shaped response. Figure 24 shows the Lorenz out-of-phase set and reset signal pulses from the LM339 comparator and have different widths at each sampling time but are made to have a constant width using the monostable devices. External resistor-capacitor components connected to the monostable set the width of the binary pulses to a constant value. The process of producing binary signals from an analogue source is a 1-bit ADC.

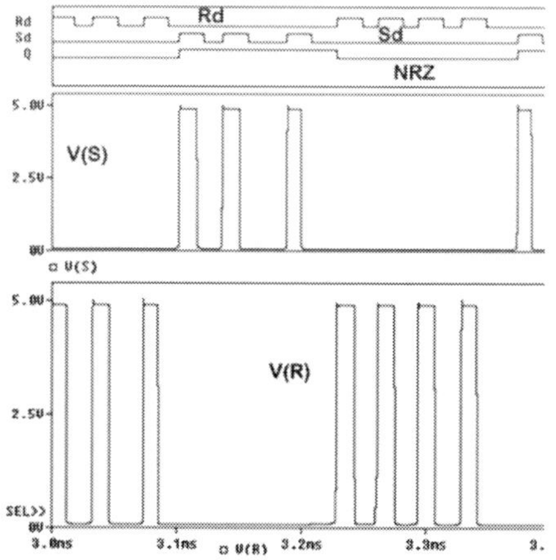

FIGURE 24. OUTPUT SET AND RESET SIGNALS FROM THE COMPARATOR.

Figure 25 illustrates how bias in the random string shows up as regular patterns in the encoded picture. This should never be allowed as any bias reduces the robustness of the OTP against attacks.

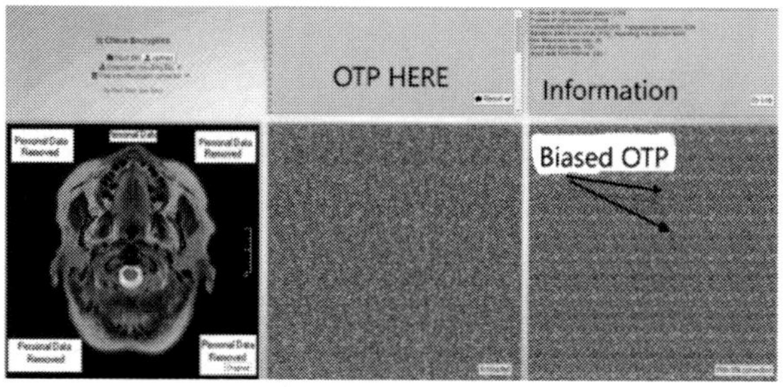

FIGURE 25. BIAS IN THE ENCODED PICTURE.

Figure 26 shows the application used to evaluate the randomness of the OTP. The parameterised tests need certain parameters inputted, as shown in the parameter boxes on the right-hand-side.

REFERENCES

[1] P. Tobin, L. Tobin, M. McKeever, and J. Blackledge, "On the Development of a One-Time Pad Generator for Personalising Cloud Security," Cloud Comput. 2017 Eighth Int. Conf. Cloud Comput. GRIDs, Virtualization, 2017, pp. 1–6.

[2] Accessed 08.12.2017. [Online]. Available: https://www.privacy-regulation.eu/en/32.htm

[3] J. P. Albrecht, "How the gdpr will change the world," Eur. Data Prot. L. Rev., vol. 2, 2016, p. 287.

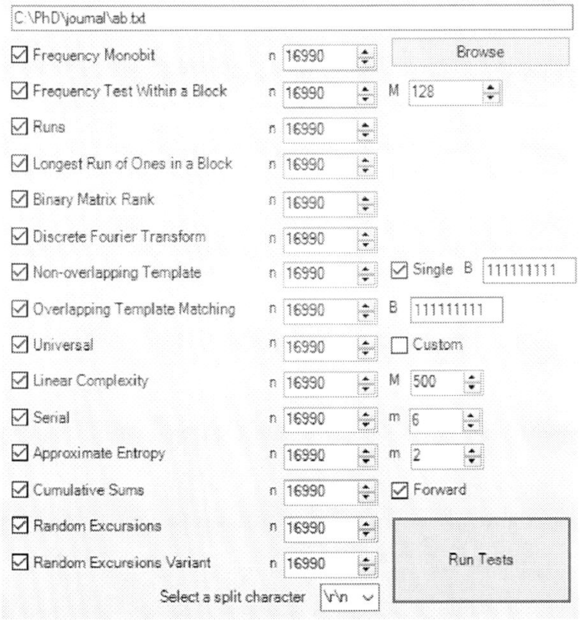

FIGURE 26. APPLICATION FOR NIST TESTING.

[4] P. Tobin, B. Duncan, M. McKeever, J. Blackledge, and M. Whittington, "UK Financial Institutions Stand to Lose Billions in GDPR Fines: How can They Mitigate This?" Cloud Comput. 2017 Eighth Int. Conf. Cloud Comput. GRIDs, Virtualization, 2017, pp. 1–6.

[5] A. Aich, A. Sen, and S. R. Dash, "A survey on cloud environment security risk and remedy," Proc. - 1st Int. Conf. Comput. Intell. Networks, CINE 2015, 2015, pp. 192–193.

[6] L. Badger, T. Grance, R. Patt-Corner, and J. Voas, "Draft cloud computing synopsis and recommendations," NIST special publication, vol. 800, 2011, p. 146.

[7] Accessed 09.12.2017. [Online]. Available: https://www.theguardian.com/media-network/media-network-blog/2014/feb/18/cloud-computing-nsa-privacy-breaches-crisis-confidence

[8] D. Shumow and N. Ferguson, "On the possibility of a back door in the nist sp800-90 dual ec prng," in Proc. Crypto, vol. 7, 2007.

[9] D. Hankerson, A. J. Menezes, and S. Vanstone, Guide to elliptic curve cryptography. Springer ScienceandBusiness Media, 2006.

[10] J. Huergo, "Nist removes cryptography algorithm from random number generator recommendations," NIST announcement, April, 2007.

[11] N. Perlroth, J. Larson, and S. Shane, "Nsa able to foil basic safeguards of privacy on web," The New York Times, vol. 5, 2013.

[12] B. Duncan and M. Whittington, "Enhancing cloud security and privacy: The power and the weakness of the audit trail," Cloud Comput, 2016, pp. 125–130.

[13] W. Blackmer, "Gdpr: Getting ready for the new eu general data protection regulation," Information Law Group, InfoLawGroup LLP, Retrieved, vol. 22, no. 08, 2016, p. 2016.

[14] S. M. Bellovin, "Frank miller: Inventor of the one-time pad," Cryptologia, vol. 35, no. 3, 2011, pp. 203–222.

[15] ——, "Vernam, mauborgne, and friedman: The one-time pad and the index of coincidence," Lecture Notes in Computer Science (including subseries Lecture Notes in Artificial Intelligence and Lecture Notes in Bioinformatics), vol. 9100, 2016, pp. 40–66.

[16] W. R. Bennett, "Secret Telephony as a Historical Example of Spread-Spectrum Communication," IEEE Trans. Commun., vol. 31, no. 1, 1983, pp. 98–104.

[17] O. Hoare, "Enigma: Codebreaking and the second world war," The True Story through Contemporary Documents, introduced and selected by Oliver Hoare. UK Public Record Office, Richmond, Surrey, 2002.

[18] J. M. Blackledge, Cryptography and Steganography: New Algorithms and Applications. Center for Advanced Studies Warsaw University of Technology, 2011.

[19] D. Rijmenants, "Is one-time pad history," Cipher maschines and cryptology, vol. 5, 2011.

[20] D.Rijmenants, "The complete guide to secure communications with the one time pad cipher," Cipher Machines & Cryptology, 2010.

[21] S. Mrdovic and B. Perunicic, "Kerckhoffs' principle for intrusion detection," in Telecommunications Network Strategy and Planning Symposium, 2008. Networks 2008. The 13th International. IEEE, 2008, pp. 1–8.

[22] B. ShreeJain, S. Chandrakar, and S. Tiwari, "An innovative approach for implementation of one-time pads," International Journal of Computer Applications, vol. 89, no. 13, 2014, pp. 35–37.

[23] G. Upadhyay and M. J. Nene, "One Time Pad Generation Using Quantum Superposition States," no. 1, 2016, pp. 1882–1886.

[24] M. Borowski and M. Lesniewicz, "Modern usage of old one-time pad," Communications and Information Systems Conference (MCC), 2012 Military, 2012, pp. 1–5.

[25] M. Borowski, "The infinite source of random sequences for classified cryptographic systems," in 2016 International Conference on Military Communications and Information Systems, ICMCIS 2016, 2016.

[26] P. Tobin, L. Tobin, M. Mc Keever, and J. Blackledge, "Chaos-based cryptography for cloud computing," 2016 27th Irish Signals and Systems Conference, ISSC 2016, 2016.

[27] P. Jees and T. Diya, "Medical image protection in cloud system," matrix, vol. 2, 2016, p. 3.

[28] J. Blackledge, A. Al-Rawi, and P. Tobin, "Stegacryption of DICOM Metadata," Irish Signals Syst. Conf. 2014 2014 China-irel. Int. Conf. Inf. Commun. Technol. (ISSC 2014/CIICT 2014). 25th IET, 2014, pp. 304–309.

[29] F. A. Mohsin, R. R. Mostafa, and H. M. El Bakry, "Design of information system for facilitating litigation procedures," International Journal of Computer Engineering and Information Technology, vol. 6, no. 1, 2015, pp. 107–112.

[30] C. E. Shannon, "Communication theory of secrecy systems," Bell Labs Technical Journal, vol. 28, no. 4, 1949, pp. 656–715.

[31] C.E, Shannon, "A mathematical theory of communication," ACM SIGMOBILE Mobile Computing and Communications Review, vol. 5, no. 1, 2001, pp. 3–55.

[32] C. Pellicer-Lostao and R. Lopez-Ruiz, "Notions of chaotic cryptography: Sketch of a chaos based cryptosystem," arXiv preprint arXiv:1203.4134, 2012.

[33] G. Alvarez and S. Li, "Some basic cryptographic requirements for chaos-based cryptosystems," International Journal of Bifurcation and Chaos, vol. 16, no. 08, 2006, pp. 2129–2151.

[34] W. Diffie and M. Hellman, "New directions in cryptography," IEEE transactions on Information Theory, vol. 22, no. 6, 1976, pp. 644–654.

[35] J. M. Blackledge, "On the Applications of Deterministic Chaos for Encrypting Data on the Cloud," in Third Int. Conf. Evol. Internet, 2011, pp. 78–87.

[36] V. Patidar, N. Pareek, and K. Sud, "A new substitution–diffusion based image cipher using chaotic standard and logistic maps," Communications in Nonlinear Science and Numerical Simulation, vol. 14, no. 7, 2009, pp. 3056–3075.

[37] E. B. Barker and J. M. Kelsey, Recommendation for the Entropy Sources Used for Random Bit Generator. US Department of Commerce, National Institute of Standards and Technology, 2012.

[38] J. Van Neuman, "Various techniques used in connection with random digits, collected works, 765–770," 1963.

[39] E. B. Barker and A. Roginsky, "Recommendation for Cryptographic Key Generation," NIST Spec. Publ. 800-133, 2012, pp. 1–26.

[40] S. Bruce, "Applied cryptography: protocols, algorithms, and source code in c," John WileyandSons, Inc., New York, 1996.

[41] P. M. Binder and R. V. Jensen, "Simulating chaotic behavior with finite-state machines," Physical Review A, vol. 34, no. 5, 1986, p. 4460.

[42] S. Li, X. Mou, Y. Cai, Z. Ji, and J. Zhang, "On the security of a chaotic encryption scheme: problems with computerized chaos in finite computing precision," Computer physics communications, vol. 153, no. 1, 2003, pp. 52–58.

[43] E. N. Lorenz, "Deterministic nonperiodic flow," Journal of the atmospheric sciences, vol. 20, no. 2, 1963, pp. 130–141.

[44] P. Tobin, PSpice for Digital Communications Engineering. Morgan & Claypool Publishers, 2007, vol. 2, no. 1.

[45] Tobin, Paul, PSpice for circuit theory and electronic devices. Morgan & Claypool Publishers, 2007, vol. 2, no. 1.

[46] M. Lakshmanan and D. V. Senthilkumar, Dynamics of nonlinear time-delay systems. Springer Science & Business Media, 2011.

[47] P. Tobin, "Pspice for digital signal processing," Synthesis Lectures On Digital Circuits and Systems, vol. 2, no. 1, 2007, pp. 1–142.

[48] M. P. Kennedy, "Three steps to chaos. i. evolution," IEEE Transactions on Circuits and Systems I: Fundamental Theory and Applications, vol. 40, no. 10, 1993, pp. 640–656.
[49] ——, "Robust op amp realization of chua's circuit," Frequenz, vol. 46, no. 3-4, 1992, pp. 66–80.
[50] P. Kennedy, "Genealogy of chuas circuit," Chaos, CNN, Memristors and Beyond: A Festschrift for Leon Chua With DVD-ROM, composed by Eleonora Bilotta, 2013, pp. 3–24.
[51] R. Kiliç, A practical guide for studying Chua's circuits. World Scientific, 2010, vol. 71.
[52] P. M. Alcover, A. Guillamón, and M. d. C. Ruiz, "A new randomness test for bit sequences," Informatica, vol. 24, no. 3, 2013, pp. 339–356.
[53] J. M. Bahi, X. Fang, C. Guyeux, and Q. Wang, "Ramdomness quality of CI chaotic generators. Application to Internet security," Science (80-.)., 2010.
[54] K. Hamano, F. Sato, and H. Yamamoto, "A new randomness test based on linear complexity profile," IEICE Trans. Fundam. Electron. Commun. Comput. Sci., vol. E92-A, no. 1, 2009, pp. 166–172.
[55] M. Haahr, "Random. org: True random number service," School of Computer Science and Statistics, Trinity College, Dublin, Ireland. Website (http://www. random. org). Accessed, vol. 10, 2010.
[56] F. D. K. Corporation, "The Evaluation of Randomness of RPG100 by Using NIST and DIEHARD Tests," Test, 2003, pp. 1–6.
[57] D. A. Cristina and B. R. Eugen, "A new method to improve cryptographic properties of chaotic discrete dynamical systems," in Internet Technology And Secured Transactions, 2012 International Conference for. IEEE, 2012, pp. 60–65.
[58] A. NIST, "Statistical test suite for the validation of random number generators and pseudo random number generators for cryptographic applications," Special Publication, 2001, pp. 800–22.
[59] J. Boyling, "Carnot engines and the principle of increase of entropy," International Journal of Theoretical Physics, vol. 7, no. 4, 1973, pp. 291–299.
[60] R. Frigg and C. Werndl, "A guide for the perplexed," Probabilities in physics, 2, p. 115.
[61] P. Tobin and J. Blackledge, "Entropy, information, landauer's limit and moore's law," in 25th IET Irish Signals & Systems Conference 2014 and 2014 China-Ireland International Conference on Information and Communications Technologies (ISSC 2014/CIICT 2014).
[62] L. Szilard, "On the Decrease of Entropy in a Thermodynamics System by the intervention of intelligent beings," Zeitschrift für Physik, vol. 53, 1929, pp. 840–856.
[63] R. Landauer, "Irreversibility and heat generation in the computing process," IBM journal of research and development, vol. 5, no. 3, 1961, pp. 183–191.
[64] R. Wackerbauer, A. Witt, H. Atmanspacher, J. Kurths, and H. Scheingraber, "A comparative classification of complexity measures," Chaos, Solitons & Fractals, vol. 4, no. 1, 1994, pp. 133–173.
[65] K. Pawelzik and H. Schuster, "Generalized dimensions and entropies from a measured time series," Physical Review A, vol. 35, no. 1, 1987, p. 481.
[66] R. Ashby, Designer's guide to the Cypress PSoC. Newnes, 2005.

PassGame: Robust Shoulder-Surfing Resistance Through Challenge-Response Authentication

Jonathan Gurary*, Ye Zhu*, Nahed Alnahash†, and Huirong Fu†
*Department of Electrical and Computer Engineering, Cleveland State University, Cleveland, Ohio
Emails: j.gurary@vikes.csuohio.edu, y.zhu61@csuohio.edu
†Department of Computer Science, Oakland University, Oakland, Michigan
Emails: nalnahas@oakland.edu, fu@oakland.edu

Abstract—**Mobile devices are constantly exposed to the risk of shoulder-surfing by prying eyes and video surveillance. In this paper, we propose *PassGame*, a shoulder-surfing resistant mobile authentication scheme based on chess. PassGame can offer extremely high shoulder-surfing resistance, even against camera attacks, at some cost to usability. PassGame works by challenging a user with a random formation of chess pieces on a game board; successful authentication requires the user to alter the board so that a set of predefined rules are satisfied. We implement PassGame on Android. Our user studies show that PassGame can achieve 100% recall rates one week after password setup. Our user studies on the shoulder-surfing resistance of PassGame show that weak PassGame passwords cannot be shoulder-surfed even after viewing 5 complete recorded password entries, and strong passwords are resilient even against camera attacks.**

Keywords–Shoulder Surfing; Challenge Response; Mobile; Graphical Password; Authentication

I. INTRODUCTION

A short, preliminary version of this work was published at ACHI 2017 [1].

Mobile devices- such as smartphones and tablets- are becoming increasingly popular because of their nearly ubiquitous Internet access through various communication capabilities such as WiFi and their numerous applications and games. While users are enjoying the benefits of ubiquitous computing enabled by mobile devices, they are also becoming more vulnerable to shoulder-surfing attacks. Consider a user on a crowded subway train: the user may want to check emails as there are a few stops before a destination. But, to check emails through a smartphone, the user has to unlock the screen with possibly several pairs of eyes watching the whole authentication process from behind. Since current authentication schemes on mobile devices are not designed to resist shoulder-surfing attacks [2], users of mobile devices are in danger of password theft and its consequences. Harbach et al. [3] suggest that mobile phone users unlock their devices an average of 48 times per day (about 3 unlocks per hour), and users perceive shoulder-surfing to be possible in 17% of these instances.

Designing an authentication scheme for mobile devices is a challenging task because the scheme should be both *secure* and *usable*. For mobile devices, a secure authentication scheme should be shoulder-surfing resistant for ubiquitous computing and the scheme should have a large password space, i.e., a large number of possible passwords. Usability of an authentication scheme is of the same importance for mobile devices: (1) The scheme should be easy to use, (2) Passwords generated by the scheme should be easy to remember.

In this paper, we are concerned primarily with knowledge-based passwords, not biometric methods such as fingerprint scanning and facial recognition. At this time, biometric authentication on Android and iOS is always backed by a knowledge-based fallback authentication scheme. Furthermore, biometric schemes face unique security and usability challenges that are outside the scope of this paper.

In this paper, we propose *PassGame*, a shoulder-surfing resistant mobile authentication scheme based on board games. PassGame is essentially a challenge-response authentication scheme. In our current design, PassGame is based on the popular game of chess. Authentication starts with a random chess board, i.e., a chess board with randomly selected game pieces on randomly selected tiles of a game board. The random chess board serves as a challenge to the user. To finish authentication successfully, the user responds to the challenge by making adjustments to the random game board so that a set of predefined rules are satisfied. The adjustments can be moving game pieces, adding new game pieces, and removing existing game pieces.

PassGame supports both rules without any requirements on chess knowledge and rules requiring only basic chess knowledge. The design consideration is to make sure every user, including those who have no knowledge of chess, can use the authentication scheme. The latter rules require only basic chess knowledge, more exactly, the knowledge of how game pieces attack. We include these rules requiring basic knowledge of chess to take advantage of the popularity of the game because we hypothesize that chess knowledge or previous experiences in chess games may improve memorability of PassGame passwords.

We hope that gamifying our scheme can make authentication better in learning, user experience, and user behavior. Hamari et al. [4] and Kroeze et al. [5] assert that gamification can lead to positive effects in learning and user behavior, and that improvements in user behavior can make the scheme more secure. We anticipate that gamifying our scheme will offset some of the usability costs associated with challenge-response authentication. Chess players are trained to analyze the game board and move pieces quickly, as moving quickly is part of normal game etiquette. In other words, chess players may already be trained to solve the challenge quickly.

Our contributions can be summarized as follows: (1) PassGame is designed to counter shoulder-surfing attacks. Our security analysis based on information theory shows that the scheme is better in shoulder-surfing resistance than previous schemes. PassGame also has a large password space to counter brute force attacks. (2) We implemented the PassGame design on the Android operating system. Our user studies with the implementation show that PassGame passwords generated with two rules can achieve 100% recall one week after setting the passwords. PassGame passwords generated with two rules already have a larger password space than 4-digit PIN, an authentication scheme widely used on mobile devices.

In general, shoulder-surfing resistant schemes incur relatively higher usability costs such as longer password entry time. We believe PassGame can be used as a shoulder-surfing resistant option for accessing high security features of the device or for authentication in public places. A user may want to access their phone when on a bus or subway, in plain view of strangers and potentially camera surveillance. There is always an intelligence cost (and thus a tradeoff for usability) when using a challenge-response scheme, so we think PassGame will be best suited as a supplementary security scheme. The user may rely on their simplier scheme when alone or for data with low security importance, and authenticate with PassGame for high security data or when in public. In a high risk environment, users may be willing to pay the usability cost.

PassGame is not designed to replace existing mobile authentication schemes, such as Google's pattern unlock and the four-digit PIN widely used on smartphones. Instead PassGame can be a supplemental scheme for use in crowded places or places with camera surveillance. PassGame can also be a choice for high security authentications on smartphone operating systems supporting different security levels in authentication such as Android.

This paper has been extended from its original version [1] in several ways: we have added a section to address our threat model (Section III), added a section to explain the functionality of our Android implementation (Section VI), added a section on security analysis- including a theoretical framework for measuring shoulder-surfing resistance and an analysis of the lower bound password space of PassGame (Section V), added analysis of user choice in PassGame (Section VII), added a new shoulder-surfing user study (Section VII), and finally extended our discussion and conclusion to address some plans for future work and to cover the new material above (Sections VIII and IX).

The rest of the paper is organized as follows: We review related work on graphical passwords and shoulder-surfing resistant authentication schemes in Section II. We introduce the threat model considered in this paper in Section III. Then, we present the design details of PassGame in Section IV. We analyze the security and theoretical shoulder surfing resistance of the scheme in Section V. We present our user studies on the usability and memorability of PassGame in Section VII. We conclude the paper in Section IX.

II. Related Work

PassGame, like most existing authentication schemes for mobile devices, can be classified as a graphical password scheme. Graphical password schemes rely on the "pictorial superiority effect" [6], the concept that humans have a much better memory for images than they do for numbers and letters, to increase memorability. Since Blonder's pioneer work [7], researchers have proposed various graphical password schemes [8], [9], [10].

Two graphical password schemes are widely available for commercial use on mobile devices. Google's pattern unlock scheme allows users to form a password by connecting dots arranged in a three by three grid (in newer versions of the Android OS, a larger grid can be used). The scheme has high usability as authentication can be finished with one long gesture. The cost of the advantage in usability is its relatively small password space [11]. Microsoft's picture password requires users to form a password by drawing gestures on top of an image that they select. A circle, line, or single touch are considered a single gesture. The gesture direction and location are recorded as a picture password. In addition to graphical password schemes for mobile authentication, 4-digit PIN and alphanumeric authentication are still available in both Android and iOS. While biometric schemes like fingerprint scanning are also available on some devices, these schemes always require a fallback password, typically a PIN. All current authentication schemes on mobile devices, including the pattern unlock scheme, the picture password scheme, and the 4-digit PIN, are vulnerable to shoulder-surfing attacks.

Research suggests that users are aware of the vulnerability of graphical schemes to observation, and perceive a greater risk of having their password observed in a graphical scheme versus a conventional keyboard based scheme [12]. Previous research also suggests that many graphical password schemes are more vulnerable to shoulder-surfing attacks than text-based password entry [2], [12].

A number of research efforts have been aimed to add shoulder-surfing resistance into existing schemes. Roth et al. [13] proposed to add shoulder-surfing resistance to the classic 4-digit PIN by splitting the PIN entry pad into two sets (black and white buttons) and asking users to choose which set their digit is in. The process is repeated several times to confirm the choice of a digit and repeats again until all the digits are chosen. Since then many schemes to add shoulder-surfing resistance to the 4-digit PIN have been proposed, including SwiPIN [14], ColorPIN [15], and The Phone Lock [16]. While these schemes can improve shoulder-surfing resistance of PIN-based schemes, they still suffer from inherently weak security strength of PINs and these schemes can be easily compromised by brute force attacks.

Zakaria et al. [17] proposed to improve the shoulder-surfing resistance of Draw a Secret [8] by erasing strokes as they are drawn. Their user study shows the improvement can reduce the rate of medium-strength passwords captured by an attacker after a single observation from 80% to roughly 40%. Lin et al. [18] proposed to add a grid to Draw A Secret. In addition to matching the Draw a Secret gesture, users in this scheme must also match the direction (e.g., up, down, left, right) in which some strokes of their gesture pass through the added grid lines. Their user study reports that 0 of 10 participants were able to shoulder surf the password after one viewing, as opposed to 7 out of 10 for plain Draw a Secret, but memorability of the scheme was impacted significantly.

Convex Hull Click (CHC) [19] is a graphical password scheme designed to counter shoulder-surfing attacks. CHC asks users to choose icons to represent their passwords. Rather than clicking the icons, users are required to click somewhere inside the triangular area bounded by their chosen icons. CHC suffers from long authentication times because multiple click sessions are required and it takes time for the user to find their icons. The CDS scheme [20], a combination of Draw a Secret [8] and Story [21], arranges a series of images randomly into a grid and asks users to draw a line through the images they choose to represent their passwords. The shoulder-surfing resistance of CDS depends largely on the behavior of the user and how many images an attacker can remember.

PicassoPass [22] asks users to choose individual elements from several layers, such as letter, color, or shape, which must then be tapped in order. The layers are superimposed over each other during authentication, so when a user taps a location, the attacker cannot tell which layer was part of the user's password. Zero out of 22 participants were able to successfully shoulder surf a PicassoPass password after a single viewing, but no usability study is available for comparison.

PassGame can be considered a multi-dimensional password, as proposed in [23]. PassGame uses many dimensions such as rule, color, piece type, and number of attacking pieces.

A. *Hardware-based Schemes*

Some approaches to mitigating shoulder-surfing propose to add hardware to the device. Adding hardware can be problematic because of additional incurred production costs, additional points of failure in the device, and additional software requirements. Back-of-Device Shapes (BoD Shapes) [24] has users authenticate by using additional touch hardware at the back of the device. A shoulder-surfer would need to look up from the floor in order to see password entry. Glass Unlock [25] puts the authentication image on the user's private near eye display (e.g., Google Glass), using the touchscreen only as a nearly blank input device. EyePassword [26] reduces shoulder-surfing by gaze-based password entry. Eye-tracking software and hardware are used to track a user's gaze on screen to input sensitive information through an on-screen keyboard. A shoulder-surfer would need to see the orientation of the user's eyes to have enough information to crack the password. A gaze-based method may not be suitable for mobile authentication because of much smaller screens on mobile devices and the requirement for additional hardware such as a high-resolution front-facing camera and IR illumination.

Bianchi et al. [16] propose to use audio cues for authentication, but audio is not always available to a user when in a public place, for example in a movie theater. De Luca et al. [27] propose VibraPass, a shoulder-surfing resistant scheme for bank terminals that uses vibration cues from a mobile phone, which relies on access to a mobile phone with vibration enabled. Biometric schemes such as facial recognition and fingerprint scanning are immune to shoulder-surfing attacks, but they are vulnerable to theft of biometric data. Chaos Computer Club defeated the Apple iPhone 5s fingerprint scanner within 48 hours of its release, using only a photograph of the fingerprint from a glass surface [28]. PassGame does not require extra hardware and it does not rely on biometric data.

B. *Gamification*

Hamari et al. [4] demonstrate that gamification generally produces positive effects in learning, user experience, and user behavior. We hypothesize that certain good behaviors from chess will carry over to PassGame. For example, common etiquette in chess is for players to analyze the board and make their moves quickly, which may encourage users to enter their passwords quickly, especially when first learning the scheme. Kroeze et al. [5] speculate that adding game elements to authentication can improve user behavior and make them more secure. We attempt to base PassGame on a game that most people are able to play. We hypothesize that increasing familiarity will improve both memorability and usability for many users.

III. Threat Model

In this paper, we consider three different threat models:

1) An observer watching over the victim's shoulder for a small amount of time, long enough to observe a small number of successful entries. This is by far the most common threat, although it can carry relatively little severity. As Harbach et al. [3] note, many users are aware of aware of threats from curious attackers such as friends, acquaintances, and children- all of which can have frequent line of sight access to the password entry. A password without shoulder-surfing resistance, such as PIN, can easily be cracked with a single clear view of the password entry.

2) An observer watching over the victim's shoulder for a longer period of time, observing many successful entries. In this case, the attack is likely premeditated. Shi et al. [29] demonstrate that in general, viewing multiple entries of a shoulder-surfing resistant password significantly increases the probability of cracking it.

3) An observer who records the victim entering the password via camera or other means, allowing infinite reviewing of recorded entries. With any scheme based on information, the password can eventually be determined if sufficient entries are recorded and the intersection between them is analyzed. In general, it is useful to know how many entries are necessary to crack a password with intersection, with typical values at 2-3 entries [30].

In all three cases, we assume the observer has the opportunity to watch one or several password entries by following the victim and observing them. We assume the observer is familiar with the scheme. We also assume that the observer is able to completely see the screen with no obstructions. Once the observer is confident in their ability to bypass the victim's authentication, they may steal the device or otherwise access it without the user knowing.

We assume the observer is not able to access data on the device by any means other than authenticating themselves as the user, due to some encryption on the device.

IV. The PassGame Design

In this section, we first present an overview of PassGame and describe the design details of PassGame.

A. Overview

The current design of PassGame is based on the popular game chess. PassGame is essentially a challenge-response authentication scheme. In PassGame, a mobile device challenges a user with a randomly generated chess board, i.e., a chess board with randomly selected game pieces placed on randomly selected tiles. The user responds to the challenge by making adjustments on the chess game board including adding new games pieces, removing existing game pieces, and moving existing game pieces. A correct response will be an adjusted game board satisfying some predefined rules. For example, one rule of PassGame is to move game pieces by n_{tile} tiles in total. Any move of a game piece, including moves that would be illegal in chess, are allowed. Moving a game piece to the right or the left by one tile increases or decreases one tile from the total. Similarly, moving a game piece up or down by one row increases or decreases eight tiles from the total, as one row on the board has 8 tiles. A user can increase or decrease the number of tiles moved by adding a new game piece to the board or removing a game piece from the board. As long as the sum total of tiles moved is equal to n_{tile}, the rule is satisfied and the user will be authenticated (if no other rules are in use). Otherwise, the authentication is unsuccessful.

PassGame supports both rules that do not require knowledge of how to play chess and rules requiring basic chess knowledge. The design is to make sure every user, including those who have no knowledge of chess, can use the authentication scheme. The other rules require only basic chess knowledge of how game pieces attack. We include these rules requiring basic knowledge of chess to take advantage of the popularity of chess because we hypothesize that chess knowledge or previous experiences in chess games may improve memorability of PassGame passwords.

A PassGame password can be formed with multiple rules. In general, using more rules to form a PassGame password can make the PassGame password more complex, and in turn more resistant to brute force attacks and shoulder-surfing attacks.

As long as the rules of a password are satisfied, PassGame allows users to make unrelated adjustments to the board. In other words, a user can add, remove, and move game pieces that are not involved in any rules used to form the password. These unrelated adjustments to a game board allow a user to further mitigate shoulder-surfing attacks as a shoulder-surfer can not tell which adjustments are involved in the rules used to form the PassGame password.

To make PassGame more usable, the design does not enforce the rules of chess. Any piece of either color can be positioned on any tile of the chess board, and multiple pieces of the same type are permitted (e.g., three kings). Any piece can move to any tile. However, some rules utilize the attack patterns of different pieces, for example by counting the number of attacks possible on a piece. In Chess, an attack on a piece can be removed by getting rid of the attacking piece, moving the defending piece, or blocking line-of-attack between the two pieces (except for knights), meaning there are many ways to add or remove attacks on a Chess board.

In the rest of this section, we describe the generation of a random game board and then the details of each rule possibly used in a PassGame password.

B. Random Board Generation

Since PassGame authentication starts with a challenge of a random board, the generation of the random board is important for both the security and usability of PassGame. On each tile, there are 13 possibilities: the tile is empty, or it is occupied by a king, queen, bishop, knight, rook, or pawn in either black or white.

PassGame randomly selects one from the 13 possibilities for each tile. Pieces appear with the same frequency as they typically appear in midgame chess. That is, empty tiles are most common, pawns are more common than knights, bishops and rooks, and kings and queens occur least frequently. Because the board is randomly generated, it is also possible to get boards which are almost completely empty or completely full. The design is to ensure most boards have enough pieces so that there are many ways to satisfy the rules of a PassGame password, and that many different kinds of PassGame passwords will be satisfiable within any sample of a few random boards.

We allow a user to request a new random board at any time during authentication. A user may request a random board for several possible reasons: (1) The user's password cannot be completed on the given random board (e.g., remove 3 black pieces from the board on a board with less than 3 black pieces), (2) The user wants a board where the password can be input more easily, (3) The user wants to find a game board where shoulder-surfing is less likely, or (4) The user has modified the random board unsuccessfully and does not remember what it initially looked like. A random board sometimes partially or completely satisfies some of a user's rules without any modifications. Thus, a shoulder-surfer may not necessarily see the user inputting all the rules that comprise the user's password, forcing them to guess remaining rules from the contents of the random board.

C. PassGame Rules

In our current design, a PassGame password can be formed with 12 rules. We present the details of the rules below. Users can, and should, pick multiple rules at the same time. In general, rules ask users to pick numerical values, locations, piece types, or color. When choosing color, a user can choose not to pick a color and instead answer "either", meaning the rule can be satisfied with a combination of black and white pieces.

To better understand the effective password space, at the end of our user study, we asked participants to tell us what was the maximum number of pieces they would use for each rule in practice. We present the average response along with the description of each rule.

The first 6 rules do not require any chess knowledge. So, any user should be able to use these rules.

Rule R1: Number of Tiles Moved in Total: The parameter of this rule is the number of tiles moved. To satisfy this rule, a user must make adjustments to a game board so that the number of tiles moved in total should be equal to a predefined number n_{tile}. The board can be considered as a numbered grid from 1 to 64, where the bottom left corner is 1, and the top right is 64. Moving a game piece to the right or to the left by one tile adds or decreases the number of tiles moved in total by one respectively. Similarly, moving a game piece up or down by one row adds or decreases the number of tiles moved in total by 8 respectively. Adding a game piece to a tile adds to the number of tiles moved in total by the number associated with that tile. On the contrary, removing a game piece from a tile decreases the number of tiles moved in total by the number associated with that tile.

For example, if a user sets $n_{tile} = 8$ in the password setup phase, the user can satisfy this rule by adding a piece to tile 8 if the tile is not occupied, or by moving a piece on tile 12 to tile 20 if the destination tile is not occupied. To mitigate shoulder-surfing attacks, a user can also combine multiple adjustments together to achieve the number of tiles in total. For example, if $n_{tile} = 8$, a user can move one piece forward by 20 tiles, move another piece backwards by 10 tiles, add a piece to tile 28, and remove a piece from tile 30 to make the number of total tiles moved be 8. In theory, the range of n_{tile} is $[-2080, 2080]$ as $\sum_{i=1}^{64} i = 2080$.

In practice, according to our user study, users would use a maximum of 17 tile moves for this rule.

Rule R2: Number of Pieces in a Row: The parameters of this rule are color, row index, and number of pieces of the selected color that must exist in the selected row. To satisfy this rule, a user must adjust a game board so that the selected row has the chosen number of pieces in it of the chosen color. This can be done adding pieces or removing pieces from the row, as a randomly generated row may have more pieces than are needed. The number of possible combinations of the parameters is $3 \times 8 \times 8 = 192$ as (1) color can be black, white, or either, and (2) a chess board has 8 rows and columns. According to our user study, users would use up to 5 pieces.

Rule R3: Number of Pieces in a Column: This rule is similar to Rule R2 and the only difference is that R3 is defined on a column. So the number of possible combinations of the parameters is also 192.

Rule R4: Number of Pieces on a Board: This rule is similar as Rule R2 and the only difference is that R4 is defined on a game board. The parameters of this rule are color and number of pieces on the board, so the number of possible combinations of the parameters is $3 \times 64 = 192$ as (1) color can be black, white, or either and (2) a board can hold up to 64 game pieces. According to our user study, a maximum of 22 pieces would be used in this rule.

Rule R5: More or Less Pieces: The parameters of this rule are color and the number of pieces added or removed from a board. To satisfy this rule, a user must add or remove the specified number of pieces in the chosen color. To further mitigate shoulder-surfing attacks, a user may want to add and remove pieces several times. As long as the final number of pieces added or removed from a board totals the specified number, the rule is satisfied. The number of possible combinations of the parameters is $3 \times 64 \times 2 = 384$ because (1) color can be black, white, or either, (2) at most 64 pieces can be added or removed from the board. According to our user study, users indicated they would use a maximum of 15 more pieces, and a maximum of 6 less pieces.

Rule R6: Specific Tile: The parameters of this rule are piece type, color, row index, and column index. The rule is satisfied when the specified piece of the chosen color is at the chosen row and column location. The number of possible combinations of the parameters is $6 \times 3 \times 8 \times 8 = 1152$ as (1) the piece type can be king, queen, bishop, knight, rook, or pawn, (2) the color can be black, white, or either color, and (3) the board has 8 rows and 8 columns. This rule is not shoulder-surfing resistant by itself. But, the rule can be used to form a shoulder-surfing resistant password by including unrelated adjustments such as placing random pieces onto randomly-selected tiles or simply being used with other rules.

The next 6 rules require only basic knowledge of attacks in chess. To add more attacks, a user can add game pieces under attack, attack existing pieces, or both. Attacks can also be added by removing pieces blocking attack paths of other game pieces. Similarly, attacks can be reduced by adding blocking pieces, removing attacking pieces, or removing the pieces under attack.

Rule R7: Number of Attacks on a Piece: The parameters of this rule are piece type, piece color, and number of attacks. This rule is satisfied when a game piece of the type and color selected is attacked by the chosen number of attackers. One example is that a bishop of either color is under attack by five pieces. If there is no such piece on a random board, a user can add it to the board. If there are multiple such pieces a board, then only one of them is required to be under attack by the specified number of pieces. The number of possible combinations of the parameters is approximately $6 \times 3 \times 16 = 288$ as (1) the piece type can be king, queen, bishop, knight, rook, or pawn, (2) the color can be black, white, or either color, and (3) the maximum number of attacks to one tile is 16 (4 diagonal attacks, 2 horizontal attacks, 2 vertical attacks, and 8 attacks by knights). Note that not every tile can have 16 attackers (e.g corner tiles can have a maximum of 5 attackers), so it may be necessary to move a piece or place a new one in order to satisfy larger numbers of attacks. Users indicated they would use a maximum of 4 attacking pieces.

Rule R8: Number of Attacks by Pieces: The parameters of this rule are piece type, piece color, and number of attacks. The rule is satisfied when a game piece of the selected type and color is attacking the chosen number of game pieces. For a king, a queen, or a knight, there are $3 \times 8 = 24$ combinations because (1) color can be black, white, or either and (2) a king, a queen, or a knight can attack a maximum of 8 pieces. For a bishop or a rook, there are $3 \times 4 = 12$ combinations because a bishop or a rook can attack 4 pieces at most. For a pawn, there are only $3 \times 2 = 6$ combinations because a pawn can only attack two pieces at most. So the total number of possible combinations is $3 \times 24 + 2 \times 12 + 6 = 102$. In our user study, users indicated they would use a maximum of 5 attacks.

Rule R9: Number of Pieces under Attack: The parameters of this are piece color and number of pieces under attack. The rule is satisfied when the selected number of game pieces of the chosen color are under attack. Since (1) the maximum number of attacks is 64 when a board is filled and every game piece is under attack, and (2) color can be black, white, or either, the number of possible combinations is $3 \times 64 = 192$. Users indicated they would use a maximum of 3 attacks.

Rule R10: More or Less Attacks on A Piece: The parameters of this rule are piece type, piece color, and number of attacks to add or remove. The rule is satisfied when the selected number of attacks are added or removed from a game piece of the chosen type and color. If there is no such piece on the board, a user can add it. As described in Rule R7, the maximum number of attacks on one tile is 16. Since (1) color can be black, white, or either and (2) the piece type can be king, queen, bishop, knight, rook, or pawn, the number of possible combinations is $3 \times 6 \times 32 = 576$. In our user studies, users indicated they would add a maximum of 4 attackers and remove a maximum of 2 attackers.

Rule R11: More or Less Attacks by A Piece: The parameters of this rule are piece type, piece color, and number of attacks to add. The rule is satisfied when the selected number of attacks are added or removed from a piece of the chosen color and type. A king, queen, or knight can attack 8 pieces at most. In other words, a user can select any of the 16 possible values between -8 and 8. The number of possible combinations for a king, queen, or knight is $3 \times 16 = 48$ since color can be black, white, or either. A bishop or rook can attack a maximum of 4 pieces, so the number of possible combinations for a bishop or a rook is $3 \times 8 = 24$. A pawn can attack up to 2 pieces, so the number of possible combinations for a pawn is $3 \times 4 = 12$. The total number of combinations is 204. Users indicated they would add a maximum of 4 attacks and remove a maximum of 2 attacks.

Rule R12: More or Less Pieces under Attack: The rule parameters are piece color and number of attacks to add or remove. This rule is satisfied when a user adds or removes the selected number of attacks to game pieces in the chosen color. A user can add or remove up to 64 attacks. The number of possible combinations of the parameters is $3 \times 128 = 384$ since color can be black, white, or either. In our user study, users indicated they would add up to 5 pieces under attack and remove up to 4 pieces.

D. Additional rules

PassGame supports only the rules above, however it is theoretically possible to come up with a near-infinite number of rules. For example, we can generate rules based on arbitrary criteria, for example "Knights which are 3 tiles left or right away from a bishop". We can also split existing rules into more detailed versions, for example "Knights in row 4", versus a more general rule such as rule 2, and similarly we can create less detailed rules such as "Pieces in rows 1-4". There is also more room for rules based on Chess, for example "Kings in check", and we can create rules which are boolean, for example "True/False there are no pieces in Row 3".

Increasing the number of available rules can make it more difficult for the attacker to iterate through all the rules and determine which are in use, potentially requiring them to obtain more password entries in order to make a successful guess. Furthermore, adding or varying rules in use can confound attackers who program tools to examine password entries, forcing them to constantly update these tools. However, including more rules may impact usability; users may feel overwhelmed when confronted with a list of hundreds of rules, even though reading through all of them is not strictly necessary as the user can simply pick a few arbitrarily.

V. Security Analysis

Our security analysis of PassGame focuses on shoulder-surfing resistance and password space. One of the major design goals is to mitigate shoulder-surfing attacks. We propose an information-theoretical measure of shoulder-surfing resistance and compare PassGame to other shoulder-surfing resistant schemes with the measure. An authentication scheme also needs a large password space to defeat brute force attacks by significantly increasing the cost of brute force attacks.

A. Shoulder-Surfing Resistance

The security of shoulder-surfing resistant schemes relies on the mapping between challenges and responses. If we denote the challenges and responses as C and R respectively, the mapping is $M : C \rightarrow R$, and M associates challenges with their valid responses. So, M is essentially the secret that a user has to memorize for authentication. A shoulder-surfer is able to observe a number of challenges and their corresponding valid responses. Based on the observation, the shoulder-surfer attempts to recover M so that the shoulder-surfer can break in by applying M to a future challenge given by a shoulder-surfing resistant scheme. So the dependency between challenges and responses indicates how a scheme is resistant to shoulder-surfing. A scheme with valid responses highly dependent on a challenge obviously is very vulnerable to shoulder-surfing attacks.

To reduce dependency, most shoulder-surfing resistant schemes mitigate shoulder-surfing attacks by allowing multiple responses to satisfy one challenge. For example, in CHC [19], a user can click any place within a convex hull formed by preselected pass-icons for a correct response. Similarly in Rule R1 of PassGame, if $n_{tile} = 10$, a user can satisfy this rule in many ways. A user can simply move 10 existing game pieces to the right by one tile, add a piece to tile 10 if not occupied, or a combination of right and left moves of existing pieces, piece additions, and piece removals as long as the total number of tiles moved is 10.

The dependency can be measured by mutual information, an information-theoretical measure of dependency between two random variables. For a shoulder-surfing resistant scheme, the dependency can be represented by $I(C; R)$, meaning the mutual information between challenge C and response R. According to information theory, $I(C; R) = H(C) - H(C|R)$ where $H(C)$ denotes the entropy of the possible challenges and $H(C|R)$ denotes the conditional entropy of challenge C given response R. If a scheme generates challenges with a uniform distribution, the entropy $H(C)$ is a constant dependent on the number of possible challenges. So, to reduce the mutual information $I(X; Y)$, i.e., the dependency between challenges and responses, we need to increase $H(C|R)$. Since the conditional entropy $H(C|R)$ measures the uncertainty of challenges given a response, it is better to make a response to be valid to as many challenges as possible to reduce the dependency.

PassGame is designed to reduce the dependency in this way. PassGame allows a user to make adjustments that are unrelated to rules used to form a PassGame password. The adjustments can be moving existing pieces, adding new pieces, and removing existing pieces. These unrelated adjustments make the corresponding response valid to other challenges as well. So the unrelated adjustments can further reduce dependency and in turn make PassGame more resistant to shoulder-surfing. According to our knowledge, PassGame is the first attempt to include unrelated adjustments to an authentication scheme for mitigating shoulder-surfing attacks. We do not quantitatively compare PassGame with other shoulder-surfing resistance schemes according to the metric $I(C; R)$ as $H(C)$ depends on the number of possible challenges and the number can be very different for different shoulder-surfing resistant schemes. A fair comparison with the information-theoretical metric will be one of our future tasks.

B. Password Space

A PassGame password can be formed with the 12 rules described in the previous section. If only one rule is used, the number of possible passwords is essentially the sum of the possible combinations of parameters in each rule. So the number of possible one-rule passwords is 5938. Among the 5938 one-rule passwords, some will not be frequently used. For example, in Rule R1, the number of tiles moved in total can be up to 2080. However, a password with $n_{tile} = 2080$ is not usable as it would require 64 gestures and a completely empty random board to satisfy. So, we also calculate the *usable password space* of PassGame based on data from our user study. We asked participants in our user studies to tell us the maximum number of pieces they would use for each feature (e.g., what is the max number of pieces in a row you would use if you picked this rule). We then took the average of these values to calculate the parameter ranges. Using the responses provided by our users, we obtain the usable range of the parameters of each rule and then calculate the usable password space to be 1931.

The size of the one-rule password space can be enlarged since more rules can be added to the current design of PassGame. For example, we can add rules like number of pieces which are two tiles apart. In theory, one-rule PassGame can have a large password space to counter brute force attacks.

The password space can be enlarged exponentially when a combination of rules are used to form a PassGame password. The number of two-rule passwords is approximately $5938^2 = 35,259,844$. But, there are certain impossible passwords included in the calculation. For example, we cannot form a password by using R2 and R4 if R2 requires more pieces in a row than R4 requires on the board. So, to calculate the lower bound on the password space, we remove rules or portions of rules that can cause contradictions. Omitting these potentially contradictory features, we find the two-rule password space is $5,585,124$ passwords. For comparison, a 4-digit PIN has a password space of $10^4 = 10,000$, and Android pattern unlock has a total password space of 389,112 when using a 3x3 grid [31].

The size of the usable password space for two rules, based on responses from our users, is approximately $1931^2 = 3,728,761$ passwords. With four rules, PassGame reaches a password space of over $1931^4 = 10^{13}$, approximately the strength of an 8 character alphanumeric password without symbols. If we only include rules that can not cause conflicts in the calculation, the lower bound of the usable two-rule password space is $3,119,262$. With four rules, the lower bound is still over 10^{12}. The lower bounds calculated above are not tight lower bounds, but we calculate them to show that two rule PassGame passwords already have a password space much larger than current mobile authentications schemes.

VI. IMPLEMENTATION

We implemented PassGame on the Android operating system. A screenshot of the implementation is shown in Figure 2. The implementation allows a user to set a PassGame password with the rules described in the previous section. When setting a password, a user is required to select rules and set the corresponding rule parameters. The user is also required to verify a new password on a game board before finishing the password setup. The verification asks the user to confirm the password. During an authentication, a user is shown the graphical user interface as in Figure 2. A user can request a new random board by tapping the "New Board" button. There is no penalty for requesting a new random board.

A. Rule Selection

During password setup, the user selects rules from a checklist. When a box is checked, a prompt appears to ask for details, for example the color, number, type, or location of pieces involved in the rule. The prompt also provides brief

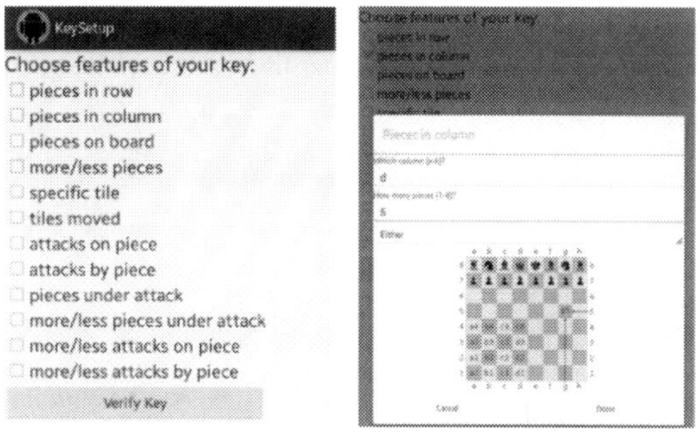

(a) Checkbox selection (b) Rule selection prompt

Figure 1. Screenshots of the password setup phase.

hints and helpful information for using the rule, for example a diagram indicating how rows and columns are labeled in chess. Figure 1 shows the password setup phase. In Figure 1(a), the user chooses from the list of rules, presented as check boxes, tapping *pieces in column* as one of their selections. The prompt in Figure 1(b) appears, asking the user to specify which column (free typing with the soft keyboard), how many pieces (free typing using the numerical soft keyboard), and which color (a drop down with black, white, and either as options). Columns are typically labeled a-h, and a maximum of 8 pieces can occupy a column. Basic hints are provided for most rules. Here, a hint figure shows how columns in chess are labeled, and hint text tells the user to use letters a-h and numbers 0-8 in their input.

When a user finishes setting the password, the user is taken to a blank board as a final sanity check against redundant passwords. An example of a redundant password could be a password that asks for 5 white pieces in row 2 but only 3 white pieces on the board. At this stage the user may also decide the password is too hard to enter, e.g., has low usability, and go back to make changes. The user has to complete the password on the blank board to finish setup. The participant can view the password during this step at any time time by pressing a "show password" button. Rules that would require removing pieces from a random board are omitted during this phase. Once the password is set, the user authenticates by entering the password on a randomly generated game board rather than a blank one.

VII. User Study

We implemented PassGame on the Android operating system. A screenshot of the implementation is shown in Figure 2. To evaluate PassGame, we conducted user studies with participants recruited from two university communities. We used a Samsumg Galaxy Tab 3 with a 7 inch 1024×600 display and the Samsung S4 with a 5 inch 1920×1080 display.

Procedure: On the first day, participants are invited to come to our controlled laboratory environment to fill out demographic information and learn how to generate a PassGame password. Participants are shown a fifteen-minute series of videos that covers the basics of PassGame and shows them how to use all the available rules. Questions about the technicalities of PassGame or the different rules are encouraged, but most participants were able to use PassGame with little to no further guidance. After learning how to use the scheme, participants are asked to generate their own PassGame passwords using one of the mobile devices. Before they leave the laboratory, participants must successfully authenticate themselves twice on two different random boards.

Figure 2. A screenshot of the PassGame application.

Similar to previous studies [32], we asked participants to use PassGame during the one-week-long user study to simulate regular use of the authentication scheme. We sent an email to participants 3-4 days after the first session then again 5-6 days after the first session. The email contains a link to an emulated version of the PassGame application hosted on the internet. The emulated version uses the same code and behaves in the same way as the version that participants used during the first session, and can be completed on any internet accessible device including a PC. We use an emulated version rather than asking participants to return to the laboratory to use the device because it is more convenient for participants and this portion of the experiment is designed solely to simulate regular use of the scheme in order to stimulate memorability. Use of the emulator is encouraged but not mandatory because (1) email responses are not reliable because of various reasons such as junk mail filtering, (2) we want to investigate the effect of regular use on the memorability of PassGame. Each participant had at most two successful authentications on the emulator and the attempts on the emulator happened within 36 hours from the sending time of the reminder emails.

One week after the first session, participants are invited back to the controlled laboratory environment for the second session. Participants are given the mobile device that they used during the first session and are asked to recall their passwords. If a participant fails to recall his or her password, the participant may try as many times as they would like for up to five minutes. At the end of the second session, participants are asked to fill out a survey rating the usability of PassGame and their favorite mobile authentication scheme.

Conditions: To evaluate the usability of PassGame with different security strengths, participants were randomly grouped into one of three conditions: (1) 1R: Participants in this condition were asked to make a password using a single rule. They were not allowed to use Rule R6 because it is not shoulder surfing resistant on its own, but otherwise had no limitations on which rules they could select. (2) 2R: Participants in this condition were asked to make a password with two rules. (3) 4R: Participants in this condition were asked to make a password with four rules.

We limit the experiment to 4 rules because in practice, we found that passwords with 5 rules or more were too difficult to create and use. This is due to the difficulty in satisfying each rule individually without contradicting others. The task would not be difficult if the same, simple rule could be used multiple times, for example Rule 2, but we wanted to see the impact of choosing different rules. Rules such as 2, 3, and 5 can be difficult to satisfy simultaneously. In our future work, we plan to study PassGame with no limits on the number of rules that can be selected and no limits on repeating the same rule multiple times.

Participants: We recruited participants for the user studies by distributing fliers and leaflet style advertisements. A $10 cash incentive was offered for completing both sessions of the user study. Thirty seven participants were recruited for the user studies and 36 successfully finished both sessions. Of those who finished, 23 participants were male and 13 were female. There were 7 participants aged 20 or younger, 22 participants aged between 21 and 25, 4 participants aged 26-30, and 3 participants over the age of 30. Participants were asked "Are you skilled at using smartphones or mobile devices." On a scale from "Strongly Disagree" (1) to "Strongly Agree" (5), participants rated their skill an average of 4.28, with 32 rating their skill at 4 or higher.

Statistical Testing: We use a significance level of .05 for our hypothesis testing in this paper. For omnibus comparisons on categorical and quantitative data, we use Chi-squared and Kruskal-Wallis respectively. If the omnibus test is significant, we perform pairwise tests with Chi-squared for categorical data and Mann-Whitney for quantitative data.

A. *Memorability Results*

As a PassGame password formed with more rules requires more rule selections and rule parameters to be memorized, we hypothesize that the recall rate of PassGame passwords decreases when the number of rules used to form PassGame passwords increases.

The recall results of the user study are shown in Table I. The results show that none of our participants had any trouble in remembering 1R or 2R passwords. The recall rate of 4R passwords is 30% lower than the rates of 1R and 2R passwords, but most participants were still able to remember their 4R passwords as well. We perform an omnibus chi-squared test on the three conditions and find a significant difference between the memorability of the conditions ($\chi^2 = 8.51$, $p = .014$). The hypothesis is supported by the data of PassGame passwords formed by 4 or less rules. We believe that the statistical difference will become more significant when the number of rules used to form a PassGame password is larger. We restrict our user study on PassGame to passwords formed with no more than 4 rules because (1) a two-rule password already has more password strength than 4-digit PIN, and (2) PassGame passwords formed with more than 4 rules are less usable.

TABLE I. PASSGAME RECALL RATES BY CONDITION

Conditions	Participants	Recall	Recall Rate
$1R$	12	12	100%
$2R$	14	14	100%
$4R$	10	7	70%

We examine the effect of the reminder emails on memorability. We hypothesize that using the emulator during the week will make participants more likely to remember their passwords at the end of the week. Five participants used the emulator only after receiving the first reminder email, 2 used the emulator only after receiving the second reminder email, 24 used the emulator both times, and 5 did not use the emulator at all. The omnibus chi-squared test reveals no significance ($\chi^2 = 1.64$, $p = .651$). All three participants who forget their passwords used the emulator both times, and were unable to finish authentication successfully either time. The results suggest that PassGame passwords are memorable after one week even with no reminders.

We hypothesize that chess knowledge has an impact on memorability. Thirty-one participants indicated that they knew how to play chess, while 5 indicated they did not know how to play chess. Among the 3 participants that forgot their passwords, 2 knew how to play chess and 1 did not. Our omnibus chi-squared test reveals that there is no significant difference ($\chi^2 = 1.04$, $p = .309$). The results are not compliant with our expectation. But, the results also indicate that the scheme is memorable even by persons who have no knowledge of chess.

B. *Password Entry Time*

Our implementation records the time users spend attempting to enter their passwords. In this section, we analyze the timing data from the final session of the user study.

TABLE II. AVERAGE ENTRY TIMES, AVERAGE NEW BOARDS AND ATTEMPTS PER SUCCESSFULL AUTHENTICATION

Conditions	Total (s)	Correct (s)	Boards	Attempts
1R	33	23	1.6	1.22
2R	110	44	1.9	2.07
4R	143	49	2.1	2.63

Table I shows the average total entry time, average entry time for successful attempts, and average attempts per successfully attempt. Users in the 1R, 2R, and 4R conditions required 33, 110, and 143 seconds respectively to authenticate themselves from the moment they started the application, including time spent thinking, requesting new boards, and making incorrect attempts. A Kruskal Wallis test between the three conditions finds no significant difference (H=4.996, p=.082). On average, users required 1.6, 1.9, and 2.1 new randomly generated boards for the 1R, 2R, and 4R conditions respectively before successfully entering their passwords. Additionally, users required an average of 1.22, 2.07, and 2.63 authentication attempts before a success for 1R, 2R, and 4R respectively. Correct attempts, measuring time from application load or the end of the previous unsuccessful attempt until the last touch in a successful attempt, required on average 23, 44, and 49 seconds for 1R, 2R, and 4R respectively. The best 4 users in 1R required less than 7s to authenticate themselves. We perform a Kruskal Wallis test on the timings for the first correct attempt and find that there is not a significant difference in the timings (H=3.741, p=.154).

We believe that these statistics will improve as users gain experience with the scheme. PassGame is effectively a short puzzle solving task. Once users become familiar with the puzzle, entry times should improve. Password entry times for a single correct attempt are already very similar between the conditions. The entry times for correct attempts are in line with other schemes such as Deja Vu (32s) [9], Delayed Oracle Choice PIN entry (25s) [13], or CDS (20s) [20] and superior to other shoulder-surfing resistant schemes like Convex Hull Click (72s) [19].

SwiPin [14], ColorPIN [15], The Phone Lock [16], and other schemes that improve on PIN or pattern unlock offer short login times, but at the cost of weak password strength and limited shoulder-surfing resistance. PassGame can be used as a supplementary high-security scheme in environments where the user is afraid of shoulder-surfing. The user may be willing to trade off entry time in exchange for security in these situations.

C. User Perception

TABLE III. USABILITY SURVEY RATINGS

Scheme	Ratings	Conve.	Speed
PassGame-1R	4	4.50	4.25
PassGame-2R	7	4.29	3.29
PassGame-4R	7	3.75	2.57
PassGame-all	18	4.06	3.22
4-digit PIN	10	5	5

At the end of the user study we asked participants to fill out a survey regarding the usability of PassGame and their current favorite authentication scheme. Participants were asked to rate the following statements (once for PassGame, and once for their favorite scheme) on a scale from "Strongly Disagree" (1) to "Strongly Agree" (5): (a) It is convenient to enter a password using this scheme. (b) The speed of entering a password with this scheme is fast. Additionally, we provide participants with the following definitions as a guideline: (a) Convenience: The scheme does not restrict you or take too much attention. (b) Speed: You can finish the scheme quickly. It usually does not need too many tries. For their favorite scheme, 10 participants chose 4-digit PIN, 2 participants chose Google's pattern unlock scheme, 3 chose fingerprint scanner. We sorted the usability results for PassGame based on which condition users were assigned to. The results of the usability survey are shown in Figure 3. The average usability rating is shown in Table III. For statistical analysis, we sort the usability ratings into the categories agree (4 or higher) or do not agree (3 or lower). We hypothesize that most users will think that PassGame is roughly as convenient as the 4-digit PIN or Google's pattern unlock scheme. We also hypothesize that the speed rating will decline as more rules are used. A chi-squared omnibus test on the three conditions of PassGame plus 4-digit PIN shows no significant difference in convenience ($\chi^2 = 4.11$, $p = .25$), however there is a significant different in speed ($\chi^2 = 11.04$, $p = .01$). Pairwise testing reveals the results are significant between 2R and 4-digit PIN ($\chi^2 = 7.47$, $p < .01$) and between 4R and 4-digit PIN ($\chi^2 = 10.12$, $p < .01$). At 2 rules and up, users perceive PassGame to be a slower scheme than the 4-digit PIN. We believe the difference is mainly caused by the shoulder-surfing resistance. A user usually repeats a 4-digit PIN without any thinking. But a user of shoulder-surfing resistant schemes needs to think out a valid response to a random challenge. Another possible reason is the difference in the familiarity to the scheme, as participants may be using 4-digit PINs on their mobile devices every day, and they only used PassGame a few times.

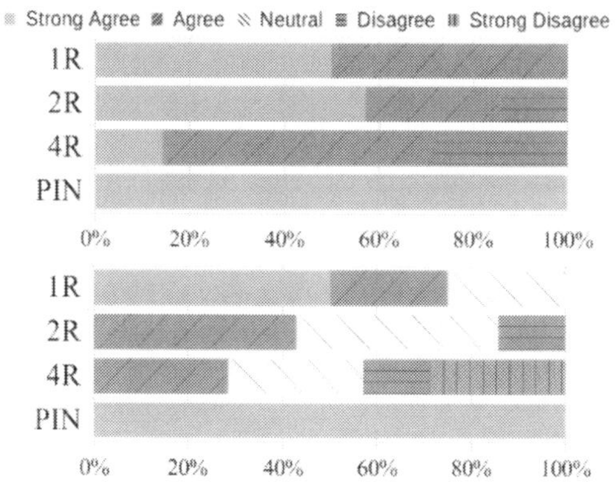

Figure 3. Usability Survey for Convenience (top), Speed (bottom).

D. User Choice in Passwords

We hypothesize that there will be hotspots in feature selection, e.g. that some features will be more common than others. Additionally, we believe that certain pieces, colors, and numbers will be more popular than others. Analyzing the data from our user study reveals several hotspots.

A total of 74 rules were selected by the 36 users in our study. A user can chose each rule only once, so the maximum number of times a rule could appear is 36 times. Figure 4 shows the number of times each rule was selected, demonstrating that

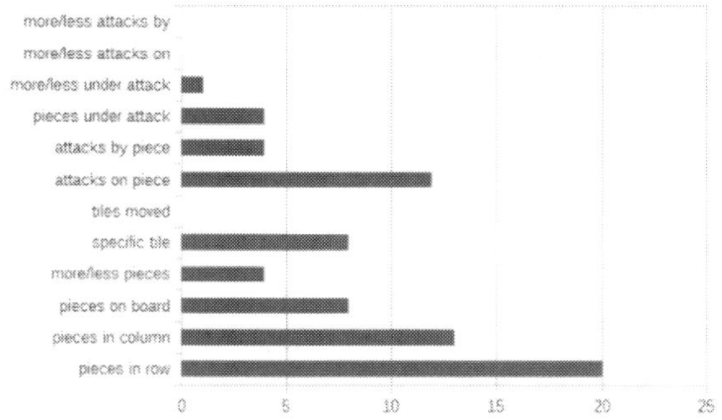

Figure 4. Number of times each feature was selected in our user study.

hotspots do exist in rule selection. For pieces in a row or column, the majority of users (85%) elected to use less than four pieces. When a piece was required to be chosen for some rule, e.g., for the specific tile rule or the attacks on piece rule, users chose the king (46%) and queen (29%) over the rook (13%), bishop (0%), knight (8%), and pawn (4%). We hypothesize that knowledge of chess leads users to prefer the most "powerful" piece, and plan to investigate the effect in games where pieces are equally balanced, such as Monopoly, in our future work.

E. Shoulder-Surfing User Study

TABLE IV. SUCCESSFULL SHOULDER-SURFING ATTEMPTS BY CATEGORY

Strength	1 Viewing	5 Viewings	Unlimited (¡1 hour)
Easy	0	5	15
Medium	0	0	3
Hard	0	0	0

We invited participants back after the first user study for a second user study on the shoulder-surfing resistance of PassGame. To ensure maximum consistency, we recorded the entry of three different PassGame passwords formed with 2 rules, 3 rules, and 4 rules. Only the 4-rule password was formed with rules requiring basic chess knowledge. Participants were told that the passwords were "easy," "medium," and "hard" respectively, that each password had between 2 and 4 rules, and that only the hard password involved chess knowledge. Five successful entries on five different random boards are recorded for each password. Participants are informed that there are no moves made during password entry that are not related to the password, i.e., no unrelated adjustments, every move made is significant to authentication and all authentication attempts are done in a natural and efficient manner.

Participants view the recordings on the same device that they used in the first user study, with no obstructions to their vision, simulating a worst case scenario for shoulder-surfing. Moves are displayed on the screen as a highly visible purple cursor that is transparent enough not to block vision of the board. Moves are executed at a relatively slower speed to allow better observation. Participants in this experiment have already been familiarized with PassGame, so only a brief recap of the rules is provided. As an additional aid, participants are provided with a sheet of paper listing all of the rules along with a brief description, and printouts of blank boards as scratch paper. If a participant thinks they have cracked the password, they can try it on the device with unlimited attempts, simulating a worst case scenario where attempts are not limited. A $100 prize pool is used to encourage participants to recover the PassGame password successfully. Participants who recover PassGame passwords successfully can split the prize, where participants who cracked the hardest password receive the majority of the pool.

Table IV shows our shoulder-surfing study results. Initially, we limit participants to a single viewing of each password entry as in [13] and [22], simulating a realistic shoulder-surfing attack by an observer. Note that in [22], participants were able to view only a single password entry, whereas we allow participants to view five. In [13], ten successful entries are shown. Zero out of fifteen participants were able to recover any of the passwords.

We investigate the effectiveness of PassGame against repeated observation, as in [33], by allowing participants 5 additional sequential viewings of each of the 5 password entries. Shi et al. [29] show that the probability of a shoulder surfer correctly guess the password in their scheme with just 2 recordings is rated at 20-25%. Chameleon [30] is considered secure against 3 or fewer captured login sessions. Our experiment allows for 5 recordings and unlimited attempts on the actual device, so the probability of a successful guess should be much higher. If an attacker has many recordings of a PassGame password, they can crack it by studying the intersection of information between the recorded entries. The number of recordings required and the probability to crack a password with a given number of recordings depends on how much intersection exists between recorded passwords. For example, an attacker could rule out the "tiles moved" rule by counting the number of tiles moved in several recordings. If the number of tiles moved does not match in just one successful authentication attempt, the attacker knows to discard this rule.

Participants were allowed to view all 5 entries an additional 5 times (a total of 6 including the previous experiment). Thus in total, participants witnessed 30 successful authentication attempts of each password. Entries were shown in sequence, that is participants saw all 5 entries, then were given time to think or take notes, then shown all 5 again. Participants chose for themselves when to move on to the next viewing, typically after a few seconds.

The easy password was shown first. After the additional viewings, 5 participants (33%) cracked the easy password with one attempt on the device.

All 15 participants moved on to the medium password. After the additional viewings, no participants were able to crack the medium password. Some participants were able to partially guess 1-2 rules (based on verbal confirmation), but none were able to crack the password entirely. We did not confirm or deny if users guessed any rules successfully during the experiment.

No participants were confident enough to opt to try inputting the password on the device.

Only 5 participants opted to try the hard password. All 5 failed to crack the password after the additional viewings. Several participants described it as "impossible" and that they felt "nobody would be able to get that."

Lastly, we allowed participants unlimited viewing of the recordings, including pause, fast forward, and rewind, along with unlimited guessing attempts on the device. Participants were also allowed to work in teams if they wished, and about 3 groups of 2 were formed. This is to simulate a worst-case situation when the attacker has captured recordings of multiple passwords, and they have considerable time and energy on their hands. All 15 participants were able to guess the easy password in this manner, but none were able to guess the medium or hard passwords after 20 minutes each (as previously, only the same 5 participants opted to attempt the hard password). Some participants opted to keep trying, and 3 participants (2 of which were grouped as a team) were able to crack the medium password after an average of 40 minutes. None were able to crack the hard password in under 1 hour, though only 1 participant attempted the hard password beyond the 20 minute mark, with the rest agreeing that it was still too difficult.

Our study shows that even a rudimentary PassGame password has good protection against shoulder surfing, and a more complicated password can be highly resistant to shoulder surfing. With a single viewing of 5 complete successful password entries, even the simple password could not be shoulder-surfed. The hard passwords was resistant to unlimited viewings, simulating a worst-case camera attack. In our future work, we plan to develop a program to crack recorded PassGame passwords to determine how many entries are needed on average to generate enough intersection for a successful guess.

VIII. Discussion

In this section, we discuss extensions of PassGame and discuss the problem of challenge-response authentication in terms of usability.

A. *Extension of PassGame with New Games*

To foil an attacker who obtains the older password through various means such as password hash cracking, interception, or simply guessing, system owners or administrators prefer expiring old passwords every a few months or weeks and asking system users to generate new passwords. While password expiration policies can possibly help secure the system by reducing the time that an attacker has to access the system, password expiration policies can cause extra burden on system users such as interruption of ongoing work and increase in login errors. Zeng et al. [34] even reported that the knowledge of old passwords can help in breaking new passwords.

PassGame can be extended to reduce or eliminate the side effects of the password expiration policies. The extension is to add a game dimension to PassGame. In other words, when a user is required to change the old password based on one game, the user can select another game and form a new password based on the new game. To better reduce or eliminate the side effects, the systems may use games that are as different as possible. For example, if the old password is based on chess, the system may suggest the user to use Monopoly for the new password.

The game change can help reduce memory interference in long term memory, which is used for continuing storage of information [35], as the new game is completely different from the old game and the passwords formed based on the different games are less likely to cause memory interference.

The addition of the game dimension can also prevent breaking new passwords based on the knowledge of old passwords. PassGame based on different games may have different sets of dimensions so no relationship between the new password and old passwords is available to assist in cracking the new password. For example chess and Monopoly have different sets of game pieces/rules and completely different game boards.

We plan to perform a user study on the extension in our future work. Since passwords usually expire every 3 months or 6 months, the user study may take a long time.

B. *Impact of Unrelated Adjustments*

As we observed in our user study, shoulder-surfing based on a recording of multiple entries is conducted by attempting to find the intersection of information between recorded passwords. Information can be gathered from 1) the initial random board, 2) the user's adjustments, and 3) success or failure of the authentication attempt. The first and third options are effectively outside the user's control when they are being recorded. To make it more difficult to deduce their password, a user can raise the overall amount of information the attacker has to parse for intersections by making unrelated adjustments. To an attacker these adjustments can be considered noise. As the amount of unrelated adjustments rises, the likelihood of intersections found by an attacker to be noise (i.e. false positives) instead of part of the actual password increases. Thus even a user that knows they are being recorded can use the scheme with some degree of protection, by trading off some usability. The more usability traded off, e.g., the more unrelated adjustments made, the harder it will be for an attacker to extract useful information from the authentication attempt.

C. *Cost of Shoulder-Surfing Resistance*

In general, shoulder-surfing resistant schemes incur relatively higher usability costs such as longer password entry time, so PassGame is designed to be a supplemental scheme for use in crowded places or places with camera surveillance. Alternatively, a user can set one or two rule PassGame passwords for medium security on Android systems, and passwords with more rules for high security.

We recognize that an inevitable shortcoming of any challenge-response scheme is the requirement of *focus*. To assess the challenge and craft an appropriate response requires intelligence and concentration which may make the scheme less suitable for some situations when users may want to check their phones (e.g., when crossing the street). Sometimes the tradeoff with usability will not be a big issue, such as when the user is sitting on a bus awaiting some destination. We believe that a scheme like PassGame would work best when used along side a faster and simpler scheme so the user can cater authentication to the situation the user is in. The user may authenticate themselves with the simpler scheme when alone or in a trusted area and defer to PassGame when in public or when accessing more sensitive data. Alternatively, the user may have a 1 or 2 feature PassGame password that is easy to input for low security, and additional features that need to be satisfied to access high security content.

IX. Conclusion

We designed PassGame to mitigate shoulder-surfing attacks on mobile authentication. We implemented PassGame on the Android operating system and conducted a user study on the memorability/usability of PassGame and the shoulder-surfing resistance of PassGame. Our user studies show that PassGame passwords, which greatly exceed the password strength of current mobile authentication schemes and feature robust shoulder-surfing resistance, can still achieve 100% recall rates when recalled one week after password setup. PassGame even offers some resistance against camera attacks.

Acknowledgment

This work was supported in part by the National Science Foundation under Grants CNS-1460897, CNS-1338105, CNS-1343141, and DGE-1623713. Any opinions, findings, and conclusions or recommendations expressed in this material are those of the authors and do not necessarily reflect the views of the funding agencies.

References

[1] J. Gurary, Y. Zhu, N. Alnahash, and H. Fu, "Passgame: A shoulder-surfing resistant mobile authentication scheme," in *Advances in Computer-Human Interactions*, Mar. 2017.

[2] X. Suo, Y. Zhu, and G. Owen, "Graphical passwords: a survey," in *21st Annual Computer Security Applications Conference*, Dec. 2005, pp. 462–472.

[3] M. Harbach, E. von Zezschwitz, A. Fichtner, A. D. Luca, and M. Smith, "It's a hard lock life: A field study of smartphone (un)locking behavior and risk perception," in *Symposium On Usable Privacy and Security*, 2014, pp. 213–230.

[4] J. Hamari, J. Koivisto, and H. Sarsa, "Does gamification work?–a literature review of empirical studies on gamification," in *47th Hawaii International Conference on System Sciences (HICSS)*, 2014, pp. 3025–3034.

[5] C. Kroeze and M. S. Olivier, "Gamifying authentication," in *Information Security for South Africa (ISSA)*, 2012, pp. 1–8.

[6] D. L. Nelson, V. S. Reed, and J. R. Walling, "Pictorial superiority effect," *Journal of Experimental Psychology: Human Learning and Memory*, vol. 2, no. 5, pp. 523–528, Sep. 1976.

[7] G. Blonder, "Graphical password," Sep. 1996, patent 5,559,961.

[8] I. Jermyn, A. Mayer, F. Monrose, M. K. Reiter, and A. D. Rubin, "The design and analysis of graphical passwords," in *Proceedings of the 8th Conference on USENIX Security Symposium*, 1999, pp. 1–14.

[9] R. Dhamija and A. Perrig, "Deja vu: A user study using images for authentication," in *Proceedings of the 9th Conference on USENIX Security Symposium*, 2000, pp. 1–4.

[10] A. De Angeli, L. Coventry, G. Johnson, and K. Renaud, "Is a picture really worth a thousand words? exploring the feasibility of graphical authentication systems," *International Journal of Human-Computer Studies*, vol. 63, no. 1-2, pp. 128–152, Jul. 2005.

[11] S. Uellenbeck, M. Dürmuth, C. Wolf, and T. Holz, "Quantifying the security of graphical passwords: The case of android unlock patterns," in *Proceedings of the ACM SIGSAC Conference on Computer Communications Security*, 2013, pp. 161–172.

[12] F. Tari, A. A. Ozok, and S. H. Holden, "A comparison of perceived and real shoulder-surfing risks between alphanumeric and graphical passwords," in *Proceedings of the Second Symposium on Usable Privacy and Security*, 2006, pp. 56–66.

[13] V. Roth, K. Richter, and R. Freidinger, "A pin-entry method resilient against shoulder surfing," in *Proceedings of the 11th ACM Conference on Computer and Communications Security*, 2004, pp. 236–245.

[14] E. von Zezschwitz, A. De Luca, B. Brunkow, and H. Hussmann, "Swipin: Fast and secure pin-entry on smartphones," in *Proceedings of the Conference on Human Factors in Computing Systems*, vol. 15, 2015, pp. 1403–1406.

[15] A. De Luca, K. Hertzschuch, and H. Hussmann, "Colorpin: securing pin entry through indirect input," in *Proceedings of the SIGCHI Conference on Human Factors in Computing Systems*, 2010, pp. 1103–1106.

[16] A. Bianchi, I. Oakley, V. Kostakos, and D. S. Kwon, "The phone lock: audio and haptic shoulder-surfing resistant pin entry methods for mobile devices," in *Proceedings of the 5th International Conference on Tangible, Embedded, and Embodied Interaction*, 2011, pp. 197–200.

[17] N. H. Zakaria, D. Griffiths, S. Brostoff, and J. Yan, "Shoulder surfing defence for recall-based graphical passwords," in *Proceedings of the 7th Symposium on Usable Privacy and Security*, 2011, pp. 1–12.

[18] D. Lin, P. Dunphy, P. Olivier, and J. Yan, "Graphical passwords & qualitative spatial relations," in *Proceedings of the 3rd Symposium on Usable Privacy and Security*, 2007, pp. 161–162.

[19] S. Wiedenbeck, J. Waters, L. Sobrado, and J.-C. Birget, "Design and evaluation of a shoulder-surfing resistant graphical password scheme," in *Proceedings of the Working Conference on Advanced Visual Interfaces (AVI)*, 2006, pp. 177–184.

[20] H. Gao, Z. Ren, X. Chang, X. Liu, and U. Aickelin, "A new graphical password scheme resistant to shoulder-surfing," in *International Conference on Cyberworlds (CW)*, 2010, pp. 194–199.

[21] D. Davis, F. Monrose, and M. K. Reiter, "On user choice in graphical password schemes," in *Proceedings of the 13th Conference on USENIX Security Symposium*, 2004, pp. 1–11.

[22] W. A. van Eekelen, J. van den Elst, and V.-J. Khan, "Picassopass: a password scheme using a dynamically layered combination of graphical elements," in *Extended Abstracts on Human Factors in Computing Systems*, 2013, pp. 1857–1862.

[23] J. Gurary, Y. Zhu, G. Corser, J. Oluoch, N. Alnahash, and H. Fu, "Maps: A multi-dimensional password scheme for mobile authentication," in *Proceedings of the 2015 International Conference on Interactive Tabletops & Surfaces*, 2015, pp. 409–412.

[24] D. Luca *et al.*, "Back-of-device authentication on smartphones," in *Proceedings of the SIGCHI Conference on Human Factors in Computing Systems*, 2013, pp. 2389–2398.

[25] C. Winkler *et al.*, "Glass unlock: Enhancing security of smartphone unlocking through leveraging a private near-eye display," in *Proceedings of the 33rd Annual ACM Conference on Human Factors in Computing Systems*, vol. 15, 2015, pp. 1407–1410.

[26] M. Kumar, T. Garfinkel, D. Boneh, and T. Winograd, "Reducing shoulder-surfing by using gaze-based password entry," in *Proceedings of the 3rd Symposium on Usable Privacy and Security*, 2007, pp. 13–19.

[27] A. De Luca, E. Von Zezschwitz, and H. Hußmann, "Vibrapass: secure authentication based on shared lies," in *Proceedings of the SIGCHI Conference on Human Factors in Computing Systems*, 2009, pp. 913–916.

[28] Frank, "Chaos computer club breaks apple touchid,"

http://www.ccc.de/en/updates/2013/ccc-breaks-apple-touchid, Sep. 2013.

[29] P. Shi, B. Zhu, and A. Youssef, "A pin entry scheme resistant to recording-based shoulder-surfing," in *Third International Conference on Emerging Security Information, Systems and Technologies (Secureware)*, 2009, pp. 237–241.

[30] W.-C. Ku, D.-M. Liao, C.-J. Chang, and P.-J. Qiu, "An enhanced capture attacks resistant text-based graphical password scheme," in *International Conference on Communications in China (ICCC)*, 2014, pp. 204–208.

[31] T. Kwon and S. Na, "Tinylock: Affordable defense against smudge attacks on smartphone pattern lock systems," *Computers & Security*, vol. 42, pp. 137–150, 2014.

[32] N. Wright, A. S. Patrick, and R. Biddle, "Do you see your password?: Applying recognition to textual passwords," in *Proceedings of the 8th Symposium on Usable Privacy and Security*, 2012, pp. 1–14.

[33] T. Takada and M. Ishizuka, "Chameleon dial: repeated camera-recording attack resilient pin input scheme," in *Proceedings of the 2015 ACM International Joint Conference on Pervasive and Ubiquitous Computing (UbiComp)*, 2015, pp. 365–368.

[34] Y. Zhang, F. Monrose, and M. K. Reiter, "The security of modern password expiration: An algorithmic framework and empirical analysis," in *Proceedings of the 17th ACM Conference on Computer and Communications Security*, 2010, pp. 176–186.

[35] R. Atkinson and R. Shiffrin, *The Psychology of Learning and Motivation*. New York: Academic Press, 1968, vol. 2.

Multi-Platform Performance of Authenticated Encryption for Payment Cards with Crypto Co-processors

Keith Mayes

Royal Holloway, University of London
Egham, Surrey, UK
Email: keith.mayes@rhul.ac.uk

Abstract—**Many security protocols rely on authentication of communicating entities and encryption of exchanged data. Traditionally, authentication and encryption have been separate processes, however, there are combined solutions, referred to as authenticated-encryption (AE). The payment card industry is revising its protocol specifications and considering AE, however, there has been uncertainty around performance and feasibility on traditional issued smart cards and when loaded as applications on security chips pre-installed within devices. It is difficult to predict and compare performance using results from generic CPUs, as typical smart card chips used in payment, have slow CPUs yet fast crypto-coprocessors, and their performance may be constrained by secured application programming interfaces. This report is based on a practical investigation, commissioned by a standards body, that compared secure platform level (MULTOS) and low-level native implementations of AE on crypto-coprocessor smart cards. The study also suggests a technology independent benchmark (TIGA) for a CPU with crypto-coprocessor. This paper extends on work first published in ICONS17/EMBEDDED2017; now describing an additional native mode implementation on a modern secured smart card chip, introducing a more precise timing measurement, and further analysing the utility of TIGA. The work has proved the feasibility of implementing various modes of authenticated encryption on appropriate smart card chips with crypto-coprocessors and has provided precise measurement results for comparison. The work has also identified a means to predict the performance of other processors and platforms not included within the practical experiments.**

Keywords–Authenticated encryption; EMV; OCB; ETM; CCM; smart card.

I. INTRODUCTION

This text describes an extended version of an ICONS 2017 conference paper [1], which measured and compared Authenticated Encryption (AE) modes on a secured smart card platform and a native mode implementation on a legacy smart card chip. In this paper we also consider the native mode implementation on a third and more modern smart card chip of the type used within the MULTOS platform. The new results give a more relevant assessment of AE mode comparative performance and allow analysis of the Technology Independent Gain Assessment (TIGA) proposed in [1]. We start by considering the background to the original study.

The EMVCo organisation [5] developed the Europay, Mastercard and Visa (EMV) standards [4] that affect billions of payment smart cards. The cards use secured microcontroller chips, designed to be strongly tamper-resistant and independently evaluated to Common Criteria (CC) [3] levels of at least Evaluation Assurance Level (EAL) 4+. Despite strong defensive capabilities, the chips lag behind the state-of-the-art in CPU performance and memory sizes. However, despite these limitations the chips excel in cryptographic operations as they incorporate relatively high-speed crypto-coprocessor hardware. The EMVCo organisation is reviewing the use of Authenticated Encryption (AE) [11] for future payment card processing. There are a number of potential modes and those originally of interest included Offset Codebook (OCB) [16], Galois Counter Mode (GCM) [21], Counter with Cipher Block Chaining Message Authentication Code (CCM) [20] and Encrypt-then-MAC (ETM) [11]. Note that a MAC in this context is a cryptographic Message Authentication Code, computed over the payload data, and used to verify its integrity and the authenticity of its source. Within this study, GCM was eventually substituted for OCB3 as the former required binary field multiplication, which was not supported by the available crypto-coprocessors. There have been previous studies of AE performance, however, they have generally focussed on more powerful generic CPUs, without dedicated crypto-coprocessors. As a starting point we take the study by Krovetz and Rogaway [15], which shows that OCB performance is faster (for the given test conditions) than alternatives; however, there are several reasons why these results cannot be immediately accepted as relevant for EMV protocols:

- The command messages in traditional smart cards are small; the data field restricted to 255 bytes; larger payloads accommodated by multiple messages.
- The results do not adequately address the case of a slow CPU with a relatively fast crypto-coprocessor.
- Support for Associated Data is not required.
- Smart cards have very restricted memory sizes with different write speeds for Random Access Memory (RAM) and Non-Volatile Memory (NVM).
- Conventional smart card interfaces are quite slow and so protocols can be communication limited rather than processing limited.

In order to gain a better appreciation of the comparative performance of AE on realistic smart card platforms, a practical study was initiated, considering first a secure platform implementation (MULTOS) [18] and then a native mode equivalent. In the original study, described in [1] the choice of native mode implementation was compromised by restrictive choice of chip and development tools, however, this extended study overcomes these restrictions.

This report describes the experimental requirements in Section II and then gives an overview of the AE modes in Section III. The platform and native results are presented and discussed in Sections IV and V respectively. Section VI discusses how implementation security may affect performance measurements, and Section VII considers communication limitations. Conclusions and suggestions for future work are presented in Section VIII.

II. Experimental Requirements

The study investigated comparative performance of AE modes implemented in both a secured smart card application platform (representative of a pre-deployed device), and as native code on a smart card chip. The selected platform was a MULTOS ML3 card, using the Infineon SLE78 chip [8], which can be CC EAL4+ certified, and includes good defences against physical, side-channel [13][14] and fault attacks. The original native mode implementation used a Samsung 16-bit smart card chip (S3CC9E8) [24], and as the crypto-coprocessor did not support AES, its performance comparisons used 3DES/DES [6]. The S3CC9E8 is a secured microcontroller with physical attack protection, fault sensors and some side-channel countermeasures, however, it would normally require added defensive measures in software; this is discussed further in Section VI. The extended study was able to add a native mode implementation on the SLE78 chip supporting both AES and 3DES/DES variants. The AE modes considered in detail were OCB (OCB2 and OCB3), CCM and ETM; with some GCM experiments.

The EMV protocol would normally have a preliminary Diffie Hellman key and nonce exchange, however, this was not modelled as would be common to all AE modes and so would not affect performance comparison. Associated Data is not needed in the EMV protocol. Communicated data is required to fit within one or more standard Application Data Protocol Units (APDU) [9], and with the exception of OCB modes, all APDU payloads that are not multiples of the encryption block-size are padded prior to encryption. The memory in smart card chips is very restricted and protocol/algorithm execution is expected to place very limited demands on it, leaving maximum space for OS and applications. For our tests, a working assumption was that 80-90% of the memory was unavailable. The RAM in smart cards is usually much faster for writing than the NVM and so critical objects/buffers are implemented in a RAM. Our application was limited to no more than 10% of the available RAM (so if 8k, we could have 800 bytes). The application was restricted to no more than 10% of the available code/data space (so if a 64k flash device then 6.4kbytes was allowed). Some implementations benefit from trading NVM space for speed using pre-computed tables, which is not well suited to smart cards, but up to 10% of the NVM space was assumed available for this. In general the imposed memory restrictions proved not to be a problem for the implemented AE modes.

Test software was in 'C', so it could be adapted and directly comparable for both MULTOS and native implementations. There is a single test application that incorporates all the AE modes plus test utilities that measure various core functions. The interface is based on APDU commands and responses, with the payload data consisting of blocks of plaintext or ciphertext. For message timing precision, commands were run at least 1024 times before response, in order to compensate for measurement tolerance. Communication delay was removed (via calibration) from the test results, although it is reconsidered in Section VII. We will now continue the discussion by providing an overview of the AE modes.

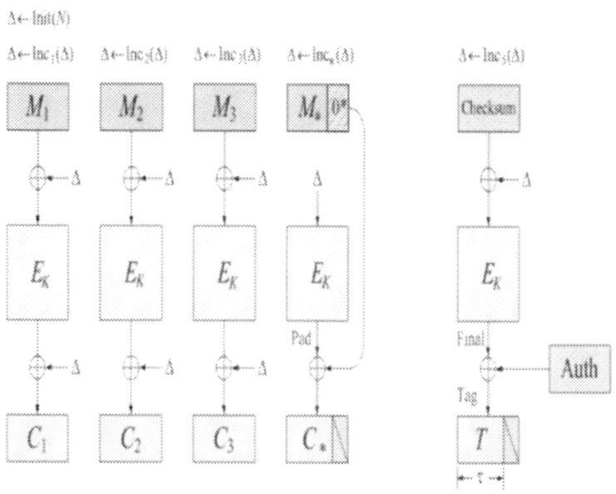

Figure 1. OCB with Incomplete Blocks [Rogaway]

III. Overview of Authenticated Encryption Modes

Offset Codebook mode is defined as mechanism 1 in ISO/IEC 19772 [11] and is also described in RFC 7253 [16]. The principles of operation are also well presented on Phil Rogaway's website [22]. For convenience, we will summarise the basic operations of OCB2 here. In Figure 1, an initialisation vector is first computed and then the plaintext message is split into blocks (M1-3, M* in example), all but the last block must be the size of the block cipher, so for AES128 we have 128 bit blocks. They are then encrypted (with modification from the input vector) to produce ciphertext blocks. The complete output is the sequence of C1-3, C* plus an extra value T. Note that because of a requirement to recompute the intialisation vector, this AE is most optimum for a 64 block message sequence and least optimum for a single block message.

CCM is mechanism 3 in ISO/IEC19772 [11] and described in NIST SP800-38C [20] and [25]. Figure 2 overviews CCM operation. Whilst the simplified diagram just shows a nonce/-counter input to the stages of the MAC calculation, the generic standard description also specifies some flag/length bit fields.

ETM scheme (see Figure 3) is mechanism 5 in ISO/IEC 19772 [11], and is a conventional approach with separate encryption and MAC processes. It does not support Associated Data, although this is not required for the study. The encryption stage uses block encryption in counter mode with key K, followed by a MAC computation on the cipher text using a different key (K') to that used for encryption. According to ISO/IEC 19772 [11] the MAC algorithm is selected from the ISO/IEC 9797 standards [12], in which there are six different MAC options, all of which have numerous variants. The selected options for the tests are listed below.

- MAC Algorithm: 1 (usually referred to as CBC-MAC)
- Padding Method: 1 (zeros)
- Final Iteration: 1 (same as other iterations)
- Output Transformation: 1 (unity = no change)
- Truncation: - (left most 64 bits)

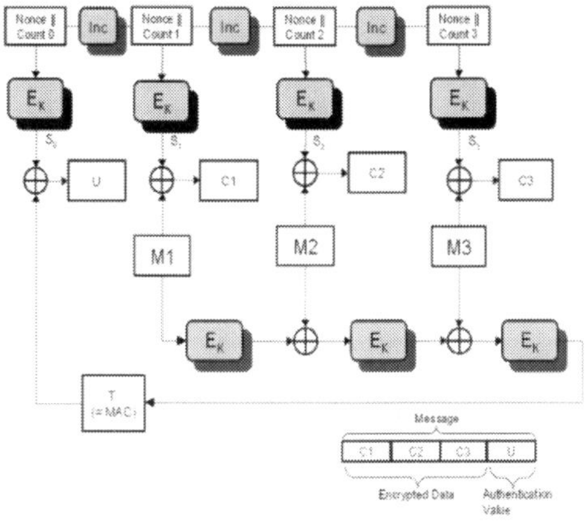

Figure 2. CCM Overview (simplified)

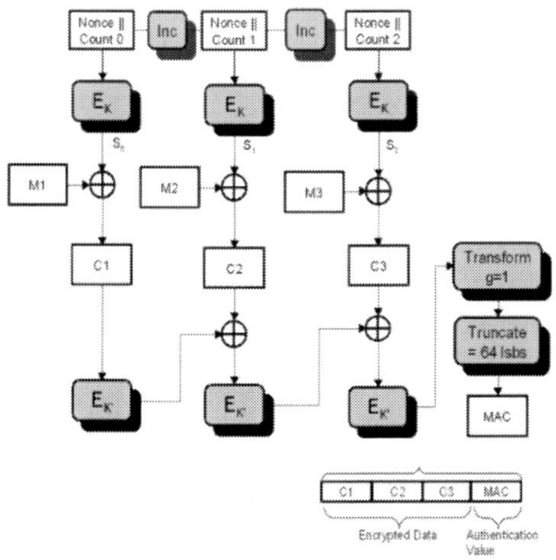

Figure 3. Encrypt then MAC

GCM (see Figure 4) mode of operation is mechanism 6 in ISO/IEC 19772 [11] and also described in NIST SP800-38D [21] and [23]. The performance of this mode could not be very usefully compared using the traditional crypto-coprocessors used for the study as GCM requires support for multiplication over Galois Field GF (2^{128}) with the hash key H, which is the encryption of all zeros under E_K.

A. *Workload Estimation*

Table I gives an indication of the underlying workload for each mode when processing the representative test message sizes (as advised by the commissioning standards body).

TABLE I. ALGORITHM WORKLOAD PER MODE

Bytes	Blks	Msgs	OCB		GCM		CCM	ETM
			E	Init	E	Mul	E	E
8	1	1	3	1	2	2	3	2
16	1	1	3	1	2	2	3	2
20	2	1	4	1	3	3	5	4
32	2	1	4	1	3	3	5	4
40	3	1	5	1	4	4	7	6
64	4	1	6	1	5	5	9	8
128	8	1	10	1	9	9	17	16
192	12	1	14	1	13	13	25	24

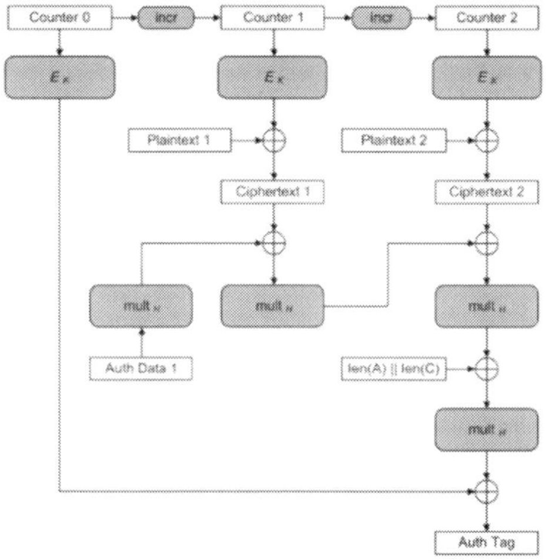

Figure 4. GCM Overview (simplified)

TABLE II. MULTOS BENCHMARK MEASUREMENTS (ms)

Function	Primitive		Application		Used
	RAM	NVM	RAM	NVM	
Block Encrypt	3.3	6.4			3.3
Block Xor	0.73	3.94	3.21	15.84	0.73
Block Shift	1.24		2.7		1.24
Block Copy	0.36		0.65		0.36
GF Multiply			199		199

IV. PLATFORM MODE RESULTS

For security, certification and reliability reasons, it is not normal to have native code access to a smart card or similar security chip once deployed. Instead the chip may offer a secure platform where added functionality is constrained to a tightly controlled application layer, using APIs to access security capabilities. The MULTOS card is such a secure platform whereby the application execution language is abstracted from the underlying hardware (see [19]), offering high standards of security, but making it difficult to predict performance of the core AE functionality. The results of initial benchmark tests are shown in Table II. It should be noted that these results are derived from the response of test commands sent to the smart card; with the tests including some control, data set-up and results extraction. Therefore the results should only be considered as rough estimates compared to the more accurate results from the method used in the extended study, and described later in this paper.

The time measured for a block encrypt with a 128-bit key was 3.3ms (confirmed by MULTOS as matching in-house results). The underlying chip crypto-engine is much faster, and the speed disparity is due to software reliability and security measures. The 3.3ms is only valid when writing encrypted data to RAM, as NVM increases the time to 6.4ms (although reading from NVM is fast); so the outputs of all functions were written to RAM. In all cases where a primitive was available, it was considerably quicker than any equivalent implemented at the application layer, although considerably slower than what might be imagined from a low-level native implementation

GCM requires a finite field multiply, but such a function did not exist as a MULTOS primitive and so was provided in a simple implementation similar to *Algorithm 1* in the standard [17]. Multiplying a single block takes 199ms, even when using primitives *multosBlockShiftRight* and *MultosBlockXor*. Other implementations are described in the standard, although they make use of time/memory trade-offs, which is not a strength for a memory limited smart card. For the initial tests, all the modes and the extra test utilities were built into a single application with the following memory requirements.

- Code Size (NVM): 5701 bytes
- Static Data (NVM): 498 bytes
- Session Data (RAM): 113 bytes

All the sizes are well within the realistic and practical design targets defined at the start of the project. For a single mode application the code size would be considerably less, and the static data is mainly internally stored test-vectors that would not normally be present. The session data could be reduced, if required.

A. Initial Tests and Optimisation

Following the MULTOS benchmark tests, the GCM mode was removed from the study (on request of the commissioning standards body) and more attention given to OCB (version 2) optimisation; and later OCB3 was also added. GCM requires specialist hardware support that was not available from the crypto-coprocessors in the test chips, whereas the other AE modes could be implemented in a straightforward manner. OCB2 was initially implemented from the published example code (see Figure 5) that was critically dependent on a function called *two_times()*.

```
//128-bit shift-left src <<= 1, XOR 0x87 if carry out
{unsigned i;
unsigned char carry=src[0]>>7;
// carry = high bit of src
for (i=0; i<sizeof(block)-1; i++) {
  dst[i]=(src[i]<<1)|(src[i+1]>>7); }
  dst[sizeof(block)-1]=(src[sizeof(block)-1]<<1)
                      ^(carry*0x87);
 }
```

Figure 5. Published Example Code for *two_times()*

This was replaced with a version (with less shifts) more suited to the MULTOS Platform (see Figure 6), which had a marked improvement on performance.

```
static void two_times(block dst, block src)
{
 unsigned char carry = src[0] & 0x80;
 multosBlockShiftLeft(AES_BLK_SZ, 1, src, src);
 if (carry) {src[AES_BLK_SZ - 1] ^= 0x87;}
 }
```

Figure 6. MULTOS Code for *two_times()*

Given the resulting speed-up (four/five times on larger messages) from improving OCB2 code, it was decided to also implement OCB3 based on the pseudo code and test vectors in RFC7253 [15].

1) OCB3 Memory considerations: At the beginning of the OCB3 encrypt pseudo code, a number of bit arrays need to be set-up, see Figure 7, noting that '_' is used to indicate subscript in the pseudo code and that *double()* is the same as the *two_times()* function used in OCB2. The array L_i to use in block processing, varies per message block using index L_[*ntz(i)*]. **L_i:** If we allow for processing 64 blocks of 128

```
L_* = ENCIPHER(K, zeros(128))
L_$ = double(L_*)
L_0 = double(L_$)
L_i = double(L_{i-1}) for every integer i > 0
```

Figure 7. OCB3 Key-dependent Variable Set-up

```
Nonce = num2str(TAGLEN mod 128,7)
        || zeros(120-bitlen(N)) || 1 || N
bottom = str2num(Nonce[123..128])
Ktop = ENCIPHER(K, Nonce[1..122] || zeros(6))
Stretch = Ktop || (Ktop[1..64] xor Ktop[9..72])
Offset_0 = Stretch[1+bottom..128+bottom]
Checksum_0 = zeros(128)
```

Figure 8. OCB3 Nonce and Pre-encrypt Variables

bits then it might appear that we need 64 of the L_i arrays. However, the *ntz(i)* index means we only need 6 ($2^6 = 64$) L_i arrays, as well as L_*, L_$ and L_0. Therefore we need 9 blocks (144 bytes), rather than 67 blocks; which is well within our target RAM limit.

ntz(): Another memory requirement arises from the ntz() function. Bit/byte manipulations at the MULTOS application layer are slow and so it is quicker to implement the function as a look up table. For a maximum 64 block message we require a 64 byte array that can be precomputed and stored in NVM. This small amount of memory is easily accommodated within a smart card.

2) OCB3 Functional Aspects: OCB3 defines a hash function for use with Associated Data, however, this is not needed in the EMV experiments. OCB3 has a preparation stage where key and nonce related data is readied prior to processing message blocks. The key data was described earlier (computation is relatively straight forward) and nonce related data is illustrated in Figure 8. This is mostly straightforward apart from the innocuous looking line showing the calculation of *Offset_0*. The variable *bottom* will have a value between 0 and 63; and it is effectively used as a bit-wise left shift. As discovered previously, application level bit-shifts are inefficient on the MULTOS test platform, however, the primitives *multosBlockShiftLeft/Right* are much quicker. Unfortunately, the primitives require a fixed constant value for the number of places to shift. Although the operation is only carried out once per message it could adversely affect efficiency, especially of small messages and so effort was directed towards optimisation. The first step was to split *bottom* into a number of byte shifts plus a smaller number (up to seven) bit shifts. Byte shifts are easy as we can just change the array index. The bit-shifts were used in a switch/case to reach primitive calls with the appropriate number of shifts. More code was needed, but the overall code space requirements are small.

B. MULTOS Platform Results

The results from testing OCB2, CCM, ETM and OCB3 are shown in Table III.

From the MULTOS results we can see OCB2 is the quickest mode for message sizes beyond 32bytes. OCB3's initial processing makes it slower than OCB2, and OCB3 only overtakes ETM for messages larger than 128 bytes. CCM is always a little slower than ETM due to the extra encryption block, and both are less efficient when working on input data that requires padding.

TABLE III. MULTOS PLATFORM RESULTS (ms)

Bytes	OCB2	CCM	ETM	OCB3
8	16.59	17.78	14.27	28.66
16	16.61	17.22	13.70	29.27
20	22.17	25.73	22.21	34.40
32	22.17	25.16	21.62	35.00
40	27.72	33.67	30.15	40.12
64	33.35	41.09	37.57	46.42
128	55.77	72.91	69.38	69.21
192	78.17	104.73	101.22	92.06

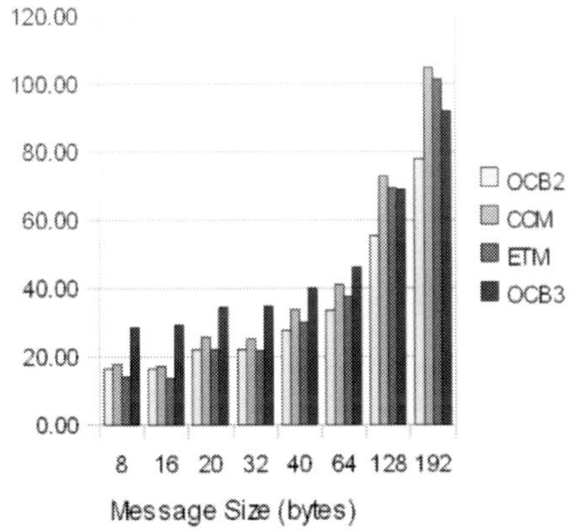

Figure 9. AE Comparative Performance on MULTOS Platform

Although OCB2 seems the faster option for the MULTOS platform (for messages 32+bytes) the relative difference in processing time is not enormous. OCB2 benefited from some optimisation, however, there is little scope for improvement in ETM and CCM as much of their time is spent encrypting, which is only possible via a MULTOS API call. The MULTOS platform (and platforms in general) add abstraction between the application layer and the underlying hardware, and so there is considerable uncertainty that the comparative results of Table III would be similar in a native mode smart card implementation. Furthermore, the absolute performance times on the MULTOS platform, would be expected to be at least one order of magnitude slower than a simple native implementation. Therefore, the AE modes were next tested on a hardware emulator for an older, but still relevant 16-bit smart card chip (Samsung S3CC9E8).

V. NATIVE MODE

During the original study, obtaining a native mode hardware emulator for a "real" smart card with crypto-coprocessor (for use in academic research) was not possible and only the S3CC9E8 emulator/chip was suitable and used in payment cards; although because it did not support AES, substitute 16 byte block encryption functions were needed. To ensure that comparative performance results would be relevant to standards, the commissioning standards body was consulted on the substitutes. The AES 16byte data block was considered as a pair of 8byte data blocks (M1 and M2) to be coded with DES or triple DES (TDES), i.e., TDES(M1)||(M2) or DES(M1)||(M2). Clearly these functions were for performance evaluation only, although TDES(M1)||TDES(M2) was also coded as a more secure, but overly co-processor intensive alternative. Following some initial experiments, TDES(M1)||(M2) was used as the AES replacement in the original study. In the follow-on study it was possible to port the native test code to a SLE78 chip that was able to support AES as well as TDES(M1)||(M2).

TABLE IV. TDES MASKED MODE AE TIMES (ms)

Bytes	OCB2	CCM	ETM	OCB3
8	3.04	2.16	1.53	5.75
16	3.07	2.12	1.49	5.81
20	4.19	3.48	2.85	6.73
32	4.24	3.43	2.80	6.81
40	5.37	4.77	4.15	7.76
64	6.57	6.04	5.42	8.81
128	11.23	11.28	10.65	12.82
192	15.89	16.51	15.89	16.82

A. *Initial Implementation (S3CC98) and Measurement*

This stage was focussed on porting the MULTOS code to the native emulator and generating early raw results for functional checking. They derive from non-optimised code, simply replacing the MULTOS primitive calls with equivalents. The performance of the AE modes (including OCB3) was measured in a similar way to the MULTOS work. The first tests used the dual TDES(M1)||TDES(M2) block encryption option (hardest to compute) and the results are in Table IV.

From these initial native results, we observe that the processing time for a single message was under 17ms, regardless of the AE mode. Although the block ciphers were of course different, the overall native execution times were significantly faster than those from the MULTOS experiments, even without optimisation. ETM was the best option for single APDU messages, although in absolute terms there was not much to choose between any of the modes. For smaller messages, ETM and CCM still seemed to have the advantage over the OCB modes. Common to both native and MULTOS implementations, ETM is always a little better than CCM and OCB3 does not seem to improve on OCB2.

B. *Optimisations*

The original source code used within the initial tests was very similar to the MULTOS code. The scope for optimisation on the MULTOS platform was limited as core functions were most efficiently carried out using platform primitives that were abstracted from the underlying hardware. Native mode programming generally offers more opportunity for optimisation as there is less hardware abstraction. Only speed optimisation was considered in this part of the study as all versions of the native code were well within our target memory bounds.

Data Block Copy and XOR: The algorithm modes make use of simple byte manipulation functions including XOR and Copy. In the MULTOS implementation these functions were provided by MULTOS primitives, which in the native code were initially replaced by simple equivalents that assumed variable sized fields and handled data byte-by-byte. However, within the authentication modes, very few operations use variable sized fields, with the majority working on 16 byte memory blocks. Knowing the field size, means that we can avoid loop counters, and by ensuring that the blocks are aligned on 4-byte boundaries we can perform operations on unsigned long integer types rather than bytes. Referring to Table V we see that as a result, BlockXor and BlockCopy have almost doubled in speed, which has also improved the overall block cipher performance. Note that functional calls are still used at this stage rather than in-line code.

TABLE V. OPTIMISATION OF CORE FUNCTION EXECUTION (ms)

Function	Original	Optimised
Block Xor	0.161	0.071
Block Copy	0.114	0.064
ECB TDES || TDES + mask	0.608	0.381
Fixed Block Shift Left	0.330	0.073

TABLE VI. OPTIMISED CORE PERFORMANCE BENCHMARKS (ms)

Functionality	Time
FixBlockXor	0.071
FixBlockCopy	0.064
FixBlockShiftLeft	0.073
DES(M1)||M2	0.128
DES(M1)||DES(M2)	0.141
DES(M1)||DES(M2) + mask XOR	0.146
DES(M1)||DES(M2) + mask XOR + key clear	0.154
TDES(M1)||M2	0.140
TDES(M1)||TDES(M2)	0.163
TDES(M1)||TDES(M2) + mask XOR	0.169
TDES(M1)||TDES(M2) + mask XOR + key clear	0.178

Block Shifts: The OCB modes use Copy and XOR operations, but also rely on the function *two_times()* (discussed earlier), which in turn makes use of a function for shifting the contents of a block to the left. The function from the first tests, *BlockShiftLeft()* was a direct replacement for the MULTOS primitive that supported variable shifts on variable sized blocks, referred to by pointer parameters. However, in practice, *two_times()* can be constrained to always use shifts of one place in a 16 byte global variable block. It was therefore possible to create a simpler *FixBlockShiftLeft()* function to use instead. The resulting speed improvement for the shift functions was very significant, as shown in Table V.

Further Refinement: When implementing the block cipher functions, further optimisation removed calls to core functions involving variable length arguments, and in some cases replaced them with simple in-line code. The block encryption function no longer called the core functions, but had faster in-line equivalents. The different block functions are handled by compile-time switches. Note that when using a crypto-coprocessor an input may be masked to reduce side-channel leakage and so a dummy mask was included in the test modes. An option was also added to clear the keys after use, however, this was not used in the main measurements. The extended set of benchmarked measurements is shown in Table VI, however, now that operations are speed optimised the absolute figures are significantly influenced by the measurement test command handling. It is more useful to consider the relative measurements, e.g., by subtracting the FixBlockCopy time from the others.

C. Native Mode Results (S3CC98)

Following the additional optimisations, the message tests were repeated for the substitute block cipher function TDES(M1)||M2. The functions are clearly intended to assess performance, rather than to ensure security of the data. The results are provided in Table VII and shown graphically in Figure 10.

D. Observations on the S3CC98 Native Tests

Considering Table VI we have significantly improved the performance of core functions. We can also use these results to estimate the achievable raw speed of the crypto-coprocessor, by cancelling out the software manipulations. For both DES and TDES operations we set-up the same keys (two are redundant for DES, but help our timing comparison), wrote in the input data once and read out the result once. The DES crypto-engine overwrites its input data with its output and so for TDES the CPU does not need to move data between the sequence of DES executions; it just refers to a different pre-stored key for each execution. Therefore, if we look at the times for an equivalent DES and TDES operation the difference should be the time taken for the extra DES executions. This time is largely dependent on the hardware although the execution has to be started and checked for completion by the CPU. We can estimate the core DES run time t_d using the following example, where $t(f)$ is the time to execute function f.

TABLE VII. S3CC98 TDES(M1)||M2 AE TIMES (ms)

Bytes	OCB2	CCM	ETM	OCB3
8	0.54	0.34	0.27	0.83
16	0.57	0.30	0.23	0.79
20	0.65	0.50	0.43	0.92
32	0.70	0.45	0.38	0.91
40	0.79	0.64	0.57	1.07
64	0.95	0.75	0.68	1.16
128	1.46	1.35	1.28	1.65
192	1.96	1.95	1.88	2.14

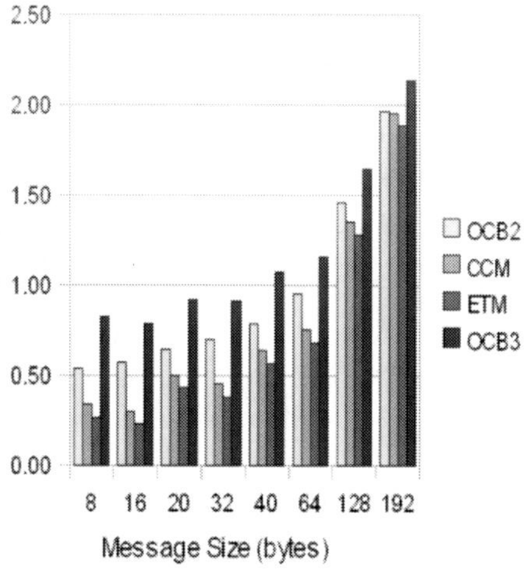

Figure 10. Optimised S3CC98 TDES(M1)||M2 AE Times (ms)

$$
\begin{aligned}
2t_d &= t(TDES(M1)||M2) - t(DES(M1)||M2) \\
&= 0.140 - 0.128 \\
&= 0.012ms
\end{aligned} \tag{1}
$$

There were two extra DES runs in the TDES version so we might suppose that each was about 6us. We can check this by calculating the following.

$$
\begin{aligned}
4t_d &= t(TDES(M1)||TDES(M2)) \\
&\quad - t(DES(M1)||DES(M2)) \\
&= 0.163 - 0.141 \\
&= 0.022ms
\end{aligned} \tag{2}
$$

The four extra DES runs take 22us, about 5.5us each; which is close to our earlier estimate. We can also see from Table VI that the dummy XOR on a 16byte block using in-line code

TABLE VIII. SLE78 BASIC PERFORMANCE BENCHMARKS (ms)

Functionality	Time
FixBlockXor	0.006
FixBlockCopy	0.004
FixBlockShiftLeft	0.006
AES	0.041
TDES(M1)||M2	0.027

TABLE IX. SLE78 Native AES AE TIMES (ms)

Bytes	OCB2	CCM	ETM	OCB3
8	0.19	0.14	0.10	0.28
16	0.19	0.14	0.10	0.27
20	0.25	0.22	0.18	0.33
32	0.25	0.21	0.17	0.32
40	0.30	0.30	0.24	0.38
64	0.36	0.37	0.31	0.42
128	0.58	0.67	0.60	0.63
192	0.81	0.97	0.89	0.82

takes about the same time, 5-6us. The key-clear, which is a 24 byte write, takes about 8-9us, so a 16byte block copy should be in a similar 5-6us range. The optimisations improved the speed of all AE modes.

E. Extended Implementation (SLE78) and Measurement

The optimised C code for the S3CC98 implementation was ported to the SLE78 chip. The code was modified to run the AES block cipher, although the capability to run TDES(M1)||(M2) was retained. To avoid a run-time switch between the block cipher modes (which might affect performance) the test card was loaded with two separate applications. Before considering the AE mode tests, some basic benchmark tests were carried out as shown in Table VIII. The measurements for XOR, copy ands shift are on the limit of accuracy for the test system, even running the command iterations over 4000 times, however, when comparing the results from Table VI, it is clear that the SLE78 is roughly an order of magnitude faster than the S3CC98 on basic processing. This result is not unexpected as the SLE78 has a much newer and faster chip and CPU than the S3CC98. The performance of the block ciphers is mainly due to the crypto-coprocessors rather than the CPUs and here the speed-up is not quite so large. Based on the approximate test command figures, the SLE78 can carry out the TDES(M1)||(M2) operation roughly five times faster than the S3CC98; and indeed 1.5 times faster than it can run the AES block cipher. The latter is due to AES being not quite so well optimised for hardware implementation as DES. If we refer back to the MULTOS results of Table II we can see that for the same SLE78 chip the MULTOS platform speed is approaching two orders of magnitude slower than is possible in native mode. This is the price to pay for a high security implementation compared to simple functional capability.

The AE mode tests were carried out on the SLE78, first using AES and then the TDES(M1)||(M2) block ciphers. The results are shown in Table IX and Table X; and graphically in Figure 11 and Figure 12. The most notable observations from the figures are that although the absolute timing is very different, the result patterns for the MULTOS implementation and the native SLE78 AES implementation have strong similarities, as do the two TDES native implementations. In the next section we will investigate if the result behaviours can be predicted in a chip and platform independent manner from simple benchmark tests.

TABLE X. SLE78 Native TDES(M1)||M2 AE TIMES (ms)

Bytes	OCB2	CCM	ETM	OCB3
8	0.15	0.11	0.08	0.24
16	0.15	0.10	0.07	0.23
20	0.20	0.15	0.13	0.28
32	0.20	0.14	0.12	0.27
40	0.24	0.19	0.17	0.32
64	0.29	0.23	0.21	0.35
128	0.46	0.41	0.38	0.50
192	0.63	0.59	0.56	0.65

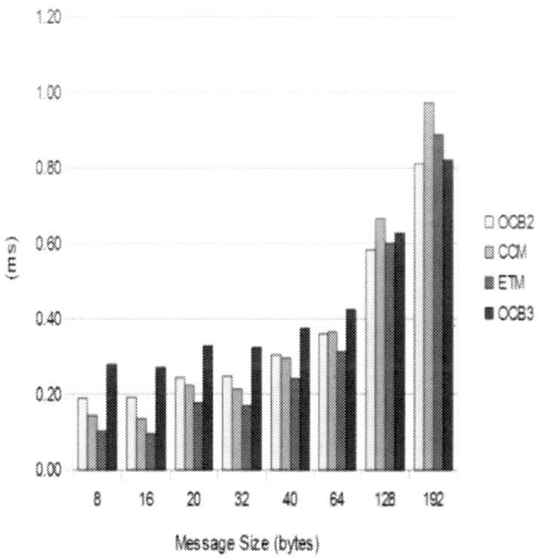

Figure 11. SLE78 Native AES AE TIMES (ms)

F. Technology Independent Gain Assessment

When considering the implementation of security algorithms and protocols on limited processors, assumptions are often made about their feasibility based on the resource intensity of the primitives with respect to the speed of the CPU. Anticipation of performance can affect the design from the outset, for example, avoiding best practice standardised algorithms in favour of simpler approaches based on hashes and XOR operations. These assumptions can be invalid if the processor can execute primitives, such as block ciphers, relatively rapidly, as in the case of a crypto-coprocessor. In fact

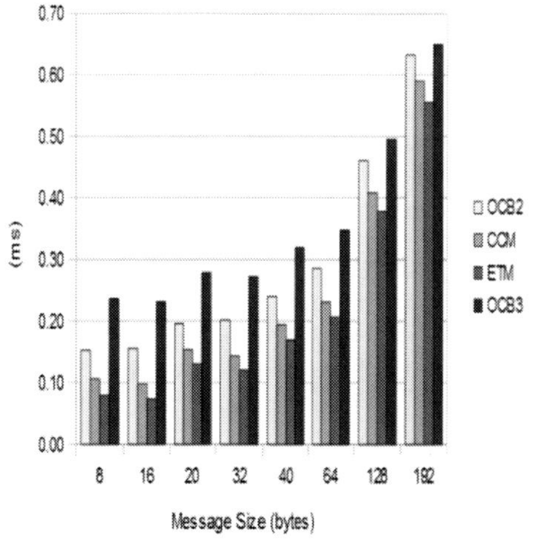

Figure 12. SLE78 Native TDES(M1)||M2 AE TIMES (ms)

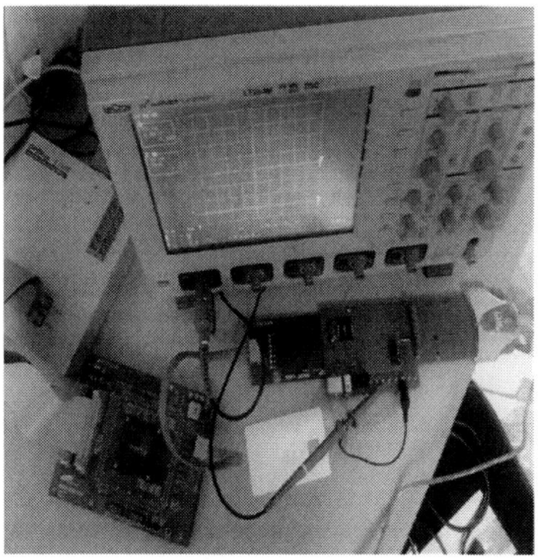

Figure 13. Measurement Equipment

in the latter case, our studies have shown that the performance results can be markedly distorted compared to a conventional CPU, so in predicting protocol performance we need some benchmark of how much distortion there will be. In the original study we proposed the use of the Technology Independent Gain Assessment (TIGA) for any CPU with a crypto-coprocessor; expressed as the percentage of the block encryption that can be completed by the crypto-coprocessor in the time it would take the CPU to compute a block XOR. For example a CPU with no co-processor would have a TIGA of 0% whereas equality of XOR and block cipher time time would give a TIGA of 100%. The general idea is that TIGA is estimated for a target platform by measuring the XOR and block cipher speeds, so performance can be reasonably predicted prior to a full protocol implementation.

The question is then how and where to measure the block cipher and XOR speeds? In the case of the MULTOS platform, knowing the raw chip-level performance is of little use as the functions are accessed through a high-level API, which includes the security protection overheads. In this case the only option was to compute TIGA at the application/API level, which produced a rough estimate value of 22%. With a variety of low-level test commands we were eventually able to establish precise measurements for the S3CC98 equating to TIGA values for DES and 3DES of 100% and 33% respectively. Although it should be noted that even with low-level code development, functionality is often accessed via simple system calls and drivers; which detract from the maximum raw speed of the hardware. Speed would be further compromised by low level software security protection measures.

In the original study, we had little option, but to compare the performance of the MULTOS AES implementation with that of TDES(M1)||(M2) on the S3CC98 chips, but now we have the native mode SLE78 results to make a proper comparison. The SLE78 exhibits two TIGA values depending on whether we use the intended block cipher (AES) or the substitute version TDES(M1)||(M2).

The benchmark measurements of the original work were not considered precise enough, by the author, to draw any solid conclusions on the usefulness of using TIGA and so a new method was designed and applied to all the test cards.

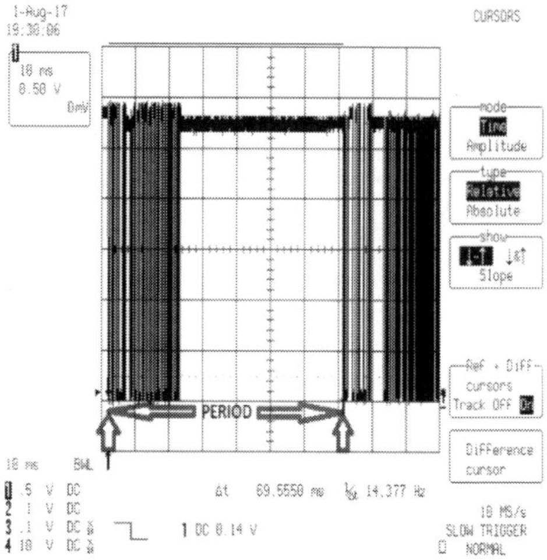

Figure 14. Improved Measurement Method

TABLE XI. TIGA Benchmarks (ms)

Platform	XOR	AES	TDES	TIGA
MULTOS SLE78	0.4695		5.3854	8.72%
Native SLE78	0.0038	0.0390		9.84%
Native SLE78	0.0038		0.0.0251	15.34%
Native S3CC98	0.0191		0.0966	19.80%

In the new method the timing measurements are obtained via an oscilloscope probing the smart card I/O line. The experimental equipment is shown in Figure 13, including the S3CC98 hardware emulator as well as one of the test cards. The sampling oscilloscope was a LeCroy LT264M, with a 350MHz bandwidth and sample speed of up to 1GS/s, although a much simpler scope would have been adequate. The PCB shown connected via the oscilloscope probe, is just a breakout board used for smart card experiments, and although it is configured for side-channel power leakage experiments, we only monitored the I/O line in this case.

One of the measurement scope traces is shown in Figure 14. The arrows have been added to clarify the measurement period, which is from the first transition of the I/O line (the start of the test command transition), to the first transition of the card response. The test command was run with a single iteration cycle giving a period P1 and then with an 'N' iteration cycle (typically 1000+) giving a period PN. The measurement was then calculated as (PN-P1)/(N-1) and thus excluded much of the fixed overhead inherent in the test command process.

These new results are presented in Table XI along with the respective TIGA calculations. Note that the TDES column implies TDES(M1)||M2.

If we consider the AES results from Table XI we see that despite more than two orders of magnitude difference in performance, the MULTOS platform and the native SLE78 have very similar TIGA values, in the range of 8-10%. When we refer to Figure 9 and Figure 11 we also see a very similar shape to the AE data measurements. Turning our attention to the TDES versions, we see they have higher gain that AES, and despite presenting a comparison of two very different chips, with a three fold difference in absolute performance, their TIGA values are quite close, in the 15-20% range. Referring to Figure 10 and Figure 12 we can see a similar shape to the AE data measurements. These results are encouraging and would suggest that the TIGA value is a reasonable estimator of performance on a crypto-coprocessor device, regardless of the level of access or API.

Although we are not always comparing like-with-like due to access restrictions, TIGA is a means to make a benchmark comparison. A high value would suggest that a designer could use block encryptions as readily as XORs and so algorithm optimisation and performance would be quite different to conventional (non crypto-coprocessor) CPUs.

At this point it should be recalled that cards/chips of interest are security sensitive and likely to be attacked. Fortunately countermeasures are quite well understood by the card industry, but they can potentially impact on performance, and so in the next section we consider how our results might be affected.

VI. Implementation Security and Performance

Payment cards safeguard financial transactions of significant value and so are required to strongly resist a wide range of attacks. EMV cards rely on the protection of various stored assets including cryptographic keys, account details and PINs, as well as on the integrity of critical functionality Adhering to information security best practice guidelines for design, (e.g., for algorithms, keys and random number generation) is not at all sufficient as many of the attacks target the implementation rather than the design. In smart cards, the attack resistance will be provided by a mix of hardware and software measures and so there is potential for performance impact. We can consider such attacks under the following three categories.

- Physical
- Fault
- Side-Channel

A. Physical Attack Resistance

Physical attack generally requires considerable expertise, equipment and time. It may for example involve decapsulating a chip, hardware reverse engineering, probing buses and memories and modifying tracks. However, smart card chips have numerous defences against such intrusions, including:

- Passive and active shields - to prevent access to a working chip
- Encrypted buses and memories - to impede direct probing
- Light sensors - to detect decapsulation
- Scrambled circuit layout - to make hardware reverse engineering difficult

Both the chips used in this study incorporate these protective measures, and because they are inherent in the hardware we do not need to degrade our performance test results.

B. Fault Attack Resistance

Fault attacks are active, in that they use means to disrupt the normal operation of the target device (chip); but without damaging it. The faults can, for example, be generated from voltage glitches, radiation pulses and operating the target outside of its operational specification. Under fault conditions the chip may reveal all kinds of information that it would not do when working normally and there are some very elegant attacks including extraction of RSA keys [2]. The hardware sensors in traditional tamper-resistant smart cards (like the S3CC9E8) are intended to detect the likely means of fault insertion and prevent a response useful to the attacker; so there may be no significant added overhead for the software. A sophisticated attack might possibly bypass the sensors, however, by adopting openly peer-reviewed algorithms and using diversified card keys, we remove motivation for such effort. Added countermeasures could be to verify a result or to run an algorithm twice and only output a response if the result is valid/consistent, however, both strategies rely on the correct outcomes of flag tests and loop counts. It is therefore good practice to add defensive coding of loop and flag tests, at the cost of some additional processing overhead,

The SLE78 chip works very differently to a traditional smart card chip as it has two CPUs working in tandem and a fault is detected if their processing does not agree. This is an innovative and effective approach, which would make it very difficult to succeed with a fault attack. As the protection is inherent in the chip hardware it should not noticeably impact our test results.

C. Side-Channel Attack Resistance

Side-channel leakage implies the leakage of sensitive information (especially keys) via an unintentional channel. This can take the form of key/data-dependent timing variations, power supply fluctuations or electromagnetic emissions. Analysis techniques are well known (see [13] [14]) and can be very powerful against unprotected implementations, including best-practice algorithm designs such as AES. Fortunately, modern smart cards are well protected against such attacks, with a range of countermeasures that mainly impede statistical averaging of signals (used to detect signals in noise) or reduce the source generation of the leakage. Attack countermeasures include:

- Power smoothing
- Noise insertion
- Randomisation of execution
- Timing equalisation
- Dual-rail logic (or Dual CPUs)

The SLE78 chip used in the MULTOS card and for the latter native mode experiments, has a sophisticated dual processing arrangement known as "Integrity Guard" that is believed to be effective at suppressing leakage at source, and this coupled with the Common Criteria certified MULTOS secured OS would suggest that no significant further performance degradation would be incurred from application level countermeasures. However, the native mode SLE78 results show us that the MULTOS protective measures have already cost two orders of magnitude in performance compared to the raw chip performance.

The S3CC9E8 used in the native implementation is a traditional secured microcontroller chip with a single CPU and so it will include some noise smoothing and execution randomisation, but will not suppress the leakage signals at source. Given the age of the chip one would expect some extra side-channel leakage protection to be required from the software, which will have a performance impact. Our tests already included a dummy XOR to represent masking the data used in the crypto-coprocessor, however, for this type of chip more help would be needed. One technique used for fast, but perhaps "leaky" crypro-processors is to run the algorithm multiple times, so that an attacker does not know which run used the correct data rather than a dummy pattern. Clearly if you hide your data in a 10 algorithm sequence, you would expect to lose an order of magnitude in performance. Hamming weight equalisation is another technique (used in non-secured CPUs) that seeks to reduce information leakage by ensuring that for each bit transition there is a complementary transition; so as a '1' changes to '0' there is also a '0' changing to '1'. In principle this should reduce leakage, however, due to electrical, timing and physical layout factors, register bits do not contribute equally to leakage, so the reduction is inferior to hardware measures and may not justify the effort. In a practical implementation this could for example be a 16-bit processor where the lower 8-bits of a register handle the normal data and the upper 8-bits handle the complementary data. This alone is not sufficient as it is necessary to also clear the registers before and after use and so rather than a two-fold reduction in performance, at least an order of magnitude should be anticipated.

D. Observations

It is likely that physical and fault attack protection can be handled by the smart card hardware without significantly degrading performance. For the MULTOS card based on the SLE78 we have sophisticated hardware coupled to an OS designed for the highest levels of security, and Common Criteria evaluation checks for strong protection against side-channel leakage. For the native implementation in the S3CC9E8 we would anticipate additional side-channel countermeasures in software and if we consider the techniques in the earlier section then even for restricted/tuned functionality, losing at least an order of magnitude in performance should be expected.

The motivation for a side-channel attack just to capture the EMV session keys is questionable, however, discovery of the keys might expose other assets or assist with sophisticated attack strategies. Therefore, it would be prudent to consider an order of magnitude speed degradation when considering the results in Table VII; although processing would still be fast, with the worst case time for a 192 byte payload being just over 21ms for the slowest mode. However, to know whether this processing is fast enough, or the bottleneck for the protocol, we need to also consider the communication speed via the smart card to Point of Sale (POS) interface.

VII. Communication Effects on Performance

Performance tests of AE, normally just focus on the processing aspects, as communication in an Internet-connected world is generally fast enough (e.g., 25-100Mbps) to cause negligible delay. However, for payment card use of AE we are dealing with interfaces that may be *much* slower and so transactions might hit communication limits before card processing limits.

A. Payment Card Interfaces

The interfaces for payment cards fall into two main categories. The contact interface is the oldest and has dominated payment card transactions using Chip & PIN, however, many cards now support the contactless interface for touch and pay (no PIN). Within the standards (contact [9] and contactless [10]) a range of interface speeds are defined, however, this does not mean the fastest modes are supported in all deployed cards, or POS terminals. Table XII shows an example range of transmission speeds and an estimation of the time to transmit the data associated with the different sized test messages. Note that the working interface speed is negotiated and agreed between the smart card and the POS terminal as part of the pre-transaction protocol and by varying clock speed as well as divider parameters the full range would be closer to 9600 - 38400 bits/s. For example the contact rates in Table XII are computed in accordance with standards, as a clock frequency (5 MHz) f_c divided by factor D (372, 512 and 512 respectively) and multiplied by a factor F (1, 8 and 32 respectively).

TABLE XII. CARD INTERFACE TRANSMISSION TIMES (ms)

Bytes	Contact (bits/s)			Contactless (bits/s)	
	13441	78125	312500	106000	424000
8	4.76	0.82	0.20	0.60	0.15
16	9.52	1.64	0.41	1.21	0.30
20	11.90	2.05	0.51	1.51	0.38
32	19.05	3.28	0.82	2.42	0.60
40	23.81	4.10	1.02	3.02	0.75
64	28.09	6.55	1.64	4.83	1.21
128	76.19	13.11	3.28	9.66	2.42
192	114.28	19.66	4.92	14.49	3.62

The speed range is very wide especially in the contact case, as the default rates maintain compatibility with very old cards and POS terminals. The command processing and transmission can be considered as separate activities; and whichever takes longer is considered the bottleneck limit. Recalling the MULTOS platform performance (Table III) we have a processing limited solution. There are some message/mode combinations that are communications limited, but only when running at the lowest default speed, which is impractically slow. If we now recall the raw native mode results (Table VII), then in practice we have a communications limited solution. At the fastest interface speeds this may not be quite the case, however, we would not normally assume that the fastest rates would be available from cards and POS terminals; and so the 78,125 bps and 106,000 bps for contact and contactless interfaces respectively would be more reasonable expectations. The future outlook is that the communication rates will get faster and the contact interface will eventually be displaced by contactless, which suggests that transactions will be processing limited. EMV implementations in mobile phones will of course have access to much faster wireless technologies such as 802.11ac that can run at 1.3 Gbits/s, however, the scope of this study is restricted to conventional smart card devices.

VIII. Conclusion and Future Work

The study investigated AE modes on existing available smart chips/platforms using conventional crypto-coprocessors. GCM was not analysed in detail as the *multH* function (or parts of it) would need to be implemented within more specialist crypto-coprocessor hardware. All the other AE modes considered, were feasible both in terms of speed and memory usage. The S3CC98 native mode implementation was much faster than the MULTOS platform and in the final tests all the modes for all single APDU test message sizes took no more than 2.14ms. The SLE78 native mode implementation was faster again with no AES AE mode taking more than 0.97ms and the slowest TDES(M1)||(M2)mode being 0.63ms.

The new results differ markedly from comparisons that have focussed on general processors, larger message sizes and the inclusion of Associated Data. For both native TDES(M1)||(M2) implementations, ETM/CCM modes were quicker than OCB for the single APDU test messages, although OCB modes would be expected to claw back the advantage for multi-APDU messages. In the SLE78 native AES implementation, OCB2 overtook ETM for message sizes around 64 bytes and upward. In all the implementations, and for a single APDU, ETM was always slightly ahead of CCM and OCB2 led OCB3.

One of the most interesting observations is that the MULTOS platform and native SLE78 AES performance results have very similar distributions, even though their absolute magnitudes differ by two magnitudes. Furthermore the two TDES(M1)||(M2) implementations also have very similar distributions albeit on very different chip platforms and with an absolute performance difference of more than three times.

At first glance, the results may seem counter-intuitive due to the extra encryptions required in ETM/CCM compared to OCB2/OCB3, however, they arise because the chip has significant crypto-coprocessor gain. The native measurements show that the core DES encryption time is comparable with a 16 byte block XOR, executed by the CPU. We suggested a new benchmark, the Technology Independent Gain Assessment (TIGA) for CPUs with crypto-coprocessors; as the percentage of the block encryption that can be completed by the crypto-coprocessor in the time it would take the CPU to compute a block XOR. We improved on our bench marking from the original study, by introducing a new method of measurement via an oscilloscope and a simple calculation to remove test command overheads. Using the new method we calculated that the MULTOS platform and SLE78 native AES had quite similar TIGA values of 8.72% and 9.84% respectively. The TIGA values for the S3CC98 and SLE78 TDES(M1)||(M2) were not too dissimilar at 15.34% and 19.80% respectively. These pairs of results account for the similarity in the related pairs of figures illustrating the data result distributions. The new TIGA measure could be valuable when comparing and predicting protocol implementation performance on various platform types, as may increasingly be the case in Internet of Things implementations.

The performance gain from the crypto-coprocessor can be eroded if more time is spent conditioning the data into and out of it. Such processing may be required for security protection, (to mask data and/or to reduce leakage), although it should be noted that any part of an algorithm running in the CPU may also require similar protection.

The processing time comparison was independent of the communications interface speed, however, both affect the overall protocol performance. The MULTOS platform is primarily processing limited, whereas the simple native implementation is mainly communications limited. If we degrade the S3CC98 native performance by an order of magnitude in anticipation of overheads to reduce side-channel leakage (e.g., repeated operations or hamming weight equalisation in software) then we approach the optimum around the 78,125bps rate; any lower than this and the protocol performance will degrade due to communication delays.

The crypto-coprocessor gain, coupled with small message sizes, means that there is not much to choose between OCB2, OCB3, ETM and CCM performance. It might be argued that ETM could be chosen for speed and efficiency of small-/medium messages or OCB if medium/large messages are the norm. It is also possible for GCM to be usable in future if supported by a specialist co-processor, however, it is unlikely to be much quicker than the other modes. As performance is unlikely to be a great differentiator for the AE modes, an option could be to standardise an AE framework around a default mode and define a negotiation process for a card and POS terminal to agree alternative AE modes. This would provide a useful mechanism if vulnerabilities were discovered in any particular AE mode, as well as a means for interworking and migration of smart cards and POS terminals having different capabilities.

A. Future Work

It would be interesting to implement the AE modes in a similar manner on other secured microcontrollers with crypto-coprocessors (although this may be difficult due to publication restrictions required by device vendors). In the first instance this should help prove the generality of the results, but also provide further evidence on the usefulness of the TIGA benchmark, which is easily determined on any processor. It is hoped that a secured smart card microcontroller chip could become available (for academic research) offering native mode programming and crypto-coprocessor support for GCM, so that a full-set of AE mode results could be generated and published. A Java Card platform has become available that would permit direct comparison with the MULTOS platform, as both are based on the SLE78 secured microcontroller.

ACKNOWLEDGMENT

The author would like to thank EMVCo for its support and guidance, and Sean Kelly (of Royal Holloway) for his valued practical assistance.

REFERENCES

[1] K. Mayes, "Performance of Authenticated Encryption for Payment Cards with Crypto Co-processors," in *Proc of ICONS17*, pp. 1-9, 2017.

[2] D. Boneh, R. Demillo, and R. Lipton, "On the importance of checking computations," in *Advances in Cryptography - Eurocrypt 97*, volume 1233, pp. 37-51, Springer Verlag, 2013.

[3] CC, "Common criteria for information technology security evaluation part1: Introduction and general model," version 3.1 release 4, September 2012.

[4] EMV, "Books 1-4," Version 4.3, 2011.

[5] EMVCo, http://www.emvco.com/ [retrieved: November, 2017].

[6] FIPS, "Federal information Processing Standards, Data Encryption Standard (DES), publication 46-3" http://csrc.nist.gov/publications/fips/fips46-3/fips46-3.pdf [retrieved: November, 2017].

[7] FIPS, "Federal Information Processing Standards, Announcing the Advanced Encryption Standard (AES), Publication 197." http://nvlpubs.nist.gov/nistpubs/FIPS/NIST.FIPS.197.pdf [retrieved: November, 2017].

[8] Infineon, "SLE78CAFX4000P(M) short product overview," v11.12, 2012.

[9] ISO/IEC, "7816 identification cards - integrated circuit(s) cards with contacts," parts 1-4, 1999.

[10] ISO/IEC, "14443 identification cards - contactless integrated circuit cards - proximity cards," parts 1-4, 2008.

[11] ISO/IEC, "19772 Information technology - Security techniques - Authenticated encryption," 2009.

[12] ISO/IEC, "9797 Information technology - Security techniques - Message Authentication Codes (MACs)," parts 1-3, 2011.

[13] P. Kocher, "Timing attacks on implementations of diffie-hellman RSA DSS and other systems," in *Advances in Cryptology - CRYPTO '96 Proceedings LNCS*, volume 1109, pp. 104-113 Springer Verlag, 1996.

[14] P. Kocher, J. Jaffe, and B. Jun, "Differential power analysis," in *Advances in Cryptology - Crypto 99 Proceedings LNCS*, volume 1666, pp. 388-397, Springer Verlag, 1999.

[15] T. Krovetz and P. Rogaway, "The software performance of authenticated encryption modes, fast software encryption, RFC 7253," in *FSE 2011 Proceedings*, pp. 306-327, Springer verlag, 2011.

[16] T. Krovetz and P. Rogaway, "The OCB authenticated-encryption algorithm, IETF RFC 7253," May 2014.

[17] D. McGrew and J. Viega, "The galois/counter mode of operation (GCM)," parts 1-3, May 2005, http://citeseerx.ist.psu.edu/viewdoc/download?doi=10.1.1.694.695&rep=rep1&type=pdf [retrieved: November, 2017].

[18] MULTOS, http://www.multos.com/ [retrieved: November, 2017].

[19] MULTOS, "The MULTOS developer's reference manual," MAO-DOC-TEC-006 v1.49, 2013.

[20] NIST, "Recommendation for block cipher modes of operation: The CCM mode for authentication and confidentiality, SP800-38C," May 2004.

[21] NIST, "Recommendation for block cipher modes of operation: Galois/-counter mode (GCM) and GMAC, SP800-38D," November 2007.

[22] P. Rogaway, "OCB mode," http://web.cs.ucdavis.edu/~rogaway/ocb/ [retrieved: November, 2017].

[23] J. Salowey, A. Choudhury, and D. McGrew, "AES galois counter mode (GCM) cipher suites for TLS, IETF RFC 5288," August 2008.

[24] Samsung, "S3CC9E4/8: 16-bit CMOS microcontroller for smart card user's manual," rev 0, 2004.

[25] D. Whiting, R. Housley, and N. Ferguson, "Counter with CBC-MAC (CCM), IETF RFC 3610," September 2003.

Privacy Token: An Improved and Verified Mechanism for User's Privacy Specification in Identity Management Systems for the Cloud

María Elena Villarreal, Sergio Roberto Villarreal, Carla Merkle Westphall, and Jorge Werner

Network and Management Laboratory
Post-Graduate Program in Computer Science
Federal University of Santa Catarina
Florianopolis, SC, Brazil
Email: maria.villarreal@posgrad.ufsc.br, sergio@lrg.ufsc.br,
carla.merkle.westphall@ufsc.br, jorge@lrg.ufsc.br

Abstract— **With the increasing amount of personal data stored and processed in the cloud, economic and social incentives to collect and aggregate such data have emerged. Therefore, secondary use of data, including sharing with third parties, has become a common practice among service providers and may lead to privacy breaches and cause damage to users since it involves using information in a non-consensual and possibly unwanted manner. Despite numerous works regarding privacy in cloud environments, users are still unable to control how their personal information can be used, by whom and for which purposes. This paper presents a mechanism for identity management systems that instructs users about the possible uses of their personal data by service providers, allows them to set their privacy preferences and sends these preferences to the service provider along with their identification data in a standardized, machine-readable structure, called privacy token. This approach is based on a three-dimensional classification of the possible secondary uses of data, four predefined privacy profiles and a customizable one, and a secure token for transmitting the privacy preferences. The applicability and the utility of the proposal were demonstrated through a case study, and the technical viability and the correct operation of the mechanism were verified through a prototype developed in Java in order to be incorporated, in future work, to an implementation of the OpenID Connect protocol. The main contributions of this work are the preference specification model and the privacy token, which invert the current scenario where users are forced to accept the policies defined by service providers by allowing the former to express their privacy preferences and requesting the latter to align their actions.**

Keywords–Privacy; Cloud Computing; Identity Management.

I. Introduction

This paper extends [1], which proposes a mechanism for users to control the secondary use of their Personally Identifiable Information (PII) based on a model to classify and represent privacy preferences and a secured token, called privacy token, by enhancing the model, and presenting a case study and an improved and more comprehensive prototype.

Cloud Computing offers infrastructure, development platform and applications as a service, on demand and charged according to usage. On the one hand, this paradigm gives users greater flexibility, performance and scalability without the need to maintain and manage their own IT infrastructure. On the other hand, it aggravates the problem of application and verification of security and causes users to lose, at least partially, control over their data and applications [2].

With the increasing amount of personal data stored and processed in the cloud, including users' Personally Identifiable Information (PII), economic and social incentives to collect and aggregate such data have emerged. Consequently, secondary use of data, including sharing with third parties, has become a common practice among Service Providers (SPs) [3]. However, since users only interact directly with SPs, which do not provide clear policies to warn them about how their PII can be used, they are usually unaware of secondary use of data and the existence of third parties [4].

According to the privacy taxonomy defined in [5], secondary use consists in the use of data for purposes other than those for which they were initially collected without the consent of the subject, e.g., the use of personal data collected on social networks for offering personalized advertising. This practice, thus, may violate the privacy of the user and cause damage since it involves using information in a non-consensual and possibly unwanted manner [5]. Nonetheless, whether certain action violates the privacy of a user depends on the perception of such user and his or her willingness to share given types of data. This, therefore, raises the need of collecting and respecting the privacy preferences of users.

An important aspect of the implementation of privacy in the cloud is Identity Management (IdM), which allows Identity Providers (IdPs) to centralize user's identification data and send it to SPs in order to enable the processes of authentication and access control [6]. IdM systems, such as OpenId Connect [7] and Shibboleth [8], allow the creation of federations, i.e., trust relationships that make possible for users authenticated in one IdP to access services provided by various SPs belonging to different administrative domains. An example is when users authenticate in different services with their Facebook accounts. In this case, Facebook acts as an IdP.

Even though there are several approaches that are intended to allow users to define their privacy preferences and organizations to express their practices, they are poorly adopted by both users and companies because they do not offer practical methods. In addition, most of them do not consider the decentralized nature of federated cloud environments. Consequently, IdM systems do not offer effective mechanisms to collect user's privacy preferences and to send them to the SP and, therefore, users are still unable to control how their PII can be used, by whom and for what purposes [2].

Werner and Westphall [9] proposed a privacy-aware identity management model for the cloud in which IdPs and SPs interact in dynamic federated environments to manage identities and ensure user's privacy. The model, while allowing users to choose and encrypt the data that can be sent to the SP, does not define a mechanism for determining users' privacy preferences and allowing them to control the use and sharing of their PII.

In order to complement the aforementioned model, this paper presents a mechanism for identity management systems that instructs users about the possible uses of their personal data by service providers and allows them to set their privacy preferences. These preferences are converted into a standardized, machine-readable structure, called privacy token, which is then sent to the SP along with other authentication data.

The remainder of this paper is organized as follows. Section II describes basic concepts relevant to the understanding of the proposal and Section III presents the main related work. In Section IV, the privacy mechanism is proposed. In Section V, a case study is presented, and, in Section VI, a prototype implementation of the mechanism is described. Finally, conclusion and future work are presented in Section VII.

II. Basic Concepts

This section presents the definitions of concepts considered important to the understanding of the proposal of this paper.

A. Identity Management (IdM)

IdM is implemented through IdM systems such as OpenId Connect [7], and is responsible for establishing the identity of a user or system (authentication), for managing access to services by that user (access control), and for maintaining user identity profiles [10].

Typical identity management systems involve three parts: users, identity providers, and service providers [10]. The user visits an SP, which, in turn, relies on the IdP to provide authentic information about the user. These systems enable the concept of federated identity, which is the focus of this work and allows users authenticated in various IdPs to access services offered by SPs located in different administrative domains due to a previously established trust relationship [11].

Some important IdM concepts are described next, as defined in [6][12][13]:

1) Personally Identifiable Information (PII): information that can be used to identify the person to whom it relates or can be directly or indirectly linked to that person. Thus, depending on the scope, information such as date of birth, GPS location, IP address and personal interests inferred by the tracking of the use of web sites may be considered as PII.

2) PII Principal: natural person to whom the PII relates.

3) Identity: computational representation of an entity active in a system, such as a person, a network device, or a programming agent.

4) Resource: entity, such as an application or a file, to which a user requires access.

5) Identity Provider (IdP): party that provides identities to subjects and is, usually, responsible for the process of authentication.

6) Service Provider (SP): party that provides services or resource access to users and, for that, requires the submission of valid credentials.

B. Privacy

Westin [14] defines privacy as the right of individuals, groups or institutions to determine for themselves when, how, and what information about them can be revealed to others.

According to the author, an essential aspect of human beings' freedom involves control over their personal information. Thus, his definition of privacy highlights the ability of people to decide on the amount, recipients, and conditions for disclosure of their personal data.

In this work, which focuses on IdM systems and federated cloud environments, privacy is considered to be the right of a user to decide if his or her PII can be used, by whom and for what purpose [5][13][15].

1) Privacy policy: set of statements that express the practices of the organizations regarding user data collection, use, and sharing.

2) Privacy preferences: preferences and permissions of a user for the secondary use of his or her PII, i.e., they determine by whom and for what purpose a PII can be used.

One way to achieve privacy in computer systems is through the implementation of Privacy Enhancing Technologies (PETs). According to ISO/IEC 2011 [13], PETs are privacy controls that consist of Information Technology measures, products or services that protect users' privacy by eliminating or reducing PII, or by preventing processing of unnecessary or unwanted PII.

III. Related Work

This section presents the work in which the proposal of this paper is based and other approaches that aim at providing privacy to users in computational environments.

A. Classification of Users by Privacy Preferences

Chanchary and Chiasson [16] performed an online survey to understand how users perceive online tracking for behavioral advertising. They demonstrated that users have clear preferences for which classes of information they would like to disclose online and that some would be more prone to share data if they were given prior control of tracking protection tools. The authors also identified three groups of users according to how their privacy attitudes influenced their sharing willingness. These groups are used as a basis for the privacy profiles of our mechanism and are presented next:

1) Privacy Fundamentalists (30.4%): consider privacy as a very important aspect and they feel very strongly about it.

2) Privacy Pragmatists (45.9%): consider privacy as a very important aspect but also like the benefits of abdicating some privacy when they believe their information will not be misused.

3) Privacy Unconcerned (23.6%): do not consider privacy an important aspect or do not worry about how people and organizations use their information.

B. Privacy Policy Languages

Platform for Privacy Preferences (P3P) [17] is a protocol designed to inform users about the practices of collecting and using data from websites. A P3P policy consists of a set of eXtensible Markup Language (XML) statements applied to specific resources such as pages, images, or cookies. When a website that has its policies defined in P3P wants to collect user's data, the preferences of that user are compared to the corresponding policy. If this is acceptable, the transaction continues automatically; if not, the user is notified and can opt-in (accept) or opt-out (reject). This work provides a basis for collecting user preferences, but it requires every user and SP to define their policies in this language and does not meet the needs of federated cloud environments.

Enterprise Privacy Authorization Language (EPAL) [18] is a formal language designed to address the industry's need to express organizations' internal privacy policies. An EPAL policy defines a list of hierarchies of data categories, user categories and purposes, as well as sets of actions, obligations, and conditions. These elements are used to formulate privacy authorization rules that allow or reject actions. Nevertheless, as it is specific for internal corporate policies, it does not consider user's preferences and is not suitable for privacy in federated identity environments.

Purpose-to-Use (P2U) [3] was proposed to provide means to define policies regarding the secondary use of the data. It is inspired by P3P, but allows the specification of privacy policies that define the purpose of use, type, retention period, and price of shared data. This language, although it enables user-editable and negotiable policies, is complex for users as it assumes that they have privacy policies and are able to define them in P2U. It also requires the SPs to have their policies defined in the same language.

C. UML Privacy Profiles

Basso et al. [19] define a Unified Modeling Language (UML) profile to assist in the development of applications and services that need to be consistent with the statements of their privacy policies. The authors identify privacy elements, such as policies and statements, through which organizations can define their policies for collecting, using, retaining, and releasing data; and organize their relationships into a conceptual model. This model is then mapped to a UML profile defined by stereotypes, attributes, and constraints that allow modeling statements of actual privacy policies. Although this profile helps application developers, it does not offer practical means for users to set their privacy preferences and transmit them to SPs.

D. Privacy Mechanisms of IdM Systems

Two of the most widely adopted identity management systems for federated environments are Shibboleth and OpenID Connect. Both IdM systems have embedded privacy mechanisms, which are described next.

Shibboleth, until its second version, had an extension for the IdP and called uApprove that added a stream to obtain user consent for the release of their data. As of the third version, with Shibboleth design changes, the consent mechanism came to be provided as standard [8].

This mechanism requires users to accept the release of attributes for service providers during authentications that include attribute data in the response [8]. Thus, users are requested to give consent for the release of attributes:

- In the first access to the resources of an SP;
- When releasing an attribute for which consent was not given before;
- When an attribute for which consent has already been given is no longer released; and
- When the value of an attribute for which consent has already been given changes.

It is possible to enable consent by attribute to allow the user to select the attributes that she or he wants to release and to define lists of attributes to which the user must always be asked to consent (whitelist), attributes for which the user should not be prompted to consent (blacklist), and attributes corresponding to a regular expression to which the user should be asked to consent (Regex).

Regarding the duration of consent for data release, users can choose between three options: to be asked for each login, to be asked if the attributes provided for a given service have changed since consent was given (standard option), and never to be asked (optional). With the last option, called global consent, all attributes are released to any service provider.

Shibboleth's mechanism, however, has some limitations. For many services, for example, the list of attributes to which the user must give consent can be very extensive, which increases complexity and often leads users to release all data and choose not to be requested in following accesses. In addition, the requested permission is only for the release of data that will be explicitly sent to the service provider by the IdP to enable the service and, therefore, this mechanism does not consider the secondary uses of such data and does not include information that may be inferred by the SP, as well as it does not make users aware about possible secondary uses of their data.

OpenID Connect (OIDC), in turn, has an integrated privacy mechanism that allows users to consent or deny the release of certain types of data to the service provider [20].

The OIDC Authorization Server, after user authentication, must obtain authorization before releasing information to the SP. The latter uses scopes to specify which access privileges are requested for a given resource, and the user uses them to determine which specific sets of attributes are available to the service provider. An application can request the specific permissions it needs through the scope parameter.

OpenID Connect defines the following scopes of data:

- *openid*: this scope is required and informs the Authorization Server that the SP is making an OpenID Connect request;
- *profile*: this scope requests access to the default attributes of the user's profile, such as name, surname, username, photo, gender, and date of birth;
- *email*: this scope requests access to the attributes related to the user's email;
- *address*: this scope requests access to the address attribute;
- *phone*: this scope requests access to attributes related to the user's phone; and

- *offline_access*: this scope requests access to the user's UserInfo even when the user is not logged in.

As the mechanism present in Shibboleth, OpenID Connect only requests the user's authorization for the IdP to provide the data requested by the SP to offer the service and, therefore, does not include information that may be induced by the service provider and does not consider the possible secondary uses of data.

E. User-Centric Privacy Architecture

Kolter [4] proposes a user-centric and SP-independent privacy architecture. This architecture comprises a collaborative privacy community and three user-side privacy management components, which are explained next.

The Privacy Community allows users to exchange information about privacy, ratings, and experiences about service providers, such as the amount of personal information needed to fill out a form, and third parties with whom the SP shares information. The Privacy Preference Generator provides a tool for users to set their privacy preferences. The Privacy Agent, on the other hand, shows relevant information from the Privacy Community, the evaluation of the privacy policy, and the reputation given by the community to the visited website, and compares the preferences generated by the Privacy Preference Generator with machine-readable privacy policies. The Data Disclosure Log component, in turn, records personal data transfers and provides an overview of past personal data streams [4].

This architecture, however, is complex and not completely independent of the SP since it demands that providers express their policies in P3P. The Privacy Agent requires the user to install an extension on their browser; the Privacy Community demands users to maintain and provide reliable information and explanations of providers' privacy policies; and the Privacy Preference Generation tool requires users to define specific preferences for the twelve types of services offered by SPs and extensively lists the data divided into nine types. If a service type is not configured, the tool understands that the user does not want to interact or make available any personal data with SPs that offer this type of service.

F. Model for IdM with Privacy in the Cloud

Werner and Westphall [9] present an IdM model with privacy for the cloud in which IdPs and SPs interact in dynamic and federated environments to manage the identities and ensure the privacy of users. They propose predefined, customizable privacy settings that help users to declare their desired level of privacy by allowing them to choose the access model, which can be anonymous, pseudonymous, or with partial attributes, and warning them about the reputation of the SP.

The interaction model defined in [9] and shown in Figure 1 proposes the registration in the IdP of the user's attributes and credentials, which may be encrypted (step 1), as well as the privacy policies to regulate the use and dissemination of their PII (step 2). Both the data and the policies are encapsulated in a package called sticky policies, which is sent to the SP along with a data dissemination model and obligations that must be fulfilled by the SP. The idea of the sticky policies is that PII is always disseminated with the policies governing their use and dissemination so that the user's privacy preferences are met

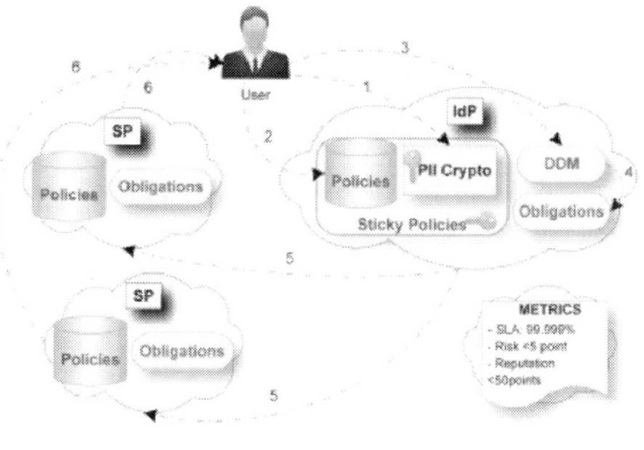

Figure 1. Interaction model between user, IdP and SP proposed in [9].

by any SP. If the policies of the SP and the sticky policies are compliant, a positive reputation assess is generated for the SP; otherwise, a low reputation score is returned. The authors, however, do not define a mechanism for collecting user's preferences, converting them into a machine-executable structure, and sending them to the SP.

IV. Proposal for a Privacy Preferences Specification Mechanism

This work aims at providing users with control over the secondary use of their PII and, consequently, protect them against the misuse of their data, through a model to classify and represent privacy preferences and a mechanism to implement such model [1].

The model consists of a comprehensive, three-dimensional classification of possible uses of PII that gives rise to a set of forty-five preferences, and four predefined privacy profiles based on these preferences.

The mechanism, in turn, enables users to select a predefined privacy profile or create a custom one. This profile is then transformed into a privacy token, a secure token similar to the ID and access tokens already used by the OpenID Connect protocol, and sent to the service provider.

A. Classification of Possible Uses of PII

Due to the large amount of possible actions and methods for collecting and sharing data, it is unfeasible to thoroughly list them. Therefore, this paper proposes a generic model that, on the one hand, is useful for users to set their privacy preferences and, on the other hand, works as a reference for SPs to assess whether the business rules of their data collection applications meet these preferences.

For this purpose, possible uses of the PII were classified in a three-dimensional structure. The dimensions, along with their respective abbreviations, are described next:

1) Data type: category of the PII to which the preference refers. The attributes of this dimension are:

- *Personal Identification (PI)*: encompasses any kind of information that represents the PII principal, such as name, national identifiers, email, cellphone number, and photo;

- *Personal Characteristics and Preferences (PCP)*: are considered to be the physical attributes of the PII principal and personal options like weight, religious or philosophical beliefs, and sexual orientation;
- *Location (LO)*: refers to any information about where the user is or has been and his or her trajectories with any precision degree and obtained by any means, such as GPS, Wi-fi networks or telecommunications systems;
- *Activities and Habits (AH)*: any activities performed by the user and habits inferred from tracking, such as web sites visited, purchases, and behavioral profile; and
- *Relationships (RS)*: people with whom the PII principal is in a specific moment or interacts through means like social networks, emails, and instant messengers.

2) Purpose: purpose for which the PII can be used. The values of this dimension are:

- *Service Improvement (SI)*: refers to the use of data for implementing improvements in the services offered, such as customization of functionalities, greater usability, and increased security;
- *Scientific (SC)*: concerns the granting of data for academic and scientific research; and
- *Commercial (CO)*: represents the use of user's PII to develop or offer new products and services with the purpose of obtaining commercial benefits.

3) Beneficiary: party that benefits with the use of the PII. The attributes are:

- *PII Principal (PP)*: corresponds to the user who accesses the service and to whom the PII is related;
- *Service Provider (SP)*: refers to the party responsible for offering the services accessed by users and for processing their data; and
- *Third Party (TP)*: represents a party interested in the data different and independent from the PII Principal and the service provider.

Table I. Configuration of the preferences of each predefined privacy profile regarding the secondary uses of PII.

PREFERENCES			PROFILES			
Data Type	Purpose	Beneficiary	F	A	P	U
Personal Identification (PI)	Service Improvement	PII Principal		✓	✓	✓
		SP			✓	✓
		Third Party				✓
	Scientific	PII Principal		✓	✓	✓
		SP		✓	✓	✓
		Third Party		✓	✓	✓
	Commercial	PII Principal		✓	✓	✓
		SP			✓	✓
		Third Party				✓
Personal Characteristics and Preferences (PCP)	Service Improvement	PII Principal		✓	✓	✓
		SP			✓	✓
		Third Party				✓
	Scientific	PII Principal		✓	✓	✓
		SP		✓	✓	✓
		Third Party		✓	✓	✓
	Commercial	PII Principal			✓	✓
		SP				✓
		Third Party				✓
Location (LO)	Service Improvement	PII Principal			✓	✓
		SP				✓
		Third Party				✓
	Scientific	PII Principal			✓	✓
		SP			✓	✓
		Third Party			✓	✓
	Commercial	PII Principal			✓	✓
		SP			✓	✓
		Third Party				✓
Activities and Habits (AH)	Service Improvement	PII Principal		✓	✓	✓
		SP		✓	✓	✓
		Third Party			✓	✓
	Scientific	PII Principal		✓	✓	✓
		SP		✓	✓	✓
		Third Party		✓	✓	✓
	Commercial	PII Principal		✓	✓	✓
		SP			✓	✓
		Third Party			✓	✓
Relationships (RS)	Service Improvement	PII Principal		✓	✓	✓
		SP		✓	✓	✓
		Third Party			✓	✓
	Scientific	PII Principal		✓	✓	✓
		SP		✓	✓	✓
		Third Party		✓	✓	✓
	Commercial	PII Principal			✓	✓
		SP			✓	✓
		Third Party				✓

The dimensions above define a structure in which each position represents a rule that expresses a user's privacy preference that must be respected by the SP. This way, each of these rules comprises three parts: the type of data the rule refers to, for what purpose it can be used, and for the benefit of whom it can be used. For example, a user can define that his or her location data can be used for the purpose of improving services for the benefit of the PII principal and, in another rule, define that the same type of information for the same purpose cannot be used for the benefit of a third party.

By using the presented classification, the user's privacy preferences can be collected in a detailed manner or through four predefined profiles, which are described in the next section.

B. *User's Privacy Profiles*

Through the classification presented in the previous subsection, the user's privacy preferences can be collected individually or through four predefined profiles. These profiles were defined based on the work in [16], presented in Section III, which classifies users into three groups according to their privacy concerns. Given that the *Privacy Pragmatist* group has the highest percentage of users and in order to offer more representative options, it has been subdivided into *Privacy Aware* and *Privacy Pragmatist*.

The four predefined profiles are described in the following paragraphs and the values of the privacy preferences for each of them are shown in Table I. In this table, the privacy profiles are represented by their initials and each row corresponds to a preference regarding the use of a type of data for a particular purpose and for the benefit of a specific part. Thus, preferences checked with a "✓" represent the user's consent to the use of the data.

1) Privacy Fundamentalist: This profile is aimed at users who have very high concerns with their privacy and do not wish their data to be used for any purpose other than the one for which they were collected. Some features, however, may not work properly or at all when this profile is chosen. In addition, any opportunities for service improvements and personalized offers of products and services will be missed.

2) Privacy Aware: This profile represents users who are concerned about their privacy but still want to enable most functionalities and service improvements, and receive some opportunities of personalized offers of products and services without sharing data with third parties.

3) Privacy Pragmatist: This profile is aimed at users who still want some privacy but also want to enable all the functionalities and service improvements. These users allow a restricted sharing of data with third parties in order to enable several personalized offers of products and services.

4) Privacy Unconcerned: This profile is for users who are not concerned about their privacy or how their PII is used, hence any data can be disclosed for any purpose and in the benefit of anyone according only to the privacy policy of each SP. All services and personalized offers of products and services are enabled with this profile.

Beside simplifying the process of setting the privacy preferences, these profiles are clarifying for the users as they inform about the possible uses of their PII and levels of risks to privacy, and, as a result, assist them in making a conscious decision. In addition, users have the possibility to customize their privacy preferences using any of the profiles above as a basis.

C. Privacy token

Once the profile is chosen or customized, the privacy preferences, along with additional information, are converted into a JSON (JavaScript Object Notation) object, which is then used as the payload for creating a JSON Web Token (JWT) signed or protected with Hash-based Message Authentication code (HMAC), and encrypted. The final object is called privacy token and is generated by the IdP and sent to the SP, which must validate it in order to verify its integrity and use its information to guide the behavior of their data usage applications.

The structure of the privacy token, illustrated in Figure 2, comprises three sections. The first one is the header, which declares that the data structure is a JWT and defines the security algorithm chosen and implemented by the IdP (in this example, SHA-256); the second section consists of the claims set, which is explained next; and the last section contains the signature of the token.

The claims set includes two parts. The first one defines the following claims inherited from the ID token: *sub*, which is the subject identifier, i.e., a sequence of characters that uniquely identifies the PII principal; *iss*, which identifies the authority issuing the token, i.e., the IdP; *aud*, which represents the intended audience, i.e., the SP; and *iat*, which declares the time at which the token was issued.

The second part of the claims set define the privacy preferences of the user. Each claim corresponds to a position of the structure presented in Section IV-A, i.e., a privacy preference, and has a boolean value. The structure of a claim is as follows: the first abbreviation represents the type of data, the second abbreviation refers to the purpose, and the last one represents the beneficiary. For example, if the value of the attribute *LO_CO_SP* is true, it means that location data can be used for commercial purpose in the benefit of the SP.

To ensure its integrity, the privacy token must be protected through an HMAC or a digital signature and then encrypted in

```
{
  "typ": "JWT",
  "alg": "HS256"
}
{
  "sub"            : "alice",
  "iss"            : "https://openid.c2id.com",
  "aud"            : "client-12345",
  "iat"            : 1486405983,

  "PI_SI_PP"       : true,
  "PI_SI_SP"       : false,
  "PI_SI_TP"       : true,
  "PI_SC_PP"       : true,
  "PI_SC_SP"       : true,
  "PI_SC_TP"       : false,
     ...
}
{
  D7SDQBpVCSRSqVUMP9PAungM0gh7JKjKgXYhU1KMr3Y
}
```

Figure 2. Structure of the privacy token.

order to protect its content and maintain its confidentiality as well as hinder its tampering. The encryption can be symmetric or asymmetric according to the choice and implementation of each identity provider. The use of digital signature or HMAC also depends on the choice of the IdP, which is responsible for sharing the secret key in the second case.

The token is secured through the Sign-then-Encrypt method to prevent attacks where the signature is removed by leaving only an encrypted message, provide privacy to the signer, and ensure that the signature is always accepted, since signatures on encrypted text are not valid in some jurisdictions.

Once signed and encrypted, the privacy token is sent to the SP via the user's browser. To perform this transmission efficiently and without compromising the system's performance, the token is encoded in a Base64 string, which can be embedded in a Uniform Resource Locator (URL). After receiving the token, the SP must send it back to the IdP and request its validation. The latter, after verifying the integrity of the privacy token, sends a validity confirmation to the service provider.

The privacy token must always be passed along with the ID token, for instance, when the ID token has expired and a new one is requested to the IdP, when passing identity to third parties or when exchanging the ID token for an access token. This is necessary to ensure that users' PII is always accompanied by the corresponding privacy preferences. This way, with the addition of the privacy token, the OpenId Connect modified flow presented in [9] would be extended, as shown in Figure 3, to encompass the following steps:

1) The user requests access to a resource in the SP;
2) The security manager at the SP asks for the user to authenticate in the IdP where she or he is registered;
3) The IdP asks for the user's credentials;
4) The user provides his or her credentials;
5) The IdP validates user's credentials and returns the ID token and the privacy token to the user, who passes it to the SP;

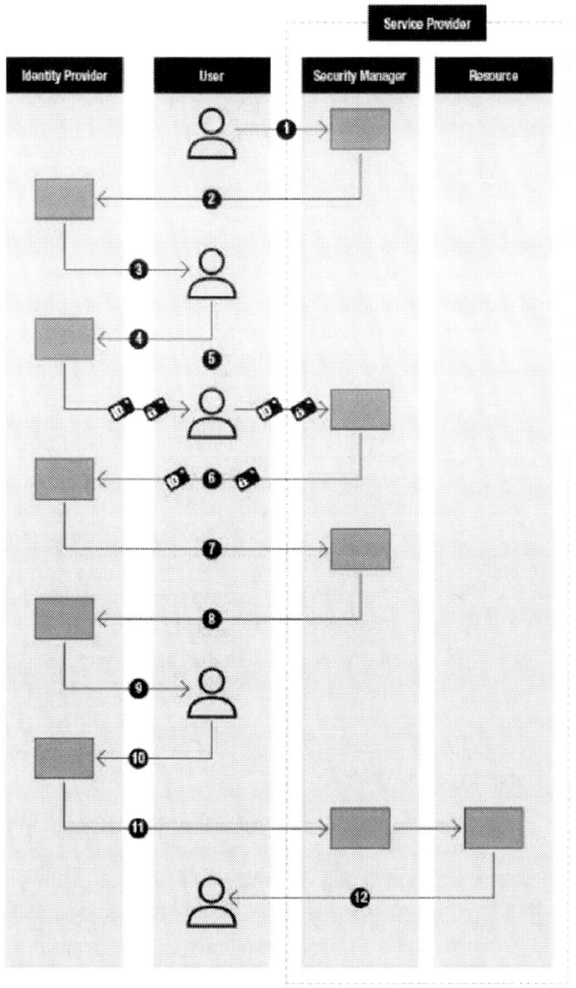

Figure 3. Extension of the IdM flow proposed in [9] with the addition of the privacy token.

6) The SP sends the ID and the privacy tokens to the IdP for the proof of validation;
7) The IdP verifies the tokens and confirms their validity to the SP;
8) The SP requests additional attributes to the IdP;
9) The IdP shows the data dissemination scopes supported by the SP for the user to choose;
10) The user chooses one of the scopes, and informs the IdP about the selected scope;
11) The IdP provides the data to the SP according to the selected scope;
12) The SP allows the user to access the desired resource.

The privacy profile that is used for generating the privacy token sent to the SP in Step 5 is chosen or customized by the user during the process of registration in the IdP. In order to offer more flexibility, users can change their choice at any moment requesting it to the IdP.

V. CASE STUDY

To demonstrate the applicability, utility and potential of the proposed model, it was applied in a hypothetical case of an online event registration service. This example shows how, despite the simplicity of the service and the small amount of data provided directly by the user, there is a great potential for secondary uses of this data, and also how the application of the model can limit the abuses by the service provider and the invasion of user's privacy.

The case analyzed consists of a service provider that offers an online event registration service. To do so, the organizers register their events and the SP provides the users with an online page with information about the event and means for registering and paying. In order to use this service, the user must be registered in an IdP belonging to the same federation as the service provider and must authenticate in the SP through this IdP. Besides, it may be necessary to provide additional data to the service provider, which keeps a record of subscriptions made by users to facilitate registration in future events.

In this case study, a street race is used as example and the SP requests the following data to the organizer of the event to register it:

- Name of the organizer;
- National identifier;
- Name of the person in charge;
- Official name of the event;
- Type of race;
- Categories;
- Location of the race;
- Date and time of the event; and
- Price of registration.

To allow the user to use the system, the service provider requires the following data, which can be obtained directly by the IdP or explicitly requested to the user:

- Full name;
- Date of birth;
- Gender;
- National identifier; and
- Email.

In order to register for the race, the user is requested to provide the following additional data to the SP:

- Cellphone number;
- Height;
- Weight;
- Distance to be run; and
- Payment data.

In addition to the data supplied by the user, the SP may collect context data at the time of the registration, such as:

- Location;
- Time of the registration;
- Device used;
- Type of connection; and

- Group of people who registered from the same device and at the same moment.

Based on the data provided and collected in the registration, on the user's registration history, and on other registrations made in the event, it is also possible to infer further information, such as:

- Time when the user usually registers for races;
- Devices and types of technology most used to make the registrations;
- Group of people who paid with the same credit card;
- Group of people who will participate together of the event (registrations made in the same context);
- Members of a family;
- Whether the user participates in races with family members;
- Frequency of user's participation in races;
- Categories preferred by the user;
- Level of physical conditioning of the user;
- User's habits of participating in outdoor activities;
- Place where the registered user will be on the date of the event;
- People who will be together at the venue on the day of the event;
- User's usual payment method;
- User's credit card brand;
- Whether the user has more than one credit card;

Finally, the collected data can be aggregated to data from other events for which the user has registered and from other sources to infer new information.

A. *Possible Secondary Uses of Data*

From both collected data and inferred information, a great number of possible secondary uses arise, some of which, defined based on actual privacy policies, are presented next classified according to the type of the data.

For the Personal Identification type of data, the following possible secondary uses have been defined:

- Add name and email to a list of notifications about the event in which the user has registered;
- Add name and email to mailing lists of the SP to promote new events;
- Add name and email to a list of valid emails to be sold to third parties; and
- Store national identifier, name, and cell phone of the participant in the database of the SP to facilitate registration in upcoming events.

The possible secondary uses defined for the Personal Characteristics and Preferences type of data are:

- Add national identifier and age to a list to be conceded to a university research project to compile statistics of participation in races by age;
- Add name and email of people who have more than one credit card to a list to be sold for advertising a real estate project;
- Add email and age to a list of people to be sold to a company that sells food supplements;
- Add email, height, and weight to a list of men and women who weigh more than certain amounts to be offered to plus-size stores; and
- Store national identifier, gender, and age of the participant in the database of the SP to facilitate registration in upcoming events.

For the Location type of data, the following possible secondary uses have been defined:

- If the registration is made from a mobile device, provide cell phone number and location to a company that specializes in offering advertising services based on location;
- Use the location of the user at the time of registration to offer tickets to other events near such location;
- When the distance between the location of the user at the time of registration and the location of the event is greater than a certain amount, offer transportation and lodging services;
- Use the location of the event to offer tickets to other events near such location; and
- Add name and email of the participant and date of the event to a list to be sold to restaurants near the location of the race.

The possible secondary uses defined for the Activities and Habits type of data are:

- Use data about the usual form of payment for automatically filling the registration form;
- Add email and preferred types of races to lists to be sold to companies that sell sporting goods; and
- If the user travels frequently to participate in events, add email and participation frequency in events to a list to be sold to home security companies.

For the Relationship type of data, the following possible secondary uses have been defined:

- Add email and family group to a list to be provided to a Ministry of Health research project about people participating in races with family; and
- Offer a collective vehicle rental to people who have registered in the same context.

B. *Application of the Model*

This subsection shows how the application of the model and the choice of the profile by users modify and restrict the behavior of the SP regarding the use of their data. Each case describes how the data usage application of the service provider acts according to the predefined privacy profile chosen by the user.

1) Case 0: No Application of the Model: If the model is not used, the SP may perform all the secondary uses aforementioned without the knowledge or the consent of the user. These uses are only conditioned by the privacy policies of the service provider, when they exist.

Table II. Possible secondary uses allowed and not allowed with the Privacy Aware profile.

PRIVACY AWARE PROFILE	
ALLOWED SECONDARY USES	**PREFERENCE**
Add name and email to a list of notifications about the event in which the user has registered.	PI_SI_PP
Store national identifier, name, and cell phone of the participant in the database of the SP to facilitate registration in upcoming events.	PI_SI_PP
Add national identifier and age to a list to be conceded to a university research project to compile statistics of participation in races by age.	PCP_SC_TP
Store national identifier, gender, and age of the participant in the database of the SP to facilitate registration in upcoming events.	PCP_SI_PP
Use data about the usual form of payment for automatically filling the registration form.	AH_SI_PP
Add email and family group to a list to be provided to a Ministry of Health research project about people participating in races with family.	RS_SC_TP
SECONDARY USES NOT ALLOWED	**PREFERENCE**
Add name and email to mailing lists of the SP to promote new events	PI_CO_SP
Add name and email to a list of valid emails to be sold to third parties.	PI_CO_TP
Add name and email of people who have more than one credit card to a list to be sold for advertising a real estate project.	PCP_CO_TP
Add email and age to a list of people to be sold to a company that sells food supplements.	PCP_CO_TP
Add email, height, and weight to a list of men and women who weigh more than certain amounts to be offered to plus-size stores.	PCP_CO_TP
If the registration is made from a mobile device, provide cell phone number and location to a company that specializes in offering advertising services based on location.	LO_CO_TP
Use the location of the user at the time of registration to offer tickets to other events near such location.	LO_CO_SP
When the distance between the location of the user at the time of registration and the location of the event is greater than a certain amount, offer transportation and lodging services.	LO_CO_SP
Use the location of the event to offer tickets to other events near such location.	LO_CO_SP
Add name and email of the participant and date of the event to a list to be sold to restaurants near the location of the race.	LO_CO_TP
Add email and preferred types of races to lists to be sold to companies that sell sporting goods.	AH_CO_TP
If the user travels frequently to participate in events, add email and participation frequency in events to a list to be sold to home security companies.	AH_CO_TP
Offer a collective vehicle rental to people who have registered in the same context.	RS_CO_SP

Table III. Possible secondary uses allowed and not allowed with the Privacy Pragmatist profile.

PRIVACY PRAGMATIST PROFILE	
ALLOWED SECONDARY USES	**PREFERENCE**
Add name and email to a list of notifications about the event in which the user has registered.	PI_SI_PP
Add name and email to mailing lists of the SP to promote new events	PI_CO_SP
Store national identifier, name, and cell phone of the participant in the database of the SP to facilitate registration in upcoming events.	PI_SI_PP
Add national identifier and age to a list to be conceded to a university research project to compile statistics of participation in races by age.	PCP_SC_TP
Store national identifier, gender, and age of the participant in the database of the SP to facilitate registration in upcoming events.	PCP_SI_PP
Use the location of the user at the time of registration to offer tickets to other events near such location.	LO_CO_SP
When the distance between the location of the user at the time of registration and the location of the event is greater than a certain amount, offer transportation and lodging services.	LO_CO_SP
Use the location of the event to offer tickets to other events near such location.	LO_CO_SP
Use data about the usual form of payment for automatically filling the registration form.	AH_SI_PP
Add email and preferred types of races to lists to be sold to companies that sell sporting goods.	AH_CO_TP
If the user travels frequently to participate in events, add email and participation frequency in events to a list to be sold to home security companies.	AH_CO_TP
Add email and family group to a list to be provided to a Ministry of Health research project about people participating in races with family.	RS_SC_TP
Offer a collective vehicle rental to people who have registered in the same context.	RS_CO_SP
SECONDARY USES NOT ALLOWED	**PREFERENCE**
Add name and email to a list of valid emails to be sold to third parties.	PI_CO_TP
Add name and email of people who have more than one credit card to a list to be sold for advertising a real estate project.	PCP_CO_TP
Add email and age to a list of people to be sold to a company that sells food supplements.	PCP_CO_TP
Add email, height, and weight to a list of men and women who weigh more than certain amounts to be offered to plus-size stores.	PCP_CO_TP
If the registration is made from a mobile device, provide cell phone number and location to a company that specializes in offering advertising services based on location.	LO_CO_TP
Add name and email of the participant and date of the event to a list to be sold to restaurants near the location of the race.	LO_CO_TP

2) Case 1: Privacy Unconcerned Profile: In this case, the profile chosen by the user is Privacy Unconcerned and therefore all permissions are enabled. Thus, the service provider can perform all the secondary uses listed previously. The difference with Case 0, however, is that users, when requested to select a profile, are made aware of possible secondary uses and, when choosing the profile, consent the use of their data, which guarantees that there will be no violation of their privacy.

3) Case 2: Privacy Fundamentalist Profile: In this case, the profile selected by the user is Privacy Fundamentalist and therefore none of the afore mentioned secondary uses is allowed. Still, the service delivery would be possible, since there is no objection to using the data for its primary purposes (registering in the race, in this example). However, if the economic benefit of the SP is based only on the secondary use of data, it may not be interesting to provide the service under these conditions. Thus, to enable the service, the SP could request specific permission to use the data or charge a fee from the user or the event organizer, for example.

4) Case 3: Privacy Aware Profile: In this case, the profile chosen by the user is Privacy Aware and the secondary uses allowed and not allowed are presented in Table II.

5) Case 4: Privacy Pragmatist Profile: With the Privacy Pragmatist profile, the secondary uses allowed and not allowed are presented in Table III.

The two last cases, which concern the application of the Privacy Aware and the Privacy Pragmatist profiles, give rise to different behaviors of the SP, since the Privacy Aware restricts the secondary use of data by third parties, even if some offers of services are missed; and the Privacy Pragmatist, on the other hand, allows for greater use of data by third parties in order to provide access to a greater amount of personalized opportunities and services.

VI. Prototype

In order to verify the technical feasibility and the correct operation of the proposed mechanism and serve as the base for a future extension of an implementation of the OpenId Connect protocol, a prototype was developed. It is a Web application implemented in Java that allows to visualize through graphical interfaces the process of generation and encryption of the privacy token, as well as the communication between the IdP and the SP.

The prototype executes the processes that must be performed by the IdP to register users, collect their privacy preferences and store them; and, when requested by the SP, generate, protect with HMAC, encrypt and validate the privacy token.

The application also represents an SP that offers an online event registration service and its data collection and use applications, in order to show the effects of different user privacy preferences on the behavior of the service provider regarding the secondary use of their PII. This functionality has been included to implement the case study presented previously.

A. Implementation of the Prototype

The application comprises classes representing the IdP, the SP, the user, the user's privacy preferences, and the privacy token. The *User* object is defined by the user's personal data collected through a registration form in the IdP and the attributes of the *PrivacyPreferences* object are set with the values corresponding to the privacy profile selected or customized by the user. The values of the *PrivacyToken* object are defined by IDs of the IdP, the SP, and the user, by the user's privacy preferences, and by a timestamp of the moment the token was generated.

The IdP class has methods to generate, protect with HMAC, encrypt, serialize, and send a *PrivacyToken* object, which are called when the user uses his or her IdP registration to authenticate in a service provider. The SP class, in turn, has methods to receive the privacy token, request its validation to the IdP, decrypt it, and use it to define which secondary uses of data are allowed.

When the user wants to use the service, the SP requests the login to the IdP, which authenticates the user and creates a *PrivacyToken* object. This object is encoded into a JSON object, according to the code snippet shown in Figure 4, with the help of the Google GSON library, which makes it possible to convert Java objects to their JSON representations, as well as convert a JSON string into an equivalent Java object [21].

To be transmitted safely and efficiently, the JSON representation of the privacy token is used as the payload to create a JSON Web Signature (JWS) with the Nimbus JOSE+JWT library, which allows the creation and verification of JWTs [22]. This JWS is protected with HMAC using the SHA-256 algorithm and a secret key. The code snippet that generates the HMAC is shown in Figure 5.

After generating the HMAC, the JWS is used as the payload to create a JSON Web Encryption (JWE), which is encrypted with the Advanced Encryption Standard (AES) in the Cipher Block Chaining (CBC) mode of operation, with Public-Key Cryptography Standards (PKCS) #7, and an Initialization Vector (IV) of 128 bits. The code responsible for this encryption process is presented in Figure 6.

Finally, the JWE is subjected to a compact serialization that transforms it into a Base64 string, so that it can be transmitted easily and efficiently to the SP through URLs, for example. The complete generation and preparation process for transmitting the privacy token can be seen in Figure 7, which shows the successive states of the token and its transitions, as well as the technologies used.

B. Graphical Interface and Usage of the Prototype

The initial screen of the prototypeis divided into two parts: one corresponding to IdP, with options that allow registering, listing and editing users; and the other corresponding to the SP, with options to log in and register in a race. The user login option starts the sequence of generation, transmission and validation of the privacy token, which is shown step-by-step by the prototype. The option of registering in a race, in turn, is enabled only when the user is already authenticated and generates a report on the data collection and secondary uses according to the profile stored in the user's privacy token.

The registration page in the IdP asks for basic data of the users and allow them to select a predefined privacy profile or create a custom one. In order to verify the utility of the model in making users aware of the secondary use of their data and to allow them to define their preferences in a simple way, the sections of profile selection and profile customization were developed with a focus on good design practices and usability, and based on the recommendations in ISO/IEC 29100 [13].

This way, each profile is represented by a number, a name, an icon and a brief but expressive description. Also, colors are used to help differentiate the profiles and represent the levels of risks to privacy in each of them, being red for the profile with the highest risks and green for the one with the lowest risks. To provide users with more information about the possible uses of their PII and the chosen profile, the *View details* button shows the complete profile, i.e., all the privacy preferences with the corresponding settings. Figure 8 shows the section of the registration screen for selecting a privacy profile.

The Custom profile option leads to the page shown in Figure 9, which displays a checkbox for each privacy preference and allows users to check the uses of their data that they want to authorize. To guide and simplify the choice, users can also select one of the four predefined profiles as a basis for personalization. This same screen is shown in the option *View details* of the predefined profiles, but with the preferences already checked and disabled for editing.

On the SP's side, the Login option initiates the user authentication process and shows, through the graphical interface, all the steps that are triggered and the results that are generated, such as the structure of the JSON object, and of the token protected with HMAC.

The second option on the service provider's side opens a page for the authenticated user to register in a race, in which some additional data is requested and context information is also collected. Once the registration has been completed, the data obtained from the IdP, the data requested to the user, and the data collected from context are shown. Following is an analysis of possible secondary uses and the result is presented as a report that lists the secondary uses of data allowed and not allowed for the profile of the logged in user.

```java
// Create GSON builder
Gson gson = new GsonBuilder().setPrettyPrinting().create();

// Create a PrivacyToken object
PrivacyToken privToken = new PrivacyToken(sp.getId(),
                                          idp.getId(),
                                          user.getId(),
                                          user.getPrivPreferences(),
                                          iat);

// Transform the PrivacyToken object into a JSON object
String tokenJsonString = gson.toJson(privToken);
```

Figure 4. Code snippet from the IdP class responsible for transforming the *PrivacyToken* object into a JSON object.

```java
// Create payload with privacy token JSON string
Payload payload = new Payload(tokenJsonStr);

// Create HMAC signer
JWSSigner signer = new MACSigner(key.getEncoded());

// Create an HMAC-protected JWS object with a JSON object as payload
JWSObject jwsObject = new JWSObject(new JWSHeader(JWSAlgorithm.HS256),
                                    payload);

// Apply the HMAC
jwsObject.sign(signer);
```

Figure 5. Code snippet from the IdP class responsible for protecting the provacy token with HMAC.

```java
// Create a JWE object with signed JWT as payload
JWEObject jweObject = new JWEObject(
    new JWEHeader.Builder(JWEAlgorithm.DIR,
            EncryptionMethod.A128CBC_HS256)
        .contentType("JWT")
        .build(),
    new Payload(jwsObject));

// Perform encryption
jweObject.encrypt(new DirectEncrypter(key.getEncoded()));
```

Figure 6. Code snippet from the IdP class responsible for encrypting the privacy token.

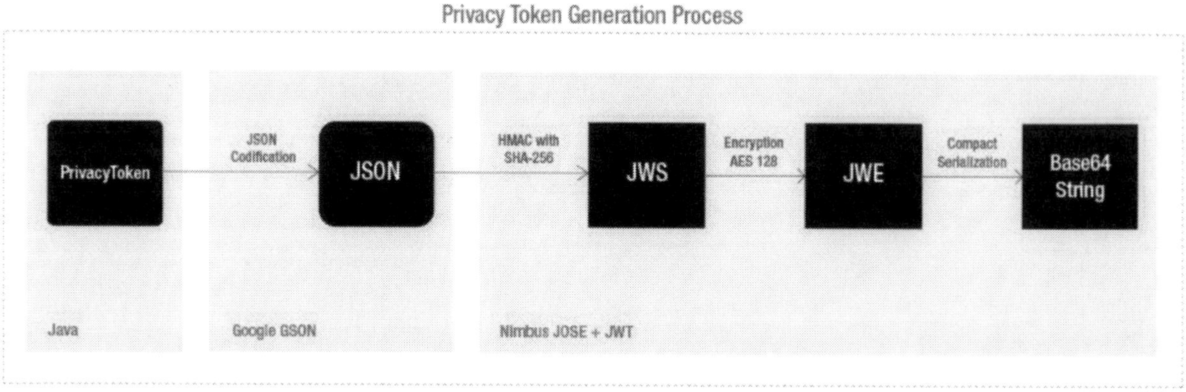

Figure 7. Generation process of the privacy token.

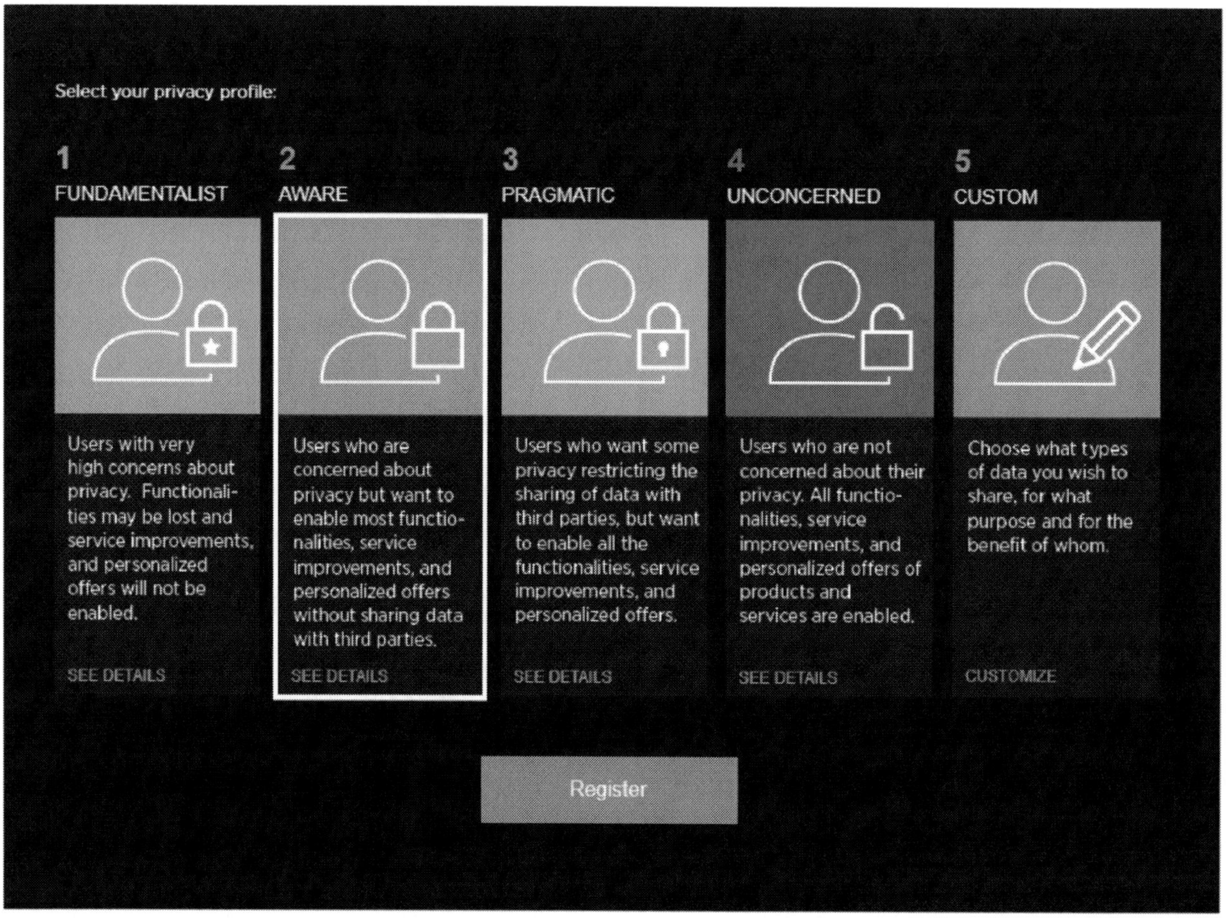

Figure 8. Prototype screen with the four predefined privacy profiles and the customizable one.

Figure 9. Part of the prototype screen that allows users to customize their privacy preferences.

VII. Conclusion and Future Work

In this paper, a practical mechanism that allows users to control how their PII can be used in a federated cloud environment was presented. The mechanism instructs them about the possible uses of PII by SPs, allows them to choose between four predefined privacy profiles or customize one, and sends their privacy preferences to the service provider.

This mechanism is based on a model that generically and comprehensively classifies the possible secondary uses of PII in three dimensions, which gives rise to a set of forty-five preferences that allow to control such uses. These preferences, which can be defined individually or through four predefined profiles, are encoded in a standardized, machine-readable format structure called privacy token, and sent to the SP along with the user's authentication data.

To the best of the authors knowledge, existing work focuses either on low-level approaches, such as privacy policy languages, which can be executed by machines; or on conceptual, high-level specifications, such as UML profiles, which provide a better understanding about privacy requirements in the development of systems and applications; or on complete architectures and models that aim to use the previous approaches to provide users with privacy. In addition, Shibboleth and OpenID Connect have privacy mechanisms that restrict the data that the user allows the IdP to send to the SP.

The aforementioned proposals, however, do not offer practical methods for users to define their preferences and send them to the SP and, in most cases, require the service provider to adopt specific technologies to represent their privacy policies. In addition, most are not suitable for federated cloud environments and do not provide resources for users to control the secondary use of their data, forcing them to accept the privacy policies established by the SPs.

The mechanism proposed in this paper, in turn, is user-centered, as it instructs users about the secondary uses of their data and helps them to control such uses. In addition, it can be easily adopted by users, IdPs, and SPs, as it does not require specific tools and knowledge from the users and is deployed with the technologies that the IdPs and SPs already use. Thus, an important feature is that it does not require service providers to use any specific standards to express and implement their privacy policies. It is only expected for SPs to adapt their data collection systems to interpret and fulfill the preferences expressed in the privacy token, which they can already read and understand once it has the same format as the other tokens used by OpenID Connect.

The applicability and the utility of the proposal were demonstrated by applying the model in a case study, and the technical viability and the correct operation of the mechanism were verified through a prototype that deploys the technologies for generation and transmission of the privacy token and implements the case study. The prototype also serves as the base for a future extension of an OpenID Connect implementation.

The proposed mechanism has the sole purpose of enabling users to control the secondary use of their PII allowing them to define their privacy preferences and sending them to the SP. Thus, it does not determine how the service provider will meet these preferences and enforce its privacy policies. For this, there are several approaches that can be used and there is no need for the SP to change those already adopted.

In addition, the mechanism does not define what data the identity provider can send to the service provider and how. Other mechanisms should be responsible for defining this, as the one proposed in [9] and the one already existing in OpenID Connect [20].

Although the use of the privacy token may create a need for negotiation between the user and the service provider, the proposed mechanism does not include methods for such a negotiation, since the latter is specific for a particular service and must be performed between the SP and the user without the need to modify the privacy token or involve the IdP.

The main contributions of this work are the preference specification model and the privacy token, which invert the current scenario where users are forced to accept the policies defined by SPs by allowing them to express their privacy preferences. These preferences are stuck together to their data and are used by the SP to align its actions or request specific permissions.

The proposal of this paper has been defined in order to extend the model presented in [9] and therefore can be incorporated into it as its mechanism for defining privacy preferences regarding the use and sharing of user's personal data. However, because of its simplicity and comprehensiveness and for using open technologies and standards, the model and the privacy token are not restricted to federated identity management systems and can be applied into any environment where it is needed to set user's privacy preferences.

As future work, we intend to extend an OpenID Connect implementation to support the proposed mechanism, as well as to analyze the impact of the token size on URL transmission and, if necessary, implement compression mechanisms. It is also proposed to perform usability tests to verify the effects of the model on users and to evaluate possible improvements in the classification of secondary uses of PII. Furthermore, it is proposed to assess the consequences for services, SPs and users of applying this mechanism in real federated cloud scenarios.

References

[1] M. E. Villarreal, S. R. Villarreal, C. M. Westphall, and J. Werner, "Privacy Token: A Mechanism for User's Privacy Specification in Identity Management Systems for the Cloud," in Proceedings of The Sixteenth International Conference on Networks - ICN 2017, Venice. IARIA XPS Press, Apr. 2017, pp. 53–58, ISBN: 978-1-612085-463.

[2] J. Zhao, R. Binns, M. Van Kleek, and N. Shadbolt, "Privacy Languages: Are We There Yet to Enable User Controls?" in Proceedings of the 25th International Conference Companion on World Wide Web, Montreal, Quebec, Canada. International World Wide Web Conferences Steering Committee, Apr. 2016, pp. 799–806, ISBN: 978-1-4503-4144-8.

[3] J. Iyilade and J. Vassileva, "P2U: A Privacy Policy Specification Language for Secondary Data Sharing and Usage," in Proceedings of the 2014 IEEE Security and Privacy Workshops, San Jose, CA, USA. IEEE Computer Society, May 2014, pp. 18–22, ISBN: 978-1-4799-5103-1.

[4] J. P. Kolter, User-Centric Privacy: A Usable and Provider-Independent Privacy Infrastructure. BoD Books on Demand, 2010.

[5] D. J. Solove, "A Taxonomy of Privacy," University of Pennsylvania Law Review, vol. 154, 2006, pp. 477–564.

[6] M. Benantar, Access Control Systems: Security, Identity Management and Trust Models. Springer, New York, 2006, ISBN: 978-0-387-27716-5.

[7] "OpenId Connect," 2015, URL: http://www.openid.net/connect/ [accessed: 2017-06-11].

[8] Shibboleth, "ConsentConfiguration," 2017, URL: https://wiki.shibboleth.net/confluence/display/IDP30/ConsentConfiguration [accessed: 2017-06-11].

[9] J. Werner and C. M. Westphall, "A Model for Identity Management with Privacy in the Cloud," in Proceedings of the 2016 IEEE Symposium on Computers and Communication (ISCC), Messina, Italy. IEEE, Jun. 2016, pp. 463–468, ISBN: 978-1-5090-0679-3.

[10] G. Alpár, J. Hoepman, and J. Siljee, "The Identity Crisis. Security, Privacy and Usability Issues in Identity Management," Computing Research Repository, vol. abs/1101.0427, 2011.

[11] D. Temoshok and C. Abruzzi, "Draft NISTIR 8149: Developing Trust Frameworks to Support Identity Federations," 2016, NIST, Gaithersburg, MD, United States.

[12] E. Bertino and K. Takahashi, Identity Management: Concepts, Technologies, and Systems. Artech House, Norwood, 2011, ISBN: 978-1-60807-039-89.

[13] "ISO/IEC 29100. International Standard - Information Technology - Security Techniques - Privacy Framework," 2011, URL: http://www.iso.org/iso/iso_catalogue/catalogue_tc/catalogue_detail.htm?csnumber=45123 [accessed: 2017-06-11].

[14] A. Westin, Privacy and Freedom. The Bodley Head, 1967.

[15] "OASIS Privacy Management Reference Model and Methodology (PMRM) Version 1.0," 2016, URL: http://http://docs.oasis-open.org/pmrm/PMRM/v1.0/PMRM-v1.0.html [accessed: 2017-06-11].

[16] F. Chanchary and S. Chiasson, "User Perceptions of Sharing, Advertising, and Tracking," in 11th Symposium On Usable Privacy and Security (SOUPS), Ottawa. USENIX Association, Jul. 2015, pp. 53–67, ISBN: 978-1-931971-249.

[17] "The Platform for Privacy Preferences 1.1 (P3P1.1) Specification," 2006, URL: https://www.w3.org/TR/P3P11/ [accessed: 2017-06-11].

[18] "Enterprise Privacy Authorization Language (EPAL 1.2)," 2003, URL: https://www.w3.org/Submission/2003/SUBM-EPAL-20031110/ [accessed: 2017-06-11].

[19] T. Basso, L. Montecchi, R. Moraes, M. Jino, and A. Bondavalli, "Towards a UML Profile for Privacy-Aware Applications," in Proceedings of 2015 IEEE International Conference on Computer and Information Technology; Ubiquitous Computing and Communications; Dependable, Autonomic and Secure Computing; Pervasive Intelligence and Computing (CIT/IUCC/DASC/PICOM), Liverpool, United Kingdom. IEEE, Oct. 2015, pp. 371–378, ISBN: 978-1-509001-552.

[20] OpenId, "OpenID Connect Core 1.0 incorporating errata set 1," 2014, URL: http://openid.net/specs/openid-connect-core-1_0.html [accessed: 2017-06-11].

[21] Google, "Google GSON," 2017, URL: http://github.com/google/gson [accessed: 2017-06-11].

[22] "Nimbus JOSE + JWT," 2017, URL: http://www.connect2id.com/products/nimbus-jose-jwt/ [accessed: 2017-06-11].

Role-based Access Control in the Digital Grid – A Review of Requirements and Discussion of Solution Approaches

Steffen Fries, Rainer Falk
Corporate Technology
Siemens AG
Munich, Germany
e-mail: {steffen.fries|rainer.falk}@siemens.com

Chaitanya Bisale
Energy Management
Siemens AG
Nuremberg, Germany
e-mail: {chaitanya.b}@siemens.com

***Abstract*—Critical infrastructures are increasingly under investigation regarding the reliable operation and resilience to ensure their provisioning of essential services to the citizens. One example for such critical infrastructures is the digital energy grid. It targets the control of increasingly fluctuating demand and generation of energy. Besides generation also the path to the final consumer has to be taken into account, resulting in the need for securing the reliable transmission and distribution of centrally and decentrally generated energy. Control is accomplished by utilizing a communication infrastructure in parallel to the actual power system infrastructure. The connection between both worlds is provided by sensors and actuators. In the past, this control communication network was mostly isolated from other communication networks, but today it is getting connected increasingly with external systems to support innovative cross-system services. This surge in connectivity also exposes the digital grid to cyber attacks. Therefore, access to resources like accumulated measurement information or control data needs to be protected to ensure a reliable operation. Legislation and operational best practice guideline activities have taken this into account and meanwhile provide the necessary framework for defining specific communication security requirements. From the technical perspective, different security counter measures exist to cope with the given requirements. However, it has to be ensured that these technical means are not only provided technically, but are in fact applied correctly in operation. This paper reviews the requirements for role-based access control (RBAC), as well as currently targeted technical approaches to achieve RBAC in the digital grid. The goal is to provide more insight into the existing application of RBAC mechanisms and to identify gaps for future enhancements. Proposals to address the identified gaps are described, which are intended to be brought to the International Electrotechnical Commission (IEC) to enhance the security standard IEC 62351 for power system automation.**

Keywords–security; user and device authentication; role-based access control; substation automation; digital grid; cyber security; critical infrastructure; IEC 62351

I. Introduction

Critical Infrastructures (CI) are technical installations that are essential for the daily life of the society and the economy of a country. Typical critical infrastructures in this context are the power grid, telecommunication, healthcare, transportation, water supply, just to state a few. Power system and communication networks even span across country borders, thereby are of multinational priority.

Digital grids, which are constantly a target of security investigations and enhancement as outlined in [1][2], are one example of CI. Especially their cyber security has gained more momentum over the last years. The increased threat level becomes visible, e.g., through reported attacks on critical infrastructure, but also through reactions in legislation, which explicitly require specific protection of critical infrastructures and reporting about serious attacks. There is a clear trend towards increased connectivity and tighter integration of systems from Information Technology (IT) in common enterprise environments with the Operation Technology (OT) part of the automation systems in the energy and industrial domains to provide enhanced services. This requires security measures to avoid negative effects of the formerly isolated OT. IT security in this context evolves to cyber security to underline the mutual relationship between the security and physical effects. Additionally, IT and OT environments have different characteristics in management and operation, which led to distinct domain specific security requirements in the past. This has to be taken into account when designing interconnected cyber-physical energy systems.

Cyber security measures typically are technical and organizational in nature. Operators of CI need to maintain their systems by complying with an Information Security Management Framework while also coping with regulatory requirements. This requires technical support in the deployment environment. Such technical requirements relate to authentication and access control, or to secure and reliable communication for example. Within this paper, the focus is placed on access control, or more specifically on Role-based Access Control (RBAC).

RBAC is already a proven concept in IT systems. It is realized by many (operating) systems to control access to system resources. RBAC for the power automation environment is already considered in several requirements standards, guidelines, and also in regulatory requirements. Beside the requirements supporting this functionality, technical standards ensuring interoperability between different vendor's products and solutions have been developed.

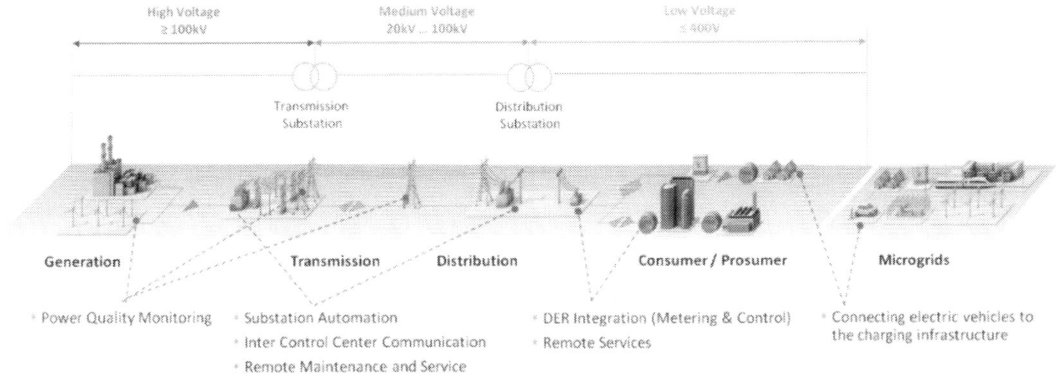

Figure 1. Overview Digital Energy Grid as Example for Critical Infrastructures

This contribution investigates into RBAC in general and specifically on the application in digital grid as depicted in Figure 1 below. Section II provides an overview of requirements from guidelines, standards, and regulations targeting access control specifically. Section III provides an overview of several state-of-the-art approaches for RBAC, while Section IV discusses the basic RBAC concept currently deployed in the digital grid. The identified shortcomings are addressed in Section V with first solution proposals that are intended to be brought to standardization. Section VI describes a realization example for the proposed migration approach. Section VII investigates further identified challenges when integrating RBAC, while section VIII concludes the document.

Note that this paper addresses first ideas to tackle identified gaps in RBAC in the Digital Grid domain. Further investigation is necessary.

II. EXAMPLES OF DOMAIN-SPECIFIC GUIDELINES/STANDARDS/REGULATIONS

IT security in communication infrastructures is not a new topic. It has been addressed specifically in office IT environments for years. Although there are some commonalities through the convergence of networks of IT and OT, specifically regarding the utilized communication protocols and networks, there are some large differences in the management and operation of these infrastructures as seen in Figure 2 below.

	Digital Grid	Office IT
Protection target for security	Generation, transmission, distribution	IT- Infrastructure
Component Lifetime	Up to 20 years	3-5 years
Availability requirement	Very high	Medium, delays accepted
Real time requirement	Can be critical	Delays accepted
Physical Security	Very much varying	High (for IT Service Centers)
Application of patches	Slow / restricted by regulation or certification	Regular / scheduled
Anti-virus	Hard to deploy, white listing	Common / widely used
Security testing / audit	Increasing	Scheduled and mandated

Figure 2: Comparison IT/OT management and operation

These differences in management and operation of the IT systems consequently lead to different security requirements as outlined in Figure 3.

	Digital Grid	Office IT
Security Awareness	Increasing	High
Security Standards	Under development, regulation	Existing
Confidentiality (Data)	Low – medium	High
Integrity (Data)	High	Medium
Availability / Reliability (System)	24 x 365 x ...	Medium, delays accepted
Non-Repudiation	Medium to High	Medium

Figure 3: Comparison IT/OT high level security requirements

As outlined in [2] for secure communication, a variety of security requirements exist for digital grids. An overview of the most relevant standards, guidelines, and regulations is shown in Figure 4 below.

As visible guidelines are available from the National Institute for Standards and Technology (NIST) of the U.S. through the "Guidelines for Smart Grid Cyber Security" in NIST IR 7628 [3] or the Report of the Smart Grid Coordination Group addressing the European Mandate M/490 [4] and the report of the successor activity, the Smart Energy Grid Coordination Group (SEG-CG) [5], which explicitly recommend the support of RBAC in the context of system configuration, operation, and maintenance. In particular, the last referenced document from the SEG-CG explicitly addresses the authentication and authorization of users and processes in the context of substation automation.

Specifically for Germany and Austria, the BDEW White Paper [6] guideline has been published, addressing RBAC in the context of user management as applied to operations of energy and water utilities. This white paper was one main source for developing ISO 27019:2013 [7] as a domain-specific profile of the Information Security Management System defined in ISO 27002 [8]. Both ISO documents address requirements for an operator regarding the handling of information security and require support for RBAC. Similar requirements can also be found in IEC 62443-2-1 for industrial environments. IEC 62443-3-3 [9] goes one step beyond by specifically defining, which foundational security requirements can be technically addressed with RBAC, without prescribing a specific technical solution. IEEE 1686 [10] is even more specific here, as it defines a minimum number of roles and also the associated rights. The last standard to be mentioned is IEC 62351-8 [11], providing specific technical means for binding RBAC information to entities in access tokens and to utilize them in communication. The latter can already be used to address some of the requirements stated before.

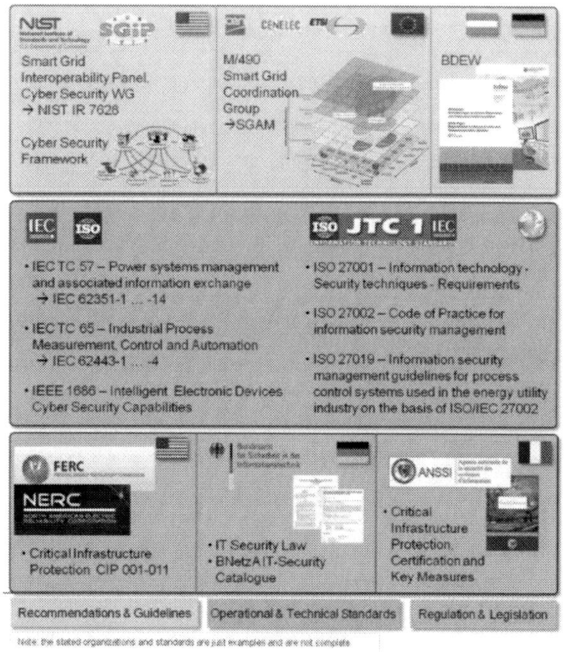

Figure 4. Examples for sources for security requirements for digital grid

From a regulatory perspective, examples are provided through the American NERC-CIP [12], the German IT-Security Act [13], and the IT security catalogue of the German network regulator group BNetzA, and the French ANSSI [14]. They all require security measures to support reliable grid operation, which are mapped in the first place to processes and organizational means, but finally, these need to be supported by appropriate technical means to operate the infrastructure appropriately. The following section elaborates technical means to address these requirements focusing on authentication and authorization to achieve access control.

III. Role Based Access Control – RBAC

This section provides an overview about the RBAC concept in general followed by an investigation into different technical approaches realizing this general concept in different ways.

Security administration is simplified through the use of roles and constraints to organize subject access levels. RBAC in general can reduce costs within an organization, as it accepts that changes in roles and responsibilities of (especially) employees occur more frequently than the changes in the rights within roles. The basic idea of RBAC is to define roles according to responsibilities within the business organization. Permissions required to perform the duties of a role are assigned to the respective role. A subject, i.e., typically human user (but may also be an application or software process or an intelligent electronic device - IED), is assigned roles according to his business responsibilities. This helps to achieve separation of duty by ensuring that a user is assigned only the roles according to his responsibilities, and possesses only the permissions required to fulfill his duties. Restrictions can be placed to prevent a single subject from being assigned to roles having a conflict of interest. RBAC also includes the concept of temporary roles to realize dynamic separation of duty: Over time, a subject may act in different roles. At any point in time, the subject only possesses the permissions of the currently active role or roles.

The general concept of RBAC is shown in Figure 5, which is the enhanced approach explained in [11]. As shown, the role separates the subject from the permissions. The permissions define certain rights on objects, like read or write operations on specific objects (e.g., files). The role itself bundles a set of permissions, which can be assigned to users. This subject assignment enables separation of duty, which is necessary to also support auditing of actions. Additionally, constraints may further be used to either restrict roles or to enable special handling in situations like emergency cases. Examples of constraints required in digital grids specifically are:

- *Area of Responsibility or scope* allows restricting the effectiveness of an issued RBAC token, e.g., to an organizational unit or a geographical location or area, or a specific communication network area (subnet).
- *Operational constraints* allow a local augmentation of the associated rights if the (hosting) object detects or is informed about specific circumstances. As an example, an Engineer may not be allowed to perform certain actions, e.g., on a protection relay, in an emergency case. Note that these constraints are typically defined and handled in a device-centric manner and may not be included in the subject specific role assignment.

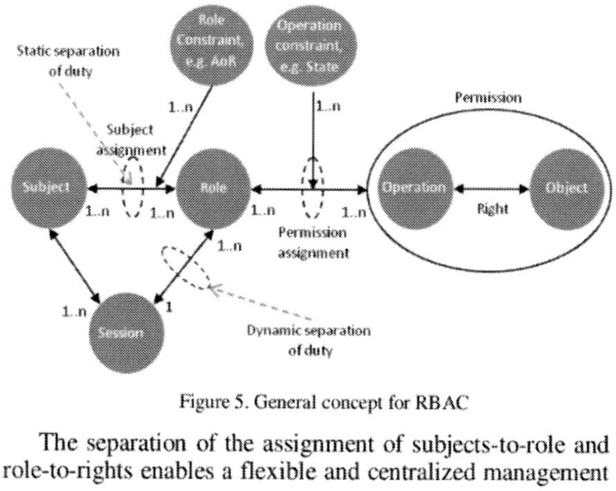

Figure 5. General concept for RBAC

The separation of the assignment of subjects-to-role and role-to-rights enables a flexible and centralized management of subject-to-role assignment that tends to be dynamic. At the same time, it can be combined with a well-defined role-to-permission-assignment that has more static character.

Figure 6 illustrates the concept of RBAC on a user base. In the upper part, the subject-role-right association is shown. Here "Tom" is assigned the role "Engineer". Acting in this role "Tom" is entitled to "view" and "control" objects. Objects may include status values or switching objects. It also shows the dynamic and static assignments between subjects, roles and rights. The example illustrates that granting the right "view" to "Mary" can be added by assigning the role "Engineer" to "Mary" without changing the associated rights on objects.

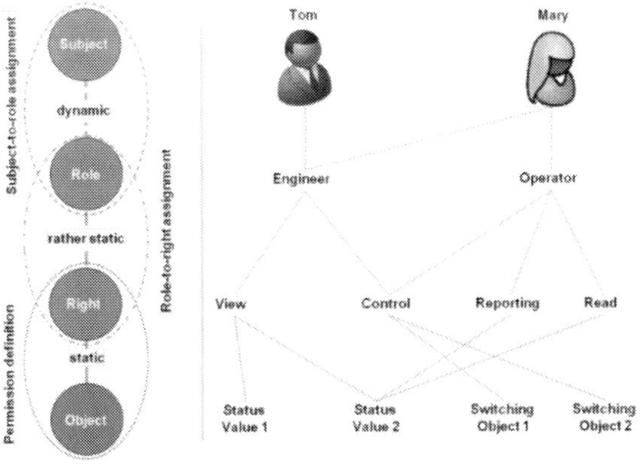

Figure 6. Basic RBAC concept applied in Digital Grids

To allow a subject to act in a distinct role, authentication is often a precondition, ensuring that the subject is who it claims to be and that it is entitled to act in this role. For this there already exist various solutions, often relying on a three-party-model, in which an identity and access server issues some form of security tokens or tickets to provide authorization information. Examples are Kerberos [15], the security assertion markup language (SAML) [16], OAuth 2.0 [17], and OpenID Connect [20]. Also domain specific approaches like X.509 certificate enhancements in IEC 62351-8 [11] for power automation have been standardized, which will be briefly introduced in the following. While they all rely on a security token mechanism, they differ, e.g., in the communication relations for the token exchange (protocols), the token format, the underlying cryptographic algorithms and the target application use cases.

A. *Kerberos*

Kerberos v5, specified in RFC 4120 [15], is a three-party system and protocol to be used for network authentication. In this system there exists a trusted third party, to which all participants authenticate as shown in Figure 7. Kerberos is widely used in different operating systems to allow access to network domain services or to realize single-sign-on.

As shown, the trusted third party grants tickets upon request to allow access to specific services or resources. Kerberos relies on symmetric cryptography for the authentication and also the ticket protection and binding and uses ASN.1 for the encoding. The Key Distribution Server is responsible for the user authentication and the granting of service specific tickets. These tickets provide an authorization of the user to utilize the services. The tickets also allow for the distribution of a session key to the user and the service to secure the service access. This is enabled by another symmetric key, which is a long term key shared between the KDC and the service component. User authentication is also done using symmetric shared secrets, like a username and password. Besides this there also exist enhancements to allow for a certificate based user authentication.

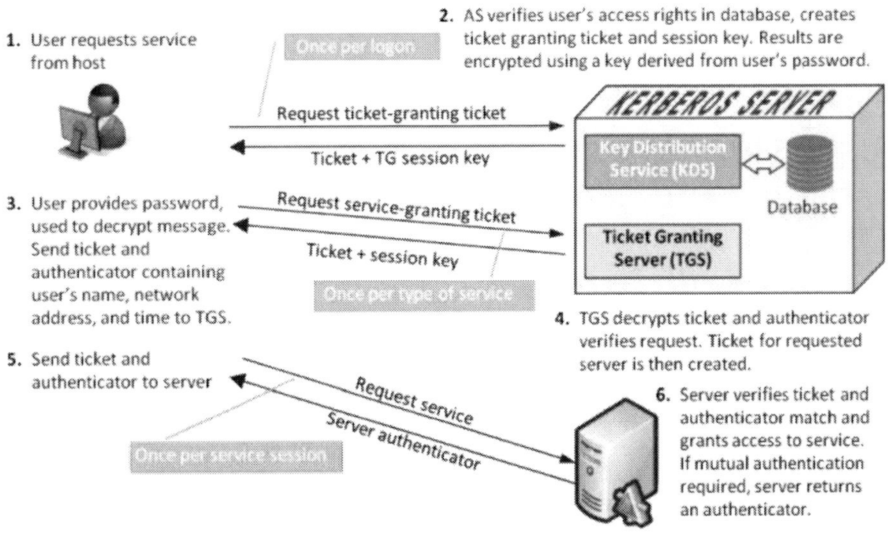

Figure 7. Kerberos authentication and authorization

B. Security Assertion Markup Language (SAML)

SAML 2.0 was defined by OASIS in [16] and is an XML based protocol to exchange authentication and authorization information between a client, an identity provider (the SAML server) and the service provider. The SAML server uses so called SAML assertions to provide statements or claims about the client. Three types can be roughly distinguished: authentication, assertions, and authorization. Especially the latter allows realizing RBAC. SAML builds on assertions symmetric and asymmetric cryptography. Hence, SAML assertions are security tokens utilizing XML signatures and XML encryption to protect the contained information. For the authentication at the identity provider, SAML does not require a specific method and thus may be used with username/password combinations or X.509 certificate based authentication or others. SAML is often used in Single-Sign-On solutions and federation scenarios. It may be used also in open authorization (OAuth 2.0) for the token realization, as described in the following subsection.

C. Open Autorization (OAuth 2.0)

The OAuth 2.0 framework is specified in RFC 6749 [17] and defines an authorization method for accessing a resource. Since OAuth 2.0, this framework can be used with various applications and protocols, whereas the original OAuth was bound to the HTTP protocol. OAuth 2.0 also relies on tokens, which are requested by a user agent, issued by an authorization server and verified at the resource server. The tokens may be provided by reference or by value. OAuth 2.0 defines the handling of the security tokens (access token), as well as the format but allows for an own definition of the token content. Beside the pure request of access tokens, a client may request for a token for a specific scope. The supplied tokens are provided according to the bearer model or the proof-of-possession (PoP) or holder of key (HoK) model. Bearer token can be used to get access to an associated resource without demonstrating possession of a cryptographic key. In contrast, the PoP/HoK token model, requires the proof of possession of a corresponding cryptographic key in order to utilize the token, as defined in RFC 7800 [18]. Note that according to [19], plain OAuth 2.0 is intended for authorization. It may support authentication, e.g., in the combination with OpenID Connect (see the next subsection). OAuth addresses typical Web-based access scenarios.

D. OpenID Connect

OpenID Connect is a security protocol to offload user authentication from a server hosting a resource to a trusted third party. It is defined by the OpenID Consortium. The core is specified in [20]. It utilizes the OAuth 2.0 protocol flows to obtain ID tokens, which are encoded as JSON web token (JWT, see also [21]). These ID tokens contain assertions about authenticated users from an authorization server. Optionally, access tokens as defined in OAuth 2.0 can be utilized to retrieve asserted user authorization information. OpenID Connect is used for web-based clients and also native clients in a variety of applications.

E. RADIUS

Remote Authentication Dial In User Service (RADIUS) [22] is a protocol used to realize access control of users and devices to networks. The protocol itself is typically applied for the communication between an authenticator and a repository performing the actual authentication.

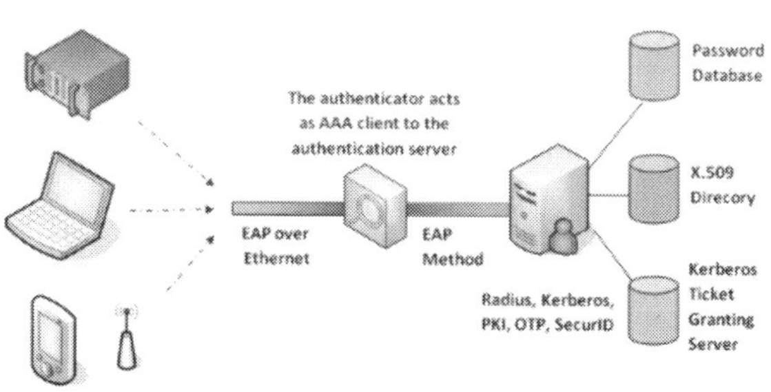

Figure 8. IEEE 802.1X Network Access Authentication

The RADIUS protocol may also be used in conjunction with the Extensible Authentication Protocol (EAP, IETF RFC 3748 [23]) to allow for direct entity authentication. EAP itself describes a container, which in turn allows for different authentication methods. Depending on the method chosen, is allows for authentication and also key establishment. This approach allows transmitting the authentication information from the accessing entity via the access node to the RADIUS server for verification. This approach is utilized for network access authentication in the context of IEEE 802.1X as shown in Figure 8.

F. Digital Grid specific X.509 Certificate Enhancements

Another option to support RBAC has been taken in IEC 62351-8 [11] for power system automation. This standard relies on the authentication based on X.509 [24] certificates and corresponding private keys. In digital grids protocols like TLS are applied, which utilize X.509 key material.

IEC 62351-8 leverages the option to enhance the ASN.1 structure of X.509 certificates with a specific extension. This extension carries information about the roles and constraints and can be added to X.509 public key certificates or X.509 attribute certificates as shown in Figure 9.

The flexibility of attribute certificates can be leveraged in use cases, in which the user to role association is rather dynamic. User-bound public key certificates typically have a longer validity, while attribute certificates may have a much shorter validity and are only valid in conjunction with the associated public key certificate. Via the corresponding private key it can be proven that a user may act in a certain role. As this approach is defined as an extension, protocols utilizing X.509 key material can directly leverage the approach. Note that for the token issuer, i.e., a certification authority, enhancements are likely to be necessary to support the RBAC extension.

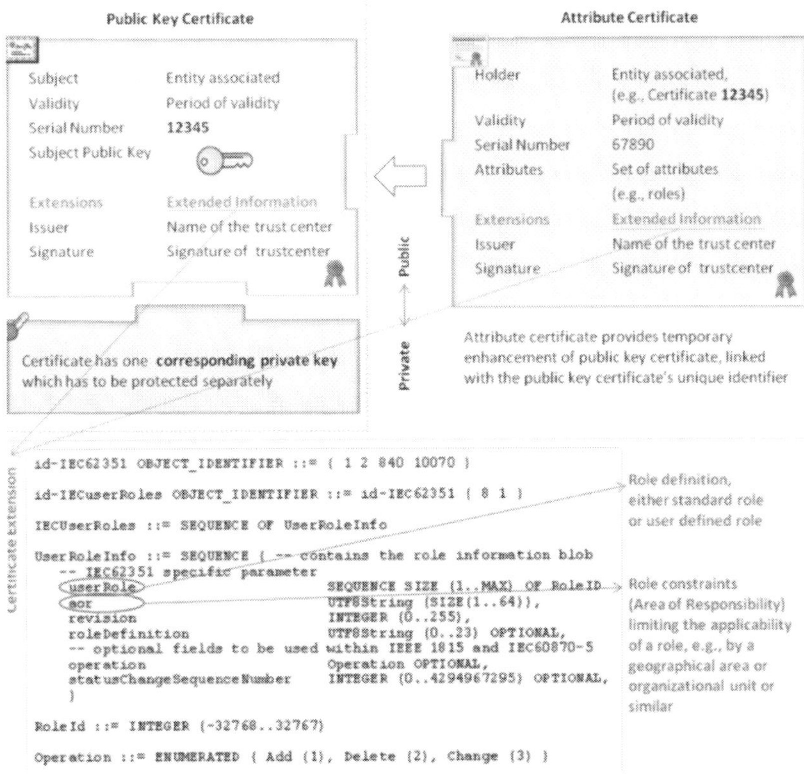

Figure 9. X.509 certificate enhancements (adopted from [11])

Besides the definition of the access token format as extension to X.509 certificates, the standard IEC 62351-8 already defines a set of mandatory roles and associated rights as shown in Figure 10.

Value	Role \ Right	VIEW	READ	DATASET	REPORTING	FILEREAD	FILEWRITE	FILEMNGT	CONTROL	CONFIG	SETTINGGROUP	SECURITY
<0>	VIEWER	X			X							
<1>	OPERATOR	X	X		X				X			
<2>	ENGINEER	X	X	X	X		X	X		X		
<3>	INSTALLER	X	X		X		X			X		
<4>	SECADM	X	X	X			X	X	X	X	X	X
<5>	SECAUD	X	X		X	X						
<6>	RBACMNT	X	X					X		X	X	
<7...32767>	Reserved	For future use of IEC defined roles.										
<-32768...-1>	Private	Defined by external agreement. Not guaranteed to be interoperable										

Figure 10. IEC 62351-8 defined roles and associated rights [11]

The definition of these roles ensures a minimum level of interoperability for different vendors' products.

IV. RBAC SPECIFICS IN THE DIGITAL GRID

As shown in Figure 9, for power systems supporting IEC 62351-8, an extension for carrying role information in X.509 certificates has been standardized, which may belong to a user, a device, or an application. This approach can be directly applied in use cases, in which protocols utilizing X.509 key material like Transport Layer Security (TLS, RFC 5246) are used. Moreover, this approach also supports application layer authentication and authorization, which can be required, if the communication link spans multiple hops. In both cases, beside the certificate validation it also involves the verification of the relying party that the applicant entity is entitled to utilize the X.509 certificate by checking the possession of a corresponding private key. This involves asymmetric cryptography for digital signature generation and verification. Compared to pure symmetric cryptography based approaches, this is costly. Hybrid methods addressing this establish a session, in which a X.509 certificate is involved in the negotiation of a symmetric session key, which is used in (different) security services to protect the session. The whole session is then executed in the context of a specific user, having an assigned role. As substation automation protocols like IEC 61850 utilize a session based approach for the transport or the application connection, this concept is immediately applicable. Note that for the generation of a digital signature, access to the private key is necessary. This private key needs to be protected accordingly, as it is necessary as proof, that the user is authorized to act in a certain role via the corresponding certificate. For devices or applications this protection may be achieved with secured memory or specific hardware modules that allow operation but not exporting of the private key. For a service technician, this protection will most likely be offered by a security token like a smart card or similar.

Current installations in digital grids often utilize a different concept by performing a local form of RBAC depending on the environment. Communication between entities in a control center for instance is performed based on either locally or centrally associated users to permission groups. This ensures that the local execution of commands can only be done if the appropriate permissions are granted, but does not necessarily provide a remote entity to verify who is going to perform a dedicated operation. This information may be necessary for audit purposes, and a complete audit trail would require having the complete chain from the remote point to the executing entity to comprehend the specific action. The approach described in IEC 62351-8 supports also a local audit trail through the capability to connect identity and access information in the access token. In substations, the local physical access may already be sufficient to get access to communicating entities.

While the approach utilizing X.509-based access tokens has its merits, it is not immediately applicable in all use cases. Also, one has to keep in mind that the infrastructure of the power grid has grown over many years and that the lifetime of installed devices is long, reaching 20-25 years.

Two examples are used here to show potential shortcomings.

1. In substation automation, field devices often feature a local human-machine-interface (HMI) handled by a service technician. These field devices typically do not feature a local interface for a smart card, but only a small screen and a number keyboard pad allowing entering a personal identification number (PIN) or a passcode. Hence, RBAC information cannot be provided directly, but may be fetched by the field device.
2. As outlined in [25] web-based services based on XMPP are specified for the integration of decentralized energy resources (DER) into the digital energy grid. These services may leverage already existing technologies that support RBAC, such as OpenID Connect or OAuth 2.0 instead of building a parallel infrastructure for handling X.509 based RBAC.

Proposals are discussed in the next section for both examples.

V. Proposals for RBAC Enhancements

In the following, solutions are proposed to handle RBAC in legacy devices and in upcoming web-based applications building on consistent RBAC information. The real-world applicability of these proposals has to be evaluated. The goal for the proposals is the enabling of a smooth migration for the enabling of RBAC from existing environments not supporting certificate-based RBAC to a public key certificate or attribute certificate-based RBAC environment. The approach taken relies on a minor reduced data structure, as defined for certificate-based RBAC and transported in a different way for the migration case. This reliance enables to establishment of processes and interfaces, which serve for both, legacy and new equipment.

A. Enabling RBAC on local HMI of legacy devices

As noted, a variety of field devices may not feature an appropriate interface to interact with a X.509 credential of a service technician. Despite the missing local interface, these devices may be enabled to work with the X.509 credentials. One approach to be used here is the fetching of the X.509 credential from a trusted third party utilizing the local login and password of the service technician. Once the service technician provides his login credentials, the field device may query a central repository for the corresponding X.509 certificate also providing the login credentials for verification. This X.509 certificate needs to be enhanced with the RBAC extension defined in IEC 62351-8 and can then be verified by the field device. The verification of the corresponding private key is neglected here, as the X.509 certificate is rather used as an assertion by the third party. By already relying on X.509 certificates with RBAC extensions, this approach may be used as a migration path without involving device-local asymmetric cryptographic operations.

The central repository may generate the credentials on demand or they may be provisioned with the X.509 certificates. In either case, the certificates may have a rather short lifetime, which simplifies the revocation handling on the field device. This approach has been considered in IEC 62351-8 with the focus on Lightweight Directory Access Protocol (LDAP) [26]. While LDAP support is typically available in control centers, it is not too widespread in substations. Mechanisms like the Remote Authentication Dial In User Service (RADIUS) [22] are rather used.

If one would want to use RADIUS out-of-the-box, access information can be provided as RADIUS allows extensions using vendor-specific attributes. The drawback is the limitation of this field to effectively 250 bytes. As X.509 certificates are typically larger (even if used with shorter ECDSA key material instead of the larger RSA key material), this field can only be used to transmit a subset of the RBAC information. A necessary subset is proposed as:

```
BEGIN-VENDOR IEC
  ATTRIBUTE RoleID             1  integer
  ATTRIBUTE roleDefinition     2  string
  ATTRIBUTE AoR                3  string
  ATTRIBUTE revision           4  integer
  ATTRIBUTE ValidFrom          5  string
  ATTRIBUTE ValidTo            6  string
END-VENDOR IEC
```

The semantic of the parameter would be kept the same as in IEC 62351-8 and therefore also supports a later processing of other token formats containing the same information. As RADIUS has some shortcomings, like missing message integrity or confidentiality or the application of the weak MD5 hash algorithm, it is recommended to use TLS according to [27] to protect the message exchange between field devices and the RADIUS server. As stated above, this approach is intended to support migration in restricted use cases without changes or enhancements to RADIUS itself.

B. *Supporting RBAC in web service scenarios*

Integration of DER into the digital grid will be supported with IEC 61850-8-2 [28]. Here XMPP is used to enable the connection of field devices (DER controller) to the control site using a publish-subscribe infrastructure. While in [28] the application of session-based end-to-end RBAC in conjunction with X.509 credentials is enabled, further services offered by the publish-subscribe infrastructure may utilize a message-based approach and may require an end-to-middle RBAC approach. Applications could be presence monitoring, notification, or discovery of resources, which may be utilized by a virtual power plant operator. Here the application of OpenID Connect is envisioned, which would need to map the existing access token information to the access token format in the OpenID Connect context.

VI. Realization Example

In order to support power system operators in taking their first step towards centrally managed RBAC in substations that applies not just to the station level (as is typically the case today) but also to the field level, technology vendors providing field equipment, such as RTUs and protection relays, should consider offering RADIUS-based centralized user management and RBAC as currently proposed for standardization in IEC 62351-8. This has the clear advantage that operators can leverage their existing RADIUS infrastructure (or install afresh with reasonable effort) in their substations and can utilize the standardized vendor-specific attribute schema to centrally assign roles and other constraints for each of the users.

As a second migration step towards centralized user management, operators may couple the RADIUS user management with substation-spanning LDAP infrastructure, which is typically realized using Windows Active Directory services. This approach enables operators to choose between a bottom-up centralization of user management and RBAC, starting first with the critical substations and then moving a level higher to incorporate multiple substations with the LDAP-RADIUS coexistence. Alternatively, a top-down approach could also be realized, with a centralized LDAP-based user management that is made available to field devices in substations over RADIUS. Both approaches do not require supporting LDAP directly on the field device but only the capability to handle the RBAC information received via RADIUS. This is seen as advantage specifically for devices with limited resources or for field devices which are in the field for a long time already. A consequent subsequent step over time would be to employ a purely LDAP-based RBAC infrastructure from the substation-spanning level down to the field device level in order to benefit from a more secure and manageable operation as described in the previous section.

Figure 11 and the following description depict a realization example for a migration path. Integrating into this centralized user management infrastructure, field device vendors can support RBAC for user interactions in substations as illustrated in figure 6 with a user-IED interaction, using the pull-model described in IEC 62351-8. When a user initiates an interactive session with the IED, his username and password are collected and sent to the IED (1).

The IED, capable of centralized user management authenticates the user with the central user management system, which may be a RADIUS or LDAP server (2). Depending on whether the user-provided credentials could be successfully verified, the central user management system responds with an authentication success or failure message to the IED (3). Also in this step, if authentication is successful, the server either additionally sends the role / authorization information in its response to the IED (as with RADIUS) or the IED retrieves this information itself from the server (as with LDAP.) The IED accordingly informs the user of the authentication status (4) and creates a new session for the user with the required authorization level and permits the user to interact with it (5). From this point on, the central user management server is no longer involved in the logged-in user's interactions with the IED.

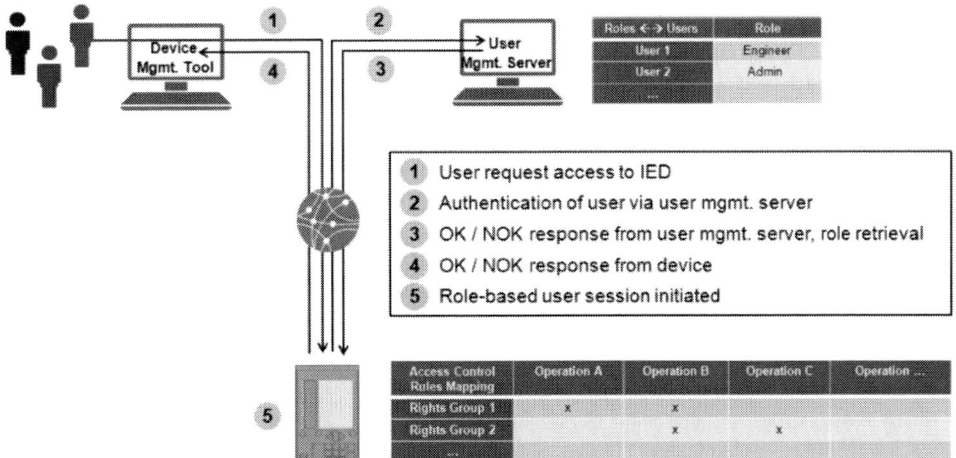

Figure 11. Central user management and RBAC as per IEC 62351-8

VII. Further identified RBAC challenges

Beside the stated solution approaches for binding RBAC information bound to a communication session and supporting migration from existing environments towards certificate supported RBAC, there are further challenges for the integration of a system spanning and vendor independent RBAC solution. These challenges relate to:

1. User- to-role assignment
   Currently, there is a heterogeneous landscape of options available to assign roles to users, which strongly depends on the target environment and on the operator assigning the roles. As in the case of information RBAC information transmission, it is expected to provide migration options between the different approaches. This is directly related with the next challenge.
2. Role-to-right assignment
   As shown in Figure 9 before, IEC 62351-8 already defines a set of mandatory roles. While these roles are intended to ensure a minimum level of interoperability, they are likely to be not flexible enough for all deployments, as an operator may have an own definition of roles and associated rights to be used. To enable a system-wide application of operator defined roles, an exchange format is necessary to describe the role to right association. This issue has also been recognized in standardization, which currently discusses the application of the eXtensible Access Control Markup Language (XACML, [29]) file format and syntax to address this.
3. Right-to-data object assignment
   The last challenge identified relates to the right to data object assignment. This is necessary to have the same interpretation and granularity of actions performed by a role on a component.

VIII. Conclusions and Outlook

This paper discusses role-based access control in the digital grid, starting from an analysis of requirements in regulation, standardization, and guideline activities. It provided an overview about existing technical approaches from other domains and discusses the specifics of the digital grid, the target domain. Feasibility of the migration of existing deployments using legacy devices to a standardized RBAC approach over multiple evolutionary steps has been shown. From an implementation and market adoption point of view, an interoperable vendor-neutral operation for central user management and RBAC according to IEC 62351-8 is yet to be seen, given the extremely hybrid and generation-spanning installed base of power system automation technologies in use today. The proposals made in this paper are intended to address these challenges in an incremental manner, leveraging existing infrastructure and paving the way for a sustainable, secure and manageable infrastructure of the years to come. The outlined proposal has been adopted by IEC for a revision of the currently revised standard IEC 62351-8 to better cope with the migration of existing installations to a future certificate supporting RBAC infrastructure. For this proposal a realization example has been discussed outlining a possible migration from RBAC in an existing environment utilizing the RADIUS protocol to a (user) certificate supported RBAC. Besides the discussion of solutions for identified integration problems also further challenges have been identified. This shows that further investigation and technical development is necessary to cope with all facets of a system spanning RBAC.

References

[1] S. Fries, R. Falk, and C. Bisale, "Handling Role-based Access Control in the Digital Grid," Proccedings IARIA Energy 2017, ISBN: 978-1-61208-556-2, pp. 27-32, https://thinkmind.org/download.php?articleid=energy_2017_2_20_30024, [retrieved July 2017].

[2] S. Fries and R. Falk, "Ensuring Secure Communication in Critical Infrastructures," Proceedings IARIA Energy 2016, June 2016, ISBN: 978-1-61208-484-8, pp. 15-20, https://thinkmind.org/download.php?articleid=energy_2016_1_30_30060, [retrieved: March 2017].

[3] NIST IR 7628, "Guidelines for Smart Grid Cyber Security," Sep. 2014, http://dx.doi.org/10.6028/NIST.IR.7628r1, [retrieved: March 2017].

[4] SGIS "Smart Grid Information Security," Dec. 2014, ftp://ftp.cencenelec.eu/EN/EuropeanStandardization/HotTopics/SmartGrids/SGCG_SGIS_Report.pdf, [retrieved: March 2017].

[5] SEG-CG "Cyber Security and Provacy," Feb. 2017, ftp://ftp.cencenelec.eu/EN/EuropeanStandardization/Fields/EnergySustainability/SmartGrid/CyberSecurity-Privacy-Report.pdf, [retrieved: July 2017].

[6] BDEW White paper "Requirements for Secure Control and Telecommunication Systems," BDEW, February 2015.

[7] ISO TR 27019: Information security management guidelines for process control systems used in the energy utility industry on the basis of ISO/IEC 27002, March 2013.

[8] ISO/IEC 27002:2005 Information technology – Security techniques – Code of practice for information security management, June 2005.

[9] IEC62443-3-3:2013, "Industrial communication networks – Network and system security – Part 3-3: System security requirements and security levels," Edition 1.0, August 2013.

[10] IEEE 1686, "IEEE Standard for Intelligent Electronic Devices Cyber Security Capabilities," December 2013.

[11] ISO/IEC 62351-8, "Role-based access control for power system management," June 2011.

[12] NERC, North American Reliability Corporation, http://www.nerc.com/pa/Stand/Pages/CIPStandards.aspx, [retrieved: March 2017].

[13] German IT Security Law, July 2015, http://www.bgbl.de/xaver/bgbl/start.xav?startbk=Bundesanzeiger_BGBl&jumpTo=bgbl115s1324.pdf, (German), [retrieved: March 2017].

[14] ANSSI Technical Note, Recommandations de sécurité concernant l'analyse des flux HTTPS, October 2015, http://www.ssi.gouv.fr/uploads/IMG/pdf/NP_TLS_NoteTech.pdf (French) [retrieved: March 2017].

[15] C. Neuman, T. Yu, S. Hartman, and K. Raeborn, "The Kerberos Network Authentication Service (V5)," RFC 4120, July 2005, https://tools.ietf.org/html/rfc4120, [retrieved: March 2017].

[16] S. Cantor, J. Kemp, R. Philpott, and E. Maier, "Assertions and Protocols for the OASIS Security Assertion Markup Language (SAML) V2.0," March 2005, http://docs.oasis-open.org/security/saml/v2.0/saml-core-2.0-os.pdf, [retrieved: March 2017].

[17] D. Hardt, "The OAuth 2.0 Authorization Framework," RFC 6749, October 2012, https://tools.ietf.org/html/rfc6749, [retrieved: March 2017].

[18] M. Jones, J. Bradley, H.Tschofenig., "Proof-of-Possession Key Semantics for JSON Web Tokens (JWTs)," RFC 7800, April 2016, https://tools.ietf.org/html/rfc7800, [retrieved: March 2017].

[19] J. Richter, "User Authentication with OAuth 2.0," https://oauth.net/articles/authentication/, [retrieved: March 2017].

[20] J. Bradley et al., "OpenID Connect Core 1.0 incorporating errata set 1," November 2014, http://openid.net/specs/openid-connect-core-1_0.html, [retrieved: March. 2017].

[21] M. Jones et al., "JSON Web Token (JWT) Profile for OAuth 2.0 Client Authentication and Authorization Grants," May 2015, https://tools.ietf.org/html/rfc7523, [retrieved: March 2017].

[22] C. Rigney et. al., "Remote Authentication Dial In User Service (RADIUS)," RFC 2865, June 2000, https://tools.ietf.org/html/rfc2865, [retrieved: March. 2017].

[23] B. Aboba et. al., "Extensible Authentication Protocol (EAP)", RFC 3748, https://tools.ietf.org/html/rfc3748, [retrieved: March 2017].

[24] D. Cooper et al., "Internet X.509 Public Key Infrastructure Certificate and Certificate Revocation List (CRL) Profile," RFC 5280, May 2008, https://tools.ietf.org/html/rfc5280, [retrieved: March 2017].

[25] S. Fries, R. Falk, H. Dawidczak, and T. Dufaure, "Decentralized Energy in the Smart Energy Grid and Smart Market – How to master reliable and secure control," International Journal on Advances in Intelligent Systems, vol 9 no 1& 2, ISSN: 1942-2679, pp. 65-75, September 2016.

[26] J. Sermersheim, "Lightweight Directory Access Protocol (LDAP): The Protocol," RFC 4511, June 2006, https://tools.ietf.org/html/rfc4511, [retrieved: March. 2017].

[27] S. Winter et al, "Transport Layer Security (TLS) Encryption for RADIUS," RFC 6614, May 2012, https://tools.ietf.org/html/rfc6614, [retrieved: March. 2017].

[28] ISO 61850-8-2: Communication networks and systems for power utility automation, Part 8-2: Specific Communication Service Mapping (SCSM) – Mapping to Extensible Messaging Presence Protocol (XMPP), Work in Progress.

[29] eXtensible Access Control Markup Language (XACML) Version 3.0, OASIS Standard, January 2013, http://docs.oasis-open.org/xacml/3.0/xacml-3.0-core-spec-os-en.html, [retrieved: July. 2017].

iaria journals

www.iariajournals.org

International Journal On Advances in Intelligent Systems
issn: 1942-2679

International Journal On Advances in Internet Technology
issn: 1942-2652

International Journal On Advances in Life Sciences
issn: 1942-2660

International Journal On Advances in Networks and Services
issn: 1942-2644

International Journal On Advances in Security
issn: 1942-2636

International Journal On Advances in Software
issn: 1942-2628

International Journal On Advances in Systems and Measurements
issn: 1942-261x

International Journal On Advances in Telecommunications
issn: 1942-2601